UNIVERSITY OF KNOWLEDGE

GLENN FRANK, B.A., M.A., Litt.D., L.H.D., LL.D., *Editor-in-Chief*

PRINTED AND BOUND IN THE UNITED STATES
OF AMERICA BY THE CUNEO PRESS, INC.

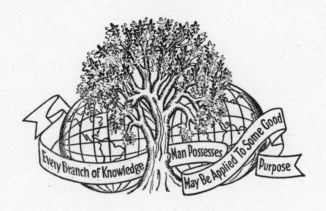

Every Branch of Knowledge Man Possesses May Be Applied To Some Good Purpose

THE SIGNING OF THE DECLARATION OF INDEPENDENCE
From the painting by John Trumbull.

THE UNIVERSITY OF KNOWLEDGE
WONDER BOOKS

GLENN FRANK, EDITOR-IN-CHIEF

HISTORY FROM THE RENAISSANCE TO NAPOLEON

By

ELIZABETH WARREN, Ph.D.

Formerly Instructor in History, The University College
Northwestern University

FRANK L. ESTERQUEST, M.A.

Lecturer in History, University College
University of Chicago

CHARLES W. PAAPE, Jr., M.A.

•

HARRIS GAYLORD WARREN, Ph.D., Editor

Instructor in History, The University College
Northwestern University

•

90-7918

UNIVERSITY OF KNOWLEDGE, INCORPORATED
CHICAGO – 1940

INTRODUCTION

The foundations of modern European civilization were evolved during the thousand years that followed the fall of the Roman Empire. Feudalism rose and flourished, only to retreat before the centralization of political authority and a new economic order. The Church extended its secular and sacred domination until there was aroused an irresistible demand for reformation. The Middle Ages were followed by a general cultural awakening which ended an era and began a new one.

Arts and sciences were given new life during the Renaissance. Printing presses multiplied incalculably the opportunities for learning. Leonardo da Vinci, Michelangelo, Rubens, and El Greco carried painting to new heights and made succeeding generations their debtors. Dante and Shakespeare wrote imperishable masterpieces. Science began its modern trend with Bacon and Newton.

Early religious reformers, like John Huss, were followed by Martin Luther, who gave impetus to a movement that divided the Church. Although Protestant denominations multiplied in number, Catholicism entered upon a new period of growth. Religion ceased to be a monopoly controlled by a narrow circle as individual desires began to be expressed in a multitude of sects. Even nationalism became imbued with religious fervor.

A commercial revolution occurred; a new world was discovered and colonized. National states engaged in gigantic contests for trade and land as empires were won and lost. Political revolutions swept through two hemispheres and new states appeared in the family of nations. Democracy won victories over absolutism. Napoleon traced his meteoric career across the page of history. These were the birth throes of the nineteenth century. This is the story of the present volume.

Dr. Elizabeth Warren, Mr. Esterquest, and Mr. Paape have given a dispassionate and detached account of the historical developments of more than three centuries. The authors acknowledge gratefully the assistance in research and composition which they received from Carl-Gustav Anthon, Pauline M. Sommer, Johan C. Te Velde, and Daniel O'Neil.

Chicago   HARRIS GAYLORD WARREN
November 5, 1937

ACKNOWLEDGMENT

The frontispiece of this volume was chosen after consultation with the editors. "The Signing of the Declaration of Independence" was a moment of universal history, so to speak. Thomas Jefferson, to whom credit is given as being the chief author of the document, probably got some ideas from the English philosopher, John Locke. He was no doubt also influenced by some French writers. Hence it may be said that "The Declaration of Independence" embodies the spirit of individualism which emerged at the time of the Renaissance and the love of liberty rampant everywhere during the latter part of the eighteenth century.

We have selected ornamentations for chapter headings that seem fitting for the times and subjects discussed. No effort or expense has been saved to make the illustrations illuminate the text.

We desire to express our gratitude to The Chicago Historical Society and The Art Institute of Chicago for their cooperation.

We have received photographs and pictures from the governments of various countries, state and city officials, chambers of commerce, and many other organizations and individuals to whom we express our thanks.

J. BRADFORD PENGELLY
Picture Editor

TABLE OF CONTENTS

PART I

RENAISSANCE AND REFORMATION

WHAT WAS THE RENAISSANCE?

UNTIL RECENTLY the Renaissance has been looked upon as a period of sudden reawakening from the "dark" Middle Ages. Renaissance, meaning rebirth, is a term used to describe the spectacular advance of culture in the fifteenth century. Principal causes for the Renaissance were held to be the revelation of ancient classical monuments in Italy, and a westward movement of numerous Greek scholars from Constantinople. These scholars, it was supposed, brought with them a knowledge of Greek literature and philosophy, and aroused a new interest in classical culture. This apparently accidental stimulus from the East was thought to have caused that magnificent outburst of cultural endeavor which characterized the fifteenth and sixteenth centuries.

More recent scholarship, however, rejects the view of a "dark" period in the Middle Ages. It regards the Renaissance as a natural consequence of gradual cultural movement that began as far back as the eleventh century with the evolution of the Romanesque style in architecture. The Renaissance, then, constitutes not only a transition, but also an inevitable stage in the growth of Western civilization.

[13]

HOUSE OF AL-
BRECHT DÜRER
IN NÜRNBERG

Great German gen-
ius of the Renais-
sance—etcher and
painter.

It is a characteristic feature of culture to make its appearance where there are aggregations of people. The rise of towns in western Europe, therefore, marks the beginning of new cultural expression. The development of urban centers did not take place simultaneously all over Europe; rather, it was conditioned by various political, social, economic, geographic, and climatic factors.

Northern Italy seems to have been most favorable to the development of towns. Here we find, in the fourteenth century, a number of flourishing, independent cities, controlling certain rural territories around them, which hence are called city-states. The paralyzing struggles between the papacy and the Holy Roman Emperors, temporary confinement of the papacy to France in the fourteenth century, the schisms that followed, and the resultant decline in the authority of the Church, all proved favorable for the independent political development of the Italian cities. Following the Crusades there arose a lively Eastern trade in spices and luxuries which brought wealth to the cities. Wealth made the brilliant achievements of the Renaissance possible; and the money economy, by now in use everywhere, facilitated intercourse between people.

VENICE—LEADER OF ITALIAN CITY-STATES

The leading city-state in northern Italy was Venice. This city was very advantageously located for commerce with the luxurious Orient, and was also sufficiently isolated to be inaccessible to invaders. During the course of the fifteenth century Venice annexed a large portion of the surrounding territory, thereby safeguarding her access to the Alpine passes which were vital to her trade with the north. The government of Venice was essentially an aristocratic one, although a republic in theory. The nominal head of the government was called the doge. He performed the duties of government with the aid of the Council of Ten, while both were subordinate to the Grand Council. This Council was supposed to represent the people at large; but actual-

VENICE—CITY OF ROMANCE
The Grand Canal and the church of Santa Maria della Salute.

ly it consisted only of members of noble families, and by 1300 all townsmen were excluded from it. In spite of the aristocratic rule, or perhaps because of it, Venice was free from popular criticism and rebellions, in contrast to Florence where all classes claimed themselves entitled to a share in the government. Venetian merchants were so absorbed in their profitable enterprises that they were very willing to leave the business of government to those competent to rule.

MILAN AND FLORENCE

The city-state of Milan displayed the principle of despotism. Under the rule of the Visconti in the fourteenth century, Milan conquered several neighboring towns until it included almost all of Lombardy. The most able ruler of the House of Visconti was Gian Galeazzo (1385-1402), who secured the title of duke of Milan from the Holy Roman Emperor. Upon the death of the last Visconti, the government was seized by Francesco Sforza, a common-born condottiere, but a vigorous and skilful ruler and a patron of the arts.

The city which exhibited the most beautiful and most versatile cultural development was Florence. Under the rule of the Medici, a wealthy banking family whose supremacy began in 1434, Florence became a powerful and prosperous state, which reached its greatest height under Lorenzo the Magnificent. This remarkable man was perhaps the most brilliant ruler of the Renaissance. He exemplified the typical Renaissance personality in versatility as well as refinement of tastes. An outstanding ruler, he was a poet of note, as well as a highly educated patron of the arts.

The Medicis ruled Florence in the manner of the modern political boss, craftily controlling the supposedly republican governmental machinery without an official title. It is surprising that, despite the unusually large number of intelligent and talented men that Florence produced, the people never succeeded in developing an efficient democratic government. On the other hand, the despotism of the Medici was not inimical to the city's welfare, since for the most part the Medici combined political craft with generosity and intellectual refinement.

LION OF ST. MARK WITH THE DOGE
Carving above the Porta della Carta of the Ducal Palace.

THE BEAUTIFUL MILAN CATHEDRAL

PORTRAIT OF DOGE
ANDREA GRITTI

BARTOLOMMEO BANDINELLI,
CALLED BACCIO

HARBOR SCENE AT NAPLES
The city of Naples was under French rule for many years.

THE PAPACY AND MINOR CITY-STATES

Of somewhat lesser importance were the States of the Church, theoretically under the authority of the pope. During and after the "Babylonian Captivity" of the popes (1309-1376) however, nearly every city succumbed to petty adventurer-despots. Upon the return of the popes to Rome, they became involved in worldly politics. In their endeavor to regain control of their territories, the ecclesiastical princes differed little from the contemporary lay princes. But the popes of the Renaissance were highly educated men and generous patrons of the arts. The papal court attracted many of the most gifted sculptors, painters, and architects; and Florence surrendered its leadership in Italian art to Rome after Leo X, a member of the Medici family, became pope in 1513.

TOWN HALL AT SIENA (ITALY)
Three centuries of rivalry with Florence
cost Siena her independence.

MODERN GENOA
Successor to the famous independent city of early Italian history.

Courtesy German Railroads Information Office

THE "CRANE GATE" IN DANZIG
Historic remnant of medieval times in the great Hanseatic city.

There were many other flourishing cities in Italy, vying with one another for supremacy, and each with a history of its own. The most important of these cities were the kingdom of Naples, for a long period under French rule; Siena, which lost its independence to Florence after three centuries of bitter rivalry; and finally, Genoa and Pisa.

PROMINENT CITIES OF NORTHERN EUROPE

While northern Italy was particularly outstanding with its large number of towns, we must not forget that in other parts of Europe there were many prosperous cities. After gaining their charters and therewith their independence from the neighboring nobles, a movement which was made possible through the increase in commerce and wealth, these cities organized democratic governments and rapidly developed into powerful commercial centers. Their positions were further strengthened by the organization of leagues, such as the Hanseatic, the Rhenish, and Swabian Leagues, which enabled the cities to resist ambitious rulers as well as rival nations.

ITALY—CRADLE OF THE RENAISSANCE

It is difficult to explain why Renaissance culture should have its beginning in the Italian city-states. The Baltic cities had a profitable trade with Scandinavia and Russia; Bruges, Ghent, Amsterdam, and a host of Flemish cities prospered in their textile industry and extensive commerce. But why were they not the cradle of the Renaissance?

The greatest advantage which Italy possessed was a certain atmosphere of freedom of thought. Scholasticism had never really taken root in Italy. This is evident in the different trends in Bologna, site of the leading university of Italy. The study of logic, so doggedly pursued in French and German universities, was unpopular in the University of Bologna. The Italian mind simply was unwilling and unsuited for the study of logic as an end in itself. Realities dealing with everyday life were of more interest to them than abstract mental acrobatics. Law was the main curriculum at Bologna, and this is an indication of the habit of calm, practical reasoning, peculiar to Italians at this time.

Furthermore, Italy enjoyed a lively contact with the Byzantine Empire in the East, an empire which still had immense wealth and prestige. The Moslem civilization, too, was bound to exert an influence on its immediate northern neighbors. Climatically, northern Italy is favored by nature with a climate very conducive to a moderate balance between activity and leisure. The northern countries were subject to a more rigorous climate, which forced people to spend more time on the mere struggle for existence. Development in northern countries was, therefore, more

THE CONDOTTIERE GATTAMELATA
Head of Donatello's statue, 1447.

ANDREA VERROCCHIO
By Lorenzo di Credi.

EQUESTRIAN STATUE OF COLLEONI
By Verrocchio.

MADONNA AND CHILD
Attributed to Luca Della Robbia, 15th century.

retarded, and even the spread of the spirit of the Renaissance from Italy continued at a much slower pace. For these reasons, we find certain phases of the Renaissance manifested one or even two centuries later in Germany, England, and Scandinavia than in Italy.

The influx of wealth into the towns naturally revolutionized the social life of the citizens. Their interests were diverted from things religious and mystical to things in this present life, earthly and real. Men began to find delight in occupations and diversions outside the realm of the Church. Commerce and the accompanying development of finance demanded a sense of objectivity, a hard, matter-of-fact common sense, as contrasted to the previous preoccupation with the hereafter. The dominance of feudal lords and that of the Church was loosening, and a new spirit of individualism arose among the people. This individualism first became apparent in the fields of learning and art; later it appeared also in the realm of religion, and led in the fifteenth and sixteenth centuries to a religious renaissance—the Reformation.

BIRTH OF NATIONAL LITERATURE IN ITALY

The new spirit appeared markedly in learning. There had been an unconditional reverence for Aristotelian logic and a blind adherence to scholastic dogmas as laid down by the medieval scholars. Toward the end of the thirteenth century there was a new tendency to study the wealth of unused sources which became available. New Greek works were found through contact with Moslem scholars; many Latin works of the Roman period, hitherto unknown, were discovered. Greek and Latin were considered the basis of a liberal education in the universities. Dante already showed a great reverence for classical writers, and a generation later Petrarch represents the first modern personality in his enthusiasm for classical literature and in his denouncement of the customary scholastic studies of his day.

It is significant too, that with Dante and Petrarch there appeared the first important literature in the Italian language. The Italian vernacular, like other dialects, was not considered suffi-

NORTH DOOR OF THE BAPTISTERY IN FLORENCE
(By Lorenzo Ghiberti)
Considered one of the finest bronze works of the Renaissance period.

SAINTONGES CHURCH, AVY, FRANCE
A splendid example of Romanesque architecture.

GIOVANNI BOCCACCIO

DANTE
(From a bronze bust by an unknown 15th
century master.)

PETRARCH

IMMORTALS OF ITALIAN
LITERATURE

Dante revered earlier classical writers;
Petrarch represents the first modern personality in literature, and Boccaccio is best
remembered for his *Decameron*.

ciently dignified by writers of the Middle Ages; but Dante loved his native dialect and had confidence in its capacity for beautiful expression. Petrarch felt disdain toward the Italian dialect, in which he wrote a few sonnets; but he wished to be remembered mainly for his Latin histories and essays. He is far better known for his Italian sonnets, although they were scorned by him. The fourteenth century also produced Boccaccio, a friend of Petrarch and a biographer of Dante. His *Decameron,* a collection of racy, bold love stories, has been a source of enjoyment to a steady, appreciative public, and has experienced a revival in recent years.

CHAUCER AND SHAKESPEARE

Geoffrey Chaucer, after a visit to Italy, used his native English enthusiastically in the *Canterbury Tales.* Thus Chaucer did for the English language what Dante and Petrarch did for the Italian. In all countries in Europe there were a vigorous assertion and development of the language of the people. In France the popular enjoyment of mystery and miracle plays, the farces, and entertainment by traveling songsters called troubadours, helped to establish the mother tongue. German *Meistersinger* and popular comedians delighted the burghers and peasantry alike; yet even Luther's translation of the Bible in the sixteenth century had a profound influence on the formation of the German language. Thus, we find local dialects forming everywhere; local forces once liberated, asserted themselves boldly.

The literature of the common people that had arisen during the later Middle Ages was for a time superseded by Latin literature of the early Renaissance. But in the sixteenth century a national literature arose in the different countries. The brilliant reign of Queen Elizabeth was accompanied by a manifestation in English literature of the new national pride. Edmund Spenser's *Faerie Queene* is classical in its form and allusions, while its theme is the praise of England's greatest queen. English drama during this period rose to a height which has not been reached for three centuries. The towering figure of this school was William Shakespeare, a dramatic genius of great versatility and an outlook on life that was universal.

PAGE OF OCCLEVE WITH PORTRAIT OF CHAUCER

Manuscript of poem written by Thomas Occleve early in the 15th century. Skeat has called this portrait of Chaucer "the best and probably the only one that can be accepted as authentic."

[30]

There were a great number of minor dramatists, such as Marlowe and Ben Jonson, who wrote during the Shakespearian age. Although we cannot mention all of them here, we must not forget the significance of their contributions to English drama. Aside from the Latin work *Utopia* by Sir Thomas More, and the treatises of Sir Philip Sidney, there is one other outstanding work of the period. This is the King James version of the Bible. Written during the reign of James I, it had great influence on subsequent English prose style, and it is still in use in the entire English-speaking world.

GROWTH OF NATIONAL LITERATURE IN FRANCE AND GERMANY

French literature, too, was temporarily checked by the polished Latin of the Humanists. But in the sixteenth century, the chapter of French literature opened with the works of two great writers. François Rabelais, although a profound classical scholar, wrote for the common people rather than for the exclusive circle of scholars. One of the greatest satirists of all time, he ridiculed the follies of men in his tale of *Gargantua and Pantagruel*, a work which found wide popular appeal. The other great writer, Montaigne, was typical of the revivifying force of the Renaissance movement. He was the first great champion of free thought and individualism. Life ought to be lived according to the law of nature, and man's reasoning power is strong enough to control all of his passions—this forms the kernel of Montaigne's philosophy which he expressed in the inimitable *Essays*. As an essayist he may be regarded the earliest, and his style exerted a strong influence on the writings of subsequent centuries.

Rabelais' satirical theme in his tale of Gargantua was taken over by Fischart in Germany, who wrote a German version of the work. The prodigious dramatic productivity of Hans Sachs, a shoemaker and *Meistersinger* of Nuremberg, was only one aspect of an already vigorous folk-literature in Germany. Folk songs and tales were popular everywhere. They flowed from rich sources of popular themes, centering in the endless fooleries of

SIR THOMAS MORE
(After Holbein)
Author of *Utopia*, Sir Thomas More was an English leader in the Humanist movement,
though not a supporter of the Reformation as interpreted by Henry VIII.

the incorrigible Till Eulenspiegel, or the tragic fate of the heretic Dr. Faustus. The days of the Thirty Years War were brought back to life in the realistic narrative of Grimmelshausen's *Simplicissimus*.

Catholic literature was represented in the profound poetry of Angelus Silesius, while Paul Gerhardt contributed his unforgettable church songs to Protestant literature. The country was alive with drama; Shakespeare's influence and wandering English comedians had imparted an impetus to the drama, and the dramatic works of Gryphius were among the best of the time. German writers were emphasizing the use of the German language, national subjects took precedence over religious ones, and in general the growing nationalizing tendency was manifested in all European literature during this century.

THE PRINTING PRESS

In this connection it is desirable to discuss an invention which was beyond doubt the most important agent in the dissemination of knowledge and opinions. Printed books are a relatively recent achievement, since until about 1400 all books had to be written and copied by hand. Books were consequently few and expensive, and could be purchased only by aristocrats or other wealthy citizens. It is clear that culture was thereby restricted to a small circle, while the large mass of people were kept in utter ignorance.

We do not know the exact origin of the printing press; but certain it is that a system of movable type was used by Johann Gutenberg in his printing shop in Germany about the year 1450. The principle of movable type was preceded by the use of wooden blocks with reversed letters carved on them. Kings and nobles used such devices for their seals or signatures; but, of course, large-scale printing was impossible with such an awkward system. The new process made use of individual letters cast in metal and arranged in the desired sequence. The very easy setting and resetting of letters enabled an unlimited variety of printing.

The new invention spread with amazing rapidity throughout the European world. Scholars and popes welcomed the improve-

GUTENBERG'S PRINTSHOP AND FOUNDRY
As reconstructed in the Gutenberg Museum at Mainz.

ment, and printing presses were built everywhere. Instead of the two books which the most skilful copyist could complete in a year, it was soon possible to produce some 2,500 volumes with one printing press in the same amount of time.

The effect of such prodigious output of books is obvious. It is impossible to overestimate the importance of the printing press in the development of modern civilization. Books and pamphlets were poured out among the people who were now financially able to buy them. Members of the middle class, in particular, assimilated the new available information, and gradually developed into the most powerful and most influential class in the nations. Not only did the ready access to knowledge create the modern intelligent public, but it also produced considerable intellectual unrest. The dissemination of knowledge aided the secularization of literature and art, the breaking down of time-proved traditions, and particularly, the democratization of culture.

HUMANISM

The great intellectual development was inaugurated by a movement called Humanism. In the fourteenth century there had been a marked interest in the study of classical literature. The Turkish conquest of Constantinople, a city which possessed a Greek culture, drove many Greek scholars to Italy. Thus they gave impetus to a movement that was already well under way. It is true that classical texts were difficult to find, and even the available ones were poor translations. The influx of Greek scholars into Italy partially remedied this lack of reliable classical texts, and exerted a refreshing and invigorating influence on Western thought.

Humanism, the study of Greek and Roman culture, is a word derived from *humanitas*, which means culture. But the word Humanism also has come to imply that new interest in man and his earthly destiny, as expressed previously by the Greeks. The main motive for Italian Humanists was a search and appreciation for beauty, and it mattered little to them whether this beauty were expressed in religious or pagan themes. Due to the renewed acquaintance with classical art and literature, there was a decided leaning toward pagan subjects, such as themes dealing with Greek and Roman mythology. This tendency was not strong in Germany, where people were more serious, and there Humanism took on a religious note. Scholars were concerned with discovering the real truth of the Bible, and with overcoming some of the shallow and corrupt practices of the Church.

The two most interesting figures involved in the religious movement were Martin Luther, the great reformer, and Erasmus of Rotterdam. The influence of these two men on the Reformation will be treated in greater length in the following chapter, but their importance as intellectual figures must be brought out here. Luther was the sturdy, bold, and stubborn rebel type in spite of caution and self-discipline in his attitude toward the Church, but Luther knew no limit in asserting his own ideas after he broke with the Church. He had no equal in courage, outspoken earnestness, and power of language.

Erasmus was a very different person. His sincere aim, too, was to reform the corrupt Church; but he was by temperament cautious to the point of timidity, diplomatic, always neutral, and extremely anxious to preserve peace. Luther was the man of action; Erasmus was hesitant, and contented himself with directing witty and stinging satires against his opponents. He did not desire to break away from the Church, but wanted to reform it from within. Erasmus was cool and calm in his reasoning, totally free from passion of any sort. He was naturally a pacifist, and much of the conflict which appeared in succeeding years might have been avoided had there been more men like Erasmus.

As a literary figure Erasmus enjoyed an enviable, widespread reputation. He was looked upon as a universal authority in intellectual matters; his judgment was final. He wrote and spoke in excellent Latin, and felt at home in any country where he could find learned men with whom to converse. Never before had there been such universal admiration for a scholar, and he was beyond doubt the "Prince of the Humanists."

The humanistic movement contained a large number of scholars in all countries. Among the German Humanists, John Reuchlin, and the passionate knight and poet, Ulrich von Hutten, were both ardent supporters of the Reformation. In England, Sir Thomas More, not a supporter of the Reformation as Henry VIII interpreted it, is best known for his idealistic work, *Utopia*. In France, we may think of Montaigne, the skeptic philosopher, as a Humanist. The movement had a widespread effect on the intellectual development of subsequent times, and many great writers and philosophers even up to the end of the seventeenth century, can be said to be a product of Humanism.

ARCHITECTURE AND SCULPTURE

ART IS ALWAYS the first medium of expression which reflects the changes and new tendencies of an age. During the Middle Ages, the arts and crafts were largely in the service of the Church, or at least under its guidance. The individual artist and craftsman was but a small link, a subordinated part of an organization, and his individual personality was almost completely obscured in the interest of the whole work. This practice had a decided advantage, for it enabled the construction of large cathedrals without the hindering forces of individual ambition and rivalry.

The whole period of Gothic art was subject to these conditions. The architect and sculptor alike did their work anonymously, and there can be little doubt that these artists were happy in their simplicity and modesty. But the consequence was a formal, stereotyped art, unsusceptible to the realities of its environment. This reality gradually penetrated the realm of art during the fourteenth century under the secularizing influence of commerce and wealth. Artists became conscious of their personalities; they found that their work was highly desired by worldly and ecclesiastical princes who offered attractive remuneration for their creations. The history of Renaissance art, therefore, becomes a history of artists.

MAIN DOOR OF STRASSBURG CATHEDRAL

During the Middle Ages, arts and crafts found their highest expression in the service of the Church. The whole period of Gothic art was subject to this influence.

The Gothic style of architecture predominated in northern Europe until the end of the fifteenth century. Italy never really adopted this style, but continued to build in a modified Romanesque form. During the fourteenth century architects began to study and experiment with the remains of classical architecture, and a new style, simplified and well balanced, emerged. Brunelleschi in Florence was a successful pioneer, and the new style found its highest expression in the works of Bramante and Palladio and, most of all, Michelangelo.

While sculpture was only a part of the architecture of the Middle Ages, it asserted itself as an independent art in the Renaissance under its resourceful artists. They prepared the world for an appreciation of the classical conception of beauty. Laws of perspective were studied, and the beauty of the human figure was boldly revealed and emphasized. Pioneers in this field were the Pisanos, who had experimented with these forms at the close of the thirteenth century. Under the encouragement of the Medici family, Florence produced a number of brilliant sculptors, among whom Lorenzo Ghiberti was the first really great master. His exquisite figures on the doors of the baptistery in Florence are still a wonder of the art world. Donatello and Verrocchio made imposing equestrian statues for their patrons, who desired to immortalize their personalities. A unique and refined art was developed by Luca della Robbia who, in addition to being an excellent marble-worker, specialized on glazed enamel and ceramics. The dominant figure in sculpture was Michelangelo. His powerful, restless figures constitute a style unique among Renaissance artists. Sculpture was his natural medium, and a sculptural element is definitely revealed also in his painting.

GREAT ITALIAN PAINTERS

The most highly developed art of the period was painting. We find the first attempt to break away from the lifeless, prescribed style of the day in the youthful, refreshing pictures of Giotto, a Florentine who was a close friend of Dante. Passion, instead of sentiment, was expressed in Giotto's painting. A delightfully fresh and joyful soul himself, he was first to give importance to expression of the human soul.

GIOTTO'S "CORONATION OF THE VIRGIN"
Close friend of Dante, Giotto is best known for the youthful and
refreshing style of his work.

Giotto's example in painting was enthusiastically pursued by
the humble Dominican monk, Fra Angelico, and by the unusually gifted Masaccio, whose technique was far in advance of
his time. Sandro Botticelli represented the graceful, aristocratic
ladies of Florence in his pagan themes. The enthusiasm for pagan-
ism went so far that it produced a popular, democratic reaction
under the leadership of the fanatic monk, Savonarola. It was
aimed against the ruling Medici family, who patronized the classical art. Penitent, Botticelli burned his exquisite nude figures and

Courtesy the A. W. Mellon Educational and Charitable Trust

BOTTICELLI: "ADORATION OF THE MAGI"

BOTTICELLI

His paintings were characterized by grace-ful, aristocratic feminine figures.

GIOVANNI BELLINI

Bellini's works show a marked Byzantine influence.

"MADONNA ALBA," BY RAPHAEL

resolved to abandon profane subjects. Nevertheless, his subsequent Madonnas continued to be elegant ladies of his refined surroundings; the new style had already taken root too deeply to be suppressed.

The papal court was far from being backward in the movement toward worldliness. The popes vied with the lay princes in securing for themselves the best artistic talents of the age. Raphael, a brilliant and prolific genius, produced his technically unsurpassed works under the patronage of Julius II and Leo X. For these popes, too, Michelangelo spent his best energy in decorating the Sistine Chapel with monumental frescoes.

DETAIL FROM MICHELANGELO: "THE LAST JUDGMENT"
In the Sistine Chapel, Rome.

FRA ANGELICO
Detail from fresco by Raphael, in the
Vatican.

Painting during the Renaissance was regional. Each community had its own peculiar school of artists, for the influences of landscape and economic pursuits made themselves felt on the style of the local masters. Venice was a wealthy commercial city with wide international relations and the Venetians were consequently less intellectual than they were sensuous and emotional. The paintings of Giovanni Bellini show a marked Byzantine influence. Later, the Venetian love for color and magnificence found its fullest expression in the famous works of Giorgione and Titian.

LEONARDO DA VINCI

The greatest personality of the period beyond a doubt was Leonardo da Vinci. In connection with Lorenzo de' Medici, reference has already been made to the great versatility of the Renaissance genius. It was the aim of artists, not only to master one art, but also to become proficient in several of them. Leonardo da Vinci was an accomplished painter, sculptor, and architect; but

LEONARDO DA VINCI

Painter, sculptor, architect, inventor, mathematician, musician, anatomist—
greatest personality of the Renaissance period.

Courtesy The Metropolitan Museum of Art
"VENUS AND THE LUTE PLAYER," BY TITIAN

his indefatigable search for the secret of life led him farther into
almost all vocations of his time. He was an ingenious inventor, a
mathematician, and musician; and his observations and sketches
in anatomy are still among the most accurate up to this day. Benvenuto Cellini was a goldsmith as well as a sculptor and a clever
writer. Michelangelo's and Lorenzo de' Medici's versatilities have
already been mentioned. Sonnet-writing became the pastime of
everyone as music became everybody's hobby a century later. But
no one man had combined so many fields of knowledge in one
personality as did Leonardo, and in this he was a typical man of
the Renaissance.

RENAISSANCE PAINTERS IN NORTHERN EUROPE

While renaissance art in Italy took on a distinctly classical
note, in northern Europe it served to give expression to the innate
Germanic spirit. There were neither Byzantine traditions nor
classical influences in the north. France and Spain accepted the

Italian style; but Germany, Scandinavia, and the Low Countries show surprisingly few effects of the classical tradition.

In Holland and Flanders painting began in the fifteenth century with the exquisite works of the Van Eyck brothers. They were followed by a number of different local schools, of which the virile, colorful peasant pictures by Pieter Bruegel are perhaps the most interesting. Dutch and Flemish painting did not come to a climax until the seventeenth century in the baroque style. This style may be regarded as a continuation of classical forms, and it is characterized by a love for movement, splendor, and ornaments.

The Low Countries had many really great painters. The voluptuous, earthly women in the pictures of Rubens express a reaction with a vengeance against the rigid Catholicism of the Spanish rule. The realistic paintings of Frans Hals show no longer any pretense of restraint and idealization. Van Dyck's style reflects the cool, aristocratic air of his refined environment. Here the artisan ceases; a worldly, elegant, and highly respected artist-personality appears—a polished gentleman, at ease with kings and

Courtesy The Metropolitan Museum of Art

WOLF-AND-FOX HUNT
Peter Paul Rubens (Flemish artist).

"PORTRAIT OF A MAN IN A FUR HAT"
Rembrandt van Rijn

nobles. The towering figure among the great number of Flemish and Dutch painters was Rembrandt van Rijn. A deeply religious man, he was misunderstood by his contemporaries. His art is lofty and noble, superior to contemporary artists in both craft and content. His etchings and paintings, largely scorned in his time, now command fabulous prices.

The art of the Low Countries was characterized by a love for subjects concerning the experiences of everyday life. It was a skil-

Courtesy Baltimore Museum of Art

"PORTRAIT OF A LADY" BY HALS
"The realistic paintings of Frans Hals show no longer any
pretense of restraint and idealization."

ful expression of a local, national feeling; always real, vivid, and
vigorous, it was unconcerned with abstractions about the hereafter.

Germany possessed very few painters in the Renaissance and
almost no baroque painters. The etchings of Dürer and the marvelous English portraits of Holbein the Younger are the most
famous works that Germany produced during this period.

French and Spanish artists imitated the Italian style. But it
was especially in Spain that Renaissance painting culminated in a
flourishing baroque style. El Greco, the chief representative, pro-

EL GRECO
Self-portrait as an evangelist.

IVAN THE TERRIBLE
By Antokolsky.

BARTOLOMÉ ESTÉBAN MURILLO

Courtesy Museum of Fine Arts, Boston

"CARLOS AND THE DWARF" BY VELASQUEZ

duced weird color and light effects which suggest visions of a dreamer. In the refined atmosphere of the Spanish court, Velasquez produced a number of magnificent royal portraits and classical subjects among which the decidedly pagan theme of Venus in the mirror is the best known. There is one other great painter to be noted in the Spanish baroque, Bartolomé Murillo, whose portraits of madonnas and saints reflect a deeper religious mind than any of his contemporaries, with the possible exception of Rembrandt.

Renaissance art decayed in a further outgrowth of the baroque into the rococo style. The art of this period lost its balance of form and content in a wholesale application of ornaments. The

"PRINCE EDWARD, AFTERWARD EDWARD VI"
By Holbein

rococo style still has a great appeal for modern generations for its utmost grace and childlike beauty; but it led in a direction where there could be no further development.

The devastating religious wars of the seventeenth century almost completely stifled any artistic endeavor. Architecture, which had experienced an encouraging revival at the beginning of the century, sank into complete stagnation during the Thirty

Years War. The condition of painting was even more depressing. Only music gave a delightful evidence of vigorous activity, and before long it became the dominant art in Germany.

MUSIC

Up to the fourteenth century music consisted of simple chants, used only in connection with the Catholic services. From the existing Greek modes there now emerged the minor and major scales of today, and a strict polyphonic style developed. In Italy this style found its highest expression in the works of Palestrina. In the north, especially in the Low Countries, it culminated in the magnificent choral works of Orlando di Lasso, Josquin Des Prés, known as the "king of music," and William Dufay.

A significant change came about with the development of musical instruments. Up to this time musical artistry had been expressed in vocal works. There were a few string and wind instruments in existence, such as the guitar, lute and harp, and the bagpipe, oboe, and a simple type of organ. Aside from church music, the improvised songs of the wandering minstrels

JOHANN SEBASTIAN BACH
Great exponent of Protestant
church music.

Ulrich H. Ellerhusen, sculptor
(University of Chicago Chapel)

in the thirteenth and fourteenth centuries flourished in early Renaissance music. Gradually, with the development of the organ, the violin, and the flute, there arose a popular desire for instrumental music. Not only professional musicians, but also the whole enthusiastic laity participated in small orchestral ensembles, as well as madrigals (short secular choral works) and religious music. The sixteenth century marks the zenith of musical activity from the point of view of popular participation, an art which was completely driven out by the brilliant performances of professional musicians. The new musical artist was now ascending from a mere craftsman to a position as protegé of the aristocracy.

In England, Purcell and Händel were developing a magnificent instrumental style, while also toying with the opera, which was then a musical innovation. This type of musical composition attempted to fuse dramatic art and music in one form, to enlarge and intensify the scope of artistic expression. It originated with Monteverdi in Italy about 1600, and was eagerly taken up by Heinrich Schütz in Germany. Schütz also developed a form of religious opera, the oratorio. This religious opera without action culminated in the works of Johann Sebastian Bach, the great exponent of Protestant Church music. An extraordinary organist, he was the most versatile and prolific composer of his day. Bach and Händel are well named "baroque musicians" and they brought music to a height that was perhaps never again attained.

ASTRONOMY RELEASED FROM ITS FETTERS

Science cannot thrive when there is domination of dogma. Under the stifling cloak of medieval scholasticism and monasticism nothing more scientific than alchemy and astrology could exist. The rise of individualism, the great sea voyages and discoveries, the relaxing domination of the Church, and the growth of free thought combined to encourage scientific development. There still persisted numerous superstitions and a belief in magic, notwithstanding the bold strides taken in the direction of scientific thought by the pioneering scientists of the fifteenth and sixteenth centuries.

NICOLAS KRATZER, A PROMINENT
EARLY ASTRONOMER
Portrait by Holbein.

Perhaps the study of astronomy exercised little direct influence on the development of practical, applied science; but it completely revolutionized man's conception of the universe and of himself. The Ptolemaic theory, originated by the Greek philosopher Ptolemy in the second century A. D., dominated throughout the Middle Ages. Ptolemy held that the earth was the center of the universe, with the sun, moon, and planets revolving around it at great speed. This theory was eagerly upheld and considered sacrosanct by the Catholic Church, for it emphasized the singular importance of the earth and with it the supreme position of man.

Notwithstanding the staunch belief in the Ptolemaic system, or the geocentric theory, there had been other conceptions of the universe. The Pythagoreans believed in a heliocentric world, the idea that the sun is the center of the system. This theory was revived by early Italian astronomers when classical culture was rediscovered.

The founder of modern astronomy was the Polish priest, Copernicus. A champion of the Pythagorean theory, he published his computations and observations in a work called *On the Revolutions of the Celestial Bodies*, and dedicated the volume to Pope Paul III. The "Copernican system," as it came to be known, displaced man's superior position in the world and placed the earth on the same level with any other planet. It is conceivable that such a revolutionary doctrine aroused widespread interest and curiosity, as well as indignation.

During the course of the sixteenth century, astronomers were busily improving their instruments for observing the skies. The most outstanding astronomical observer to test the Copernican theory was the Danish astronomer, Tycho Brahe. He set up an elaborate observatory, a veritable "Castle of the Heavens," as he called it, on a small island in the Baltic Sea. Here he diligently and systematically collected scientific data under the patronage of his king, until, falling into disrepute, he became official astronomer to the Holy Roman Emperor.

Kepler, who succeeded Tycho Brahe, continued the studies of his predecessor. His main contribution to the new theory was his establishment of the elliptical path of the planets around the sun, in contrast to the notion of a circular movement of the planets. Kepler witnessed the trial of his mother for witchcraft, and it was popularly believed that Kepler was not free from the inspiration of Satan. It is not surprising, therefore, that Kepler catered to the superstitions of people by casting horoscopes for his customers, among whom the eminent Wallenstein was the most frequent caller.

The Copernican hypothesis was brilliantly expounded and popularized by the gifted Italian scientist, Galileo. A true Renaissance mind in his diverse talents, he was a classical scholar, an able musician, and an eloquent writer as well. Galileo made permanent contributions to physics and celestial mechanics. He discovered the equal velocities of falling bodies subject to gravity, and the oscillations of a pendulum. Mechanics, existing up to this time only as a diffuse collection of a few laws and theorems, was definitely established as a science by Galileo. He invented a telescope, which is similar to the modern opera glass, but with it he discovered the satellites of Jupiter, the sun-spots, and the substance of the Milky Way. His publications evoked the suspicion of the Inquisition, an ecclesiastical court devised to suppress heresy. Found guilty by the tribunal, he was forced to abjure the

STATUE OF GALILEO IN FLORENCE
(By Costoli.) Galileo discovered the equal velocities of falling
bodies, and definitely established the science of mechanics.

heliocentric theory. Nevertheless, Galileo's work survived the
fanatic persecutions of the Inquisition, and his discoveries in mechanics and dynamics furnished a basis for the great formulations
of Newton.

MATHEMATICS, PHYSICS, AND METALLURGY

While modern astronomy received inspiration from classical theories, the science of mathematics developed on European ground from the crude beginnings of medieval science. A stimulus was provided by the current happenings in navigation, in warfare, and, most of all, by the needs of commerce. The use of Arabic numerals and elementary algebra had been taken over from the Moslems; geometry and arithmetic had been inherited from the Greeks; but on these elementary foundations, European scholars built the magnificent structure of modern mathematics.

Under the pressure of commerce and finance, mathematicians labored to devise accurate and efficient methods for calculating prices, weights and measures, wages, and coinage. Treatises were written on military science, on bookkeeping, and a somewhat roguish physician named Cardan even reckoned the calculus of possibilities in gambling.

In the field of physics, the name of Galileo again appears as a leading figure. He had made studies of motion and sound phenomena. As an inventor, he contributed the air thermometer and the architect's level. The first microscope was probably devised by the Dutch inventor, Jansen, and the invention was of utmost significance for the development of biological sciences. At this point we might also take note of the experiments of William Gilbert, who observed certain "electrical" phenomena in magnetic bodies, a discovery which ultimately led to the electromagnetic motor.

The growth of mining enterprises, made possible through the rise of capitalism, created a need for the study of minerals and metals. A German student of natural sciences, George Agricola, made a beginning in this field by his visits to mines in Bohemia and Bavaria. He summed up his observations in his *Twelve Books on Metals*, and with this work became the founder of the sciences of mineralogy and metallurgy.

BENVENUTO CELLINI
(From the engraving by Francesco Allegrini)

Distinguished no less for his fine craftsmanship as a worker in precious metals than for his sculpture and writings, Cellini designed for the papal state some of the most beautiful coins the world has ever known.

ROGER BACON
(From a 15th century manuscript)

PAPER AND GUNPOWDER

In addition to the inventions already named, there were two others of epoch-making consequences, paper and gunpowder. Modern paper has been in use for not more than five centuries. Books and manuscripts had been written largely on papyrus rolls in Egypt, on parchment or vellum in Europe. A type of linen paper was in use in the thirteenth century, but parchment was preferred because of its greater durability. With the invention of printing in the middle of the fifteenth century, it was necessary to manufacture a type of paper which was cheap enough for large-scale printing. Cotton and linen were previously used in the making of paper; but, with the shifting of the industry to northern countries, woolen rags were used in a synthetic process. The problem of a cheap paper having been solved, printing was enabled to embark on a mass publication of writings.

Of tremendous importance was the invention of gunpowder. Crossbows, longbows, and pikes had been the main weapons of infantry. In a manuscript dated 1220, gunpowder had been mentioned. Roger Bacon gave a detailed description of it, after studying various forms. But it was not until the invention of the cannon that the explosion of gunpowder could be controlled. Cannons throwing iron projectiles were mounted on wheels and were used by the end of the fourteenth century. Smaller guns fired by powder were beginning to displace the longbows and cross-bows. These guns were relatively crude and the method of ignition was inefficient, so that the bow and arrow was still in use in Cromwell's army. Military tactics were revolutionized considerably with the use of firearms, although, in comparison with the mass slaughter of modern times, wars up to the nineteenth century were still rather mild affairs.

NATURAL SCIENCES

The name Paracelsus is a symbol for natural sciences in the sixteenth century. He was a remarkable man—a versatile student of nature, a musician, physician, and mystic philosopher. A restless and quarrelsome soul, he spent most of his life denouncing the prevailing notions of Aristotle and the Roman physician Galen, and demanded recognition of individual, contemporary research. He visited mining families in the Fugger mines in Tyrol, and studied the diseases to which they were subject. Most important of all, he insisted that functions in the human body are chemical in nature, and can be treated with chemical processes. During his time, Paracelsus was considered a "quack," but modern science gives recognition to many of his revolutionary beliefs.

Another noted physician to break away from the Galen tradition, which dominated medical science throughout the Medieval Ages, was the eminent Netherlander, Vesalius. Up to his time surgery had been performed by barbers. Nevertheless, barbers were not always incompetent, and valuable contributions had been made by barber-surgeons in wars when devising artificial limbs for injured soldiers. Vesalius denounced surgery performed by inexperienced barbers, and advocated the thorough study of anatomy as a basis for training surgeons and physicians. His long treatise on anatomy was a study on the digestive and circulatory systems, the muscles, lungs, and brain. It constitutes an important stepping stone in the history of medical science. However, the actual processes of the circulatory system were not known until William Harvey published, in the beginning of the seventeenth century, his learned work, a discovery of prime significance to medicine.

RENAISSANCE PHILOSOPHY

It was natural that, with such revolutionizing discoveries in all fields of science, there should emerge new systems of philosophy. Men like Galileo and Kepler were philosophers as well as scientists. The Italian philosopher, Tommaso Campanella, developed a philosophy of nature with which he combined social and political ideas. In his *City of the Sun* he visualized a socialistic Utopia, for which he was persecuted by the Church and imprisoned for twenty-five years. The most interesting and first "modern" philosopher, however, was the Neapolitan, Giordano Bruno.

Beginning his interesting career in a Dominican monastery and brought up in the time-honored Aristotelian tradition, he soon came under the influence of Neo-Platonism. He became thoroughly imbued with the scientific spirit of his day and gradually became an enthusiastic supporter of the Copernican system. Realizing that conflicts with the Church were imminent, he threw off his ecclesiastic robe and undertook the endless wanderings that led him through France, Switzerland, Germany, and even far-off England. He sought the company of broad-minded scientists and scholars, conversed with Sidney and Shakespeare, and won the admiration of kings and princes. But he possessed a rash, irritable temper that led him into frequent troubles. Bruno was the first prophet of pantheism, the philosophy which conceives God to be embodied in nature. Naturally, such a philosophy was regarded by the Church as "heretical," and upon Bruno's return to Italy he was imprisoned and committed to the flames. Besides possessing all the qualities that characterize the modern intellectual man, Bruno is significant for being the first monistic philosopher and a predecessor to Spinoza.

Contemporaneous with Bruno, but living under more favorable circumstances, Francis Bacon was philosophizing about natural science. A student of law at the University of Cambridge, he embarked on a brilliant political career and finally became lord chancellor to King James I. He was an ambitious man, striving for wealth and fame, and he spent most of his life in the company of nobles and royal personages. Bacon, like so many of his contemporaries, definitely broke away from Aristotle and Scholasticism, and devoted most of his time to the study of the physical sciences and to the writing of philosophical works. Divorcing belief from science, he founded empirical philosophy, that is, philosophy based on experience. Yet, in spite of the work of mathematicians like Galileo and Kepler, Bacon failed to apply mathematics to philosophy. This step was finally taken by the great Frenchman, René Descartes.

GENERAL EFFECTS OF THE RENAISSANCE

The intellectual revolution, as this age may well be called, gave an impetus to all fields of knowledge. The science of philosophy flourished in the Netherlands and the University of Leyden was still the center of philology in Europe. Scientific history began with the increasing appreciation for historical and political questions, while the practice of systematically recording and collecting source material was gaining wide usage. Works like Machiavelli's *Prince* exemplify the new tendencies in history and political science.

It is clear from the evidence in all phases of Western civilization that the Renaissance embodied forces that broke up religious, political and social traditions. But the same disintegrating forces contained the seeds of a general awakening and advancement. It is erroneous to regard the Renaissance as only a revival of classical civilization. Nor is it tenable to consider the Renaissance merely as the continuation of a steady advance of humanity, an advance interrupted by an unfortunate period of darkness. Progress was made before and during the Renaissance, to be sure; but the intermediate period, ineptly termed the "Dark Ages," also made its contributions. New, definitely original and indigenous seeds were germinating in Europe between the eighth and thirteenth centuries. Intentionally or not, the conscious imitation of the classics led to a cultural development which bears characteristics distinct from those of any previous civilization.

Courtesy German Railroads Information Office

WARTBURG CASTLE NEAR EISENACH IN THURINGA, GERMANY
It was here that Martin Luther translated the New Testament into German, a work which exerted profound influence on the new High German language.

MARTIN LUTHER AND THE PROTESTANT REFORMATION

SCANDALS WITHIN THE CHURCH

THE PROTESTANT REFORMATION has been looked upon as the northern version of the Renaissance. Protestants, in the eyes of the Church, were no more and no less than heretics. The word heresy, meaning "choosing for one's self," gives us an admirable suggestion as to what characterized the spirit of the Protestant. Here again, the innate drive for individual assertion, the same force that gave impetus to the Renaissance, manifested itself in the northern countries.

The story of the Reformation is a dynamic drama. We can definitely recognize feeble beginnings many centuries before the actual issue came to a climax, and it took many years before the opposing factions settled their difficulties in a compromise.

The thirteenth century, which produced a Dante, also carried the germs of religious differences and opposition to the Church. The resentment of heretics was founded particularly on the appalling abuses and scandals within the Church. The clergy were forsaking more and more the religious and social virtues that were requisites for their sacred profession. They were giving free rein to selfish and greedy motives, shocking to the laity. High officers of the Church, bishops, cardinals, and popes alike, no longer made

[65]

pretenses about their worldly ambitions and desire for luxury. We find the reaction of the common people to the state of affairs in the Church vividly reflected in many medieval literary works.

HERESY AND THE GREAT SCHISM

Heresy was manifested in various religious sects that were particularly prominent in the twelfth and thirteenth centuries. The Waldensians and Albigensians in southern France took some of their doctrines from mystic cults of eastern Europe and the Orient. Although most members of these sects were massacred or scattered by cruel persecutions, they are important because of their stubborn persistence even up to the nineteenth century. They are of even greater immediate significance due to their influence on such early reformers as Wyclif and Huss.

The Church met these infidels in two ways. There was the possibility of remedying the chief abuses by reform within the Church. The establishment of the Dominican and Franciscan orders revived what once were the monastic ideals of Christian poverty and humility, while the various councils of the fifteenth century had attempted to alleviate the worst evils. Another method of suppressing heresy was the resort to plain force and persecution. The Inquisition, an efficient institution for persecution, was devised to eradicate heresy by persuasion or brute strength. Finally, the notorious crusades against the Albigensians and Waldensians, being nothing but wholesale slaughter, were far from successful. They injured the reputation of the Church, and in the end were instrumental in renewing the vigor and resistance of the heretics.

Nothing contributed more to the loss of prestige by the Church than the Great Schism, created by the double papal elections in the fourteenth century. A council held in Pisa in 1409, intended to clarify the situation, only added insult to injury by adding a third pope. The consequent indignation of the whole Christian world demanded an instant settlement of the issue; and the resultant Council of Constance, while it healed the Schism, only succeeded in further stirring the passion of the opponents, by its condemnation and burning of Huss.

THE BAPTISTERY, CATHEDRAL AND LEANING TOWER OF PISA

In connection with the Council of Constance, there was a point of great significance to be noted. The main issue involved in the meetings of the council was whether or not a council's decision was superior to that of the pope. The council's superiority would have meant representative government in the Catholic Church. But the national rivalry and differences among the members of the council effected the triumphant emergence of the pope. The pope had therefore retained his absolute authority, a victory of tremendous consequence throughout the following centuries. After the adjournment of the Council of Constance, the papacy consolidated its worldly possessions and proceeded to extract all possible revenue from its subjects.

Meanwhile, the martyrdom of Huss had aroused violent resentment among the Bohemians. A revolt broke out in Prague, and the imperial troops were driven back by the Hussites. Emperor Sigismund was ignominiously defeated and the surrounding territory plundered. At the Council of Basel peace was made with the moderate faction of the Hussites, while the more radical groups were suppressed.

These various happenings illustrate the decline of the authority of the Church between the eleventh and sixteenth centuries. And yet, despite all these attacks on the Church, despite the heretical movements, despite schisms and scandals—at the close of the fifteenth century the Church still dominated the life of the people. Religion was the unifying force, the one common interest which had an intensity totally foreign to the present generation.

The Catholic Church at that time practically determined the course of a person's social and spiritual life. Children of Christian parents were born into the Church, as they are born into the state today. The state assumed the enforcement of the people's adherence to the rules and doctrines of the Church. Support of the Church was effected by taxes on individuals, taxes which were compulsory, not optional. In short, it was through the Church alone that man could organize his life in this world and attain eternal happiness hereafter.

RESENTMENT AGAINST PAPAL POLICIES

In the meantime, abuses and scandals were increasing. Pope Alexander VI shocked the whole Christian world with his immoral life and his equally immoral daughter, Lucrezia Borgia. His successor, Julius II, was concerned primarily with the centralization of the papal states in central Italy. The highly educated Medici pope, Leo X, who embodied the artistic traditions of his famous family, was nevertheless guilty of gross malpractices in his efforts to finance extravagant projects. He was a generous patron of the arts—the greatest artists, including Michelangelo, were in his employ—and he was imbued with the Renaissance desire for art and learning. His ambitious project, the building of St. Peter's in Rome, was a heavy burden on his resources. Funds were procured through loans, through sale of ecclesiastical offices and worst of all, through sales of "indulgences."

The indulgences were an innovation of the sixteenth century. In consideration for a sum of money, an individual was granted an indulgence, which promised to remit all or part of the punish-

POPE ALEXANDER VI
Detail from a fresco by Pinturicchio, in the Vatican.

ments which were dealt out to a sinner after his death. Indulgences did not forgive nor permit sins, and they were granted by
the pope only on the assumption that the transgressor in question
had sincerely shown penitence for his sin. True penitence was
shown by doing good works, and good works were primarily those
which involved money payment to the pope.

The church controlled various other methods of obtaining
money. Besides the ordinary revenues, such as Peter's Pence,
feudal dues, and court expenses, there were "annates" from the
subordinate clergy. It had been customary for every clergyman
to derive his support from the proceeds of a tract of land, called
the "benefice." After receiving the benefice, the clergyman—

POPE LEO X
(From a crayon drawing by del Piombo, in the collection of
the Duke of Devonshire.)

priest, abbot, or bishop—usually paid the first year's revenue, the annate, to his ecclesiastical superior. But a vicious practice developed when the pope handed out benefices in all parts of the Christian world to Italian favorites, who drew the revenues from far-off lands and remained in their luxurious homes as absentee landlords. Germany was particularly exploited by the papacy and absentees, and the German people were loath to see so much money flow out of their country into Italy. It aroused an actual nationalistic resentment in Germany and served to put the papacy further into disgrace.

ERASMUS OF ROTTERDAM
(From the painting by Holbein the Younger in the Louvre
Museum)

THE RISING TIDE OF CRITICISM

While the Catholic Church had been able to resist criticisms
and suppress heretics for so many centuries, by the opening of the
sixteenth century new forces had appeared which were too
strong to be dealt with easily. The vice and weakness of the
clergy came to popular attention, particularly through the writings of humanist scholars. Erasmus and Reuchlin made profound
studies of the Bible and early Christian documents. Emphasis was
laid on a purer Christian organization, on the true message of the
Gospel, and on a humble clergy. The works of these writers

were popularized by various pamphleteers who ridiculed the Church in more coarse and drastic terms.

More radical in their effects were the changes that took place in the economic world. Commerce had increased the supply of money; industries and crafts were freeing themselves from ecclesiastical dominance; a general shift of emphasis from agriculture to urban life and urban occupation was apparent. People became money-minded, and followed pursuits that promised pecuniary enrichment. They cast envious looks on the wealth which the Church possessed, and they were easily won to a movement which promised eventual gains in lands and money. These capitalistic burghers showed great interest in a scheme which entailed the confiscation of Church property, and gladly co-operated with princes to bring about such seizures.

Not only did growing capitalism stir the greed of merchants and manufacturers, but also it further accentuated their comparative freedom of movement and individual strength. They became largely indifferent to their churches, and grew aggressive, vigorous, and assertive.

CONFLICT WITH NATIONALISM

Along with economic and social changes, there came considerable transformation on the political horizon as well. For centuries the Church had been a political power of strong caliber. Its clergy claimed immunity from civil duties, and in spiritual matters held themselves superior to the government. Church property was exempt from civil taxation, while the Church itself levied taxes on all its subjects without interference by the state. All cases involving clergymen, and a few special cases involving outsiders, were tried by the Church's own courts. While such political jurisdiction by the Church proved a blessing in the days of feudalism, it was bound to conflict with the ambitions of worldly rulers when feudalism disintegrated. The growth of national pride and the emergence of nations were accompanied by a desire for absolutism on the part of kings and princes. The Church proved to be the great rival to and hindrance from complete national sovereignty, and rulers realized that not until they had succeeded in subordinating the Church to the state would they be sole heads of their nations.

Under Emperor Maximilian I, the Holy Roman Empire had become particularly strong. Because of significant concentration of power in the Hapsburg family, and due to some very marked territorial additions made by Maximilian, the Hapsburgs were established as sole and undisputed rulers. The days of rivalry among princes for the imperial throne were definitely over. On the other hand, an important counterpart appeared with the development of the imperial diet into a real representative body. Not only the princes but the cities, too, now obtained a vote in

EMPEROR MAXIMILIAN I
(From the painting by Bernhard Strigel)

the diet, and all important imperial issues were fought in this new and strong assembly. No longer was the Emperor awarded the imperial crown by the pope; he was now *elected* by seven high princes, the Electors. With Maximilian the old dualism, the opposition between nobles and the crown, became especially marked. The Emperor's position was materially and politically strengthened by the addition of Bohemia and Hungary through shrewd marriage arrangements. The inheritance of the duchy of Burgundy and the Netherlands provided the Empire with two buffer states against France, a situation which determined the political history of Europe for the next three centuries. A more doubtful blessing was the later annexation of Spain under Charles V, for it decentralized the imperial power, and became of considerable consequence in determining the course of the Reformation.

Thus we notice radical changes in the religious, social, economic, and political atmosphere of Europe. The ground was prepared for a movement that would give prominent expression to indignation and discontent, sentiments which previously had been hidden and suppressed. It would give vent to ambitions, greed, and envy—finally to break forth in an immeasurable and uncontrollable movement which shook the Christian world to its core. It would become an organized protest as soon as there would appear one man, sufficiently convinced, able, and courageous—a vigorous leader. At the end of the sixteenth century such a leader appeared in the person of Martin Luther. He was soon to lead the army of *protesters* into a general *protestant revolution*.

LUTHER

There was nothing unusual about the fact that Luther showed disobedience to his father when he sought admittance to the Augustinian order in Erfurt. The following years in the monastery gave the young and serious monk the usual theology and philosophy taught throughout Europe in his day. In these early years, Luther was driven to search for the real meaning of the Gospel, the real message of God, and his longing for clarity was so great that he felt himself drawing away from the clergy around him. He became convinced of the permanence of his own

ROOM IN WHICH MARTIN LUTHER WAS BORN AT EISLEBEN, GERMANY

sinful nature through Adam and Eve, and he felt that his penitence, however sincere, was hopelessly inadequate to receive God's
grace. He drew on the mystics for inspiration, and suddenly it
became clear to him: only by faith, by blindly believing, could
man win the grace of God. Desperate had been the struggles
before he arrived at this conclusion; joyful was the message of
the Gospel, now that the divine light had shown him the true
meaning.

THE NINETY-FIVE THESES

This was Luther's mental and spiritual state when the issue of
indulgences came up. He had already become a reformer from
within, so it is erroneous to believe that the arrogant sale of indulgences—an external factor—led Luther to oppose the church.
But the effrontery of the salesmen shocked Luther. He believed
that the pope was unaware of the corruption of these clerical
vendors, and he was resolved to draw the Holy Father's attention
to this lamentable state of affairs. He did not know the financial
crookedness involved in the sales—the personal enrichment of
the archbishop of Mainz, his bribing of the papal officers, and his
loans from the Fuggers—his only concern was the corruption of
the clergy and the blessing of Jesus.

It was not so much the idea of "selling" indulgences which
Luther resented, but rather the conception that pardon or grace
could be obtained for any good deeds whatsoever, without having
complete faith, was the intrinsic objection. Firm in the belief
that it could not possibly be the pope's intent to offer indulgences
so promiscuously, and determined to bring the truth of "indulgences" to public attention, on October 31, 1517, he posted the
famous ninety-five theses on the door of the court church in Wittenberg.

The theses, or assertions, were written in Latin and signified a
challenge to a theological debate. Being translated into German,
they were widely read and aroused great popular interest. Luther
still had no intentions of breaking from the Church; he would

have been deeply insulted to be termed a heretic in the sense in which John Huss had been condemned. When the news of Luther's action reached Rome, Pope Leo X summoned the monk to appear before his judges in Rome. However, the pope was prevailed upon by Luther's protector, Frederick of Saxony, to transfer the trial to Germany.

LUTHER'S BREAK WITH ROME

A year after the theses had been posted in Wittenberg, Luther, in his indigent monk's attire, undertook his pilgrimage to Augsburg where the trial was scheduled to take place. He appeared before the papal legate, a cardinal imbued with enough Erasmian learning to be a broadminded and modern prelate. The legate found Luther to be a far more learned and profound theologian than he had expected, but between the two men there was an unbridgeable gap in their respective doctrines. Luther refused to recant, and fled into seclusion.

Following his trial in Augsburg, Luther went one step further in his new theology. In a debate with the celebrated Catholic theologian, John Eck, he admitted openly that certain points of his doctrine coincided with those of John Huss, and expressed his doubt as to the infallibility of the pope and of the Church councils. Having thus identified himself with a notorious heretic, Luther had definitely broken his connection with the Church

Now Luther was convinced that open revolt, not by force but by preaching and writing, was the only way of succeeding in a reform of the Church. He penned a series of vigorous attacks on the Church, pamphlets persuading the nobles to revolt, and other works expounding the new belief. Leo X promptly excommunicated him, and a summons was sent to him by the Emperor commanding his presence at the Diet of Worms. Luther, armed with a writ of protection from Charles V, presented himself to the assembly of all ecclesiastical and lay princes of the Empire. And here too, in his bold, stubborn, German manner, he refused to recant, and consequently was pronounced an outlaw. Luther then retired to the Wartburg, the castle of the elector of Saxony. There he undertook a new translation of the Bible, a work which exerted profound influence on the new High German language.

THE REFORMATION AND GERMAN ECONOMICS

The next few decades witnessed the development of Luther's rebellion into a national movement. We must bear in mind that the new Emperor, Charles V, had his hands full in disciplining his many distant lands. He was kept occupied in the Netherlands, in Spain, and in Italy, and thus could not easily carry out a concentrated suppression of the German heretics. The ranks of the latter swelled with the new support of men from all classes and regions, but especially from the urban centers in the north. The prospect of taking over Church properties appealed to nobles, merchants, and peasants alike. It was relatively easy for powerful princes to lend protection to the movement, since the imperial government was weak and inefficient. Peasants, who had felt miserably oppressed for centuries, were eager to gain improvement of their lot by joining a promising movement.

A contributory cause was the nationalistic feeling that became apparent among the German people during the sixteenth century. Not only was there resentment that so much money flowed into Italy, but Germans actually felt that they were being tyrannized by a foreign power. Slogans were coined which reminded the people of the victory of the German armies under the heroic Arminius against the Roman oppressors. The time had come for the descendants of Arminius again to repel the dominance of the descendants of Varus, the commander of the legion of Rome.

Before long the Reformation seemed to be taking on a distinctly revolutionary character, and the various uprisings that occurred in southern and western Germany did not exactly contribute to the prestige of the movement among the upper classes. One of the most ardent supporters was the poet-knight, Ulrich von Hutten, who wrote a number of pamphlets and poems against the Catholic Church. He was a prophet of the new nationalism, but not in favor of using force.

CITY HALL, AUGSBURG, GERMANY

It was in the city of Augsburg that the treaty was signed which gave the German princes the right to choose Catholicism or Lutheranism as their state religion.

Quite different was the temperament of Franz von Sickingen, an adventurous army leader equal to the most unscrupulous, bold condottiere of the fourteenth century. He laid siege to the city of Trier with the largest army he ever had; but here was a case where the ecclesiastical power, the archbishop of Trier, was fully equal to the worldly knight. Sickingen was forced to leave Trier, was pursued by the armies of the warlike bishop, and finally defeated and killed in his fortress in 1523.

THE PEASANTS' REVOLT

Of much greater magnitude and of a grave nature was the Peasants' Revolt that came in the next year. Most important among the motives of the uprising were economic grievances. The dominant cause was the encroachment upon their old rights by petty nobles, rights which the peasants were determined to defend. They justified their action on grounds of the new teachings of Luther; the divine justice, promised in the Gospel, they chose to take into their own hands. Even the Twelve Articles which they published did not express their real grievances, and were only a "party program" under which they could organize.

The revolt spread through Swabia and Franconia, and was characterized by barbarous roughness. Luther was indignant. He went south to preach obedience and non-violence. But he was shouted down and almost attacked by the wild mobs, whereupon he encouraged the nobility to "smite, strangle, or stab" the rebels. His words were hardly necessary, for the revolt was crushed with the utmost cruelty in 1525. As many as fifty thousand people were slaughtered in the war, and the nobles emerged stronger than ever.

PROTESTANTISM TRIUMPHANT

Meanwhile, another imperial diet at Speyer, while not recognizing the legal status of the new faith, had declared that "each prince should so conduct himself as he could answer for his behavior to God and to the Emperor," a vague declaration but rather favorable to the reformers. When a subsequent diet revoked this declaration by the decision that laws against heretics should be enforced, the Lutherans presented a formal protest. The name Protestant was derived from this protest.

Conciliation between the Catholic and Lutheran princes becoming impossible, Philip Melanchthon, humanist and close friend of Luther, drew up and presented a statement of the Lutheran principles to the diet at Augsburg in 1530. The "Augsburg Confession," as it was called, was rejected by the diet, and conciliation was henceforth out of the question.

The Emperor, becoming vexed by the disobedience of his subjects, planned to exterminate heresy by military force. The Protestant princes responded by uniting in the Schmalkaldic League for effective resistance. A series of conflicts, known as the Schmalkaldic Wars, ensued during which neither the imperial forces nor the Protestants achieved any decisive results. The Peace of Augsburg which followed granted to the Lutheran princes freedom of worship and the right to introduce their own faith within their territories.

Thus, the treaty of Augsburg marked the actual establishment of the Protestant faith. The new church ignored all papal authority, as well as any worship of saints, the Virgin, or relics. Services were now in German, while belief in purgatory, indulgences, and pilgrimages was rejected. In general, it was decided to retain everything in the church organization and services that was not, in their judgment, forbidden by the Bible.

The Reformation did not confine itself to Germany alone. Conditions which favored the Reformation in that country were also largely present in other countries, and the movement spread very rapidly into all parts of northern and central Europe. Due to the varying local conditions, it took on a different character in different countries. Furthermore, the new faith was often used for political purposes. In Denmark, Frederick I and Christian III introduced Lutheranism because it broke the authority of the Catholic Church which rivaled the royal power. The sympathy of Swedish Catholics for union with Denmark moved the king, Gustavus Vasa, to introduce Protestantism into Sweden. The Protestants embodied the national cause, and it was not long until the new faith pushed out the old. In western European countries the Reformation evolved a new type of Protestantism, which, taken as a whole, is known as Calvinism.

KING HENRY VIII OF ENGLAND

Henry cared little if anything about religion, but his marital affairs brought the issue
of England versus the Roman Church to the fore. (From the painting by Holbein the
Younger in Windsor Castle.)

PROTESTANT SECTS AND
COUNTER-REFORMATION

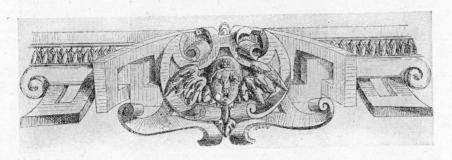

ZWINGLI AND RELIGIOUS WAR IN SWITZERLAND

THE FORERUNNER of the Reformation in Switzerland was Ulrich Zwingli, a contemporary of Luther, and a Catholic priest in the small town of Einsiedeln. His early opposition to the papacy was confined to criticism on certain political abuses in which the papacy was involved. Upon his appointment as a preacher in the Zurich Cathedral, he came out boldly with a denial of papal supremacy, advocating the Bible as the sole source for guidance. The canton of Zurich supported its preacher and declared complete independence from the Catholic Church. Other cantons followed rapidly, and a general revolt turned most of Switzerland to the new doctrine of Zwingli.

Attempts were made to co-operate with the parallel movement led by Luther in Germany. But there existed some insurmountable differences between the doctrines of the two men. Zwingli urged far more radical reforms: he insisted on the reform of the government as well as of the Church. His aim was an ideal state, in which democratic practices in politics and religion would prevail. When five of the Swiss cantons still remained Catholic, he agitated for military coercion by Protestant armies. Civil war ensued between the two factions, with the result that the Protestants were defeated and Zwingli was killed in 1531. The peace that followed provided that each canton could determine its own religion, and consequently Switzerland became partly Catholic, partly Protestant, and has remained so to this day.

CALVIN, "REFORMER OF GENEVA"
The Frenchman after whom the Swiss
reform movement was named.

JOHN CALVIN

Deprived of its founder, the movement was continued under the Frenchman John Calvin, after whom the Swiss reform movement was named. He had been "converted" in a vague way in his early years, and desired to organize a purer Christian church. There had been no formal revolt away from the Church; but France, like other countries, was filled with humanists and religious critics. Lutheran doctrines had penetrated into the country and there was a widespread discontent with the Church.

When it became known that Francis I, king of France, intended to persecute the religious dissenters in his kingdom, Calvin thought it expedient to leave the country. He went to Geneva and aided the citizens in their struggle for liberty against the Catholic duke of Savoy. As a reward he was given the post of chief pastor of the city, a position which came to be a high civil and religious office.

Calvin came to be the head of a theocracy, a government by religious leaders, that exerted a rigid rule on the city of Geneva.

Radical reforms were inaugurated under Calvin's despotism, and Geneva became famous throughout Europe. Worldly amusements, such as dances, theaters, music, and, to some extent, art were looked upon as works of the devil, and were banned from the life of the people. A cloud of austerity hung over the community, while Calvin was busy issuing numerous treatises, as well as a French translation of the Bible. He founded the University of Geneva, which soon enrolled students from France, the Netherlands, Germany and Scotland, and was responsible for the diffusion of Calvinism to many foreign countries.

Calvinists in France came to be known as Huguenots. Although Protestant doctrines did not have nearly as many supporters in France as in Germany, large numbers of middle-class people embraced Calvinism. Here too, it appealed to the moneyed classes and to a large portion of the lower nobility. The civil law courts contained a particularly large element of Protestants, and here it was where royal power was most effectively opposed.

GENEVA, WHERE CALVIN RULED

The theocracy headed by Calvin exerted a rigid rule over the city, in which many "worldly" amusements were banned.

RELIGIOUS WARS IN FRANCE

A period of religious wars began in the middle of the sixteenth century when Catherine de' Medici became regent of France. It was a long internal struggle, interspersed with sporadic attempts at conciliation. Powerful nobles, among them the Bourbons, had taken up the Huguenot cause. On August 24, 1572, there began a series of massacres, initiated by Catherine de' Medici, directed toward the annihilation of the Huguenots. The first of these massacres is known as the St. Bartholomew's Day Massacre. It is estimated that perhaps 10,000 were killed during the frightful period.

War continued with Henry of Navarre leading the Huguenot cause. Henry aspired to become king. Realizing that being a Protestant would prevent the achievement of his ambition, he abjured Protestantism. In 1594, he ascended the throne as Henry IV, although he had actually ruled since 1589. In spite of his defection, Henry came to the aid of the Huguenots. In the Edict of Nantes (1598) he granted them toleration and a degree of self-government.

SPREAD OF CALVINISM ON THE CONTINENT

The Swiss reform movement radiated from Geneva to all adjoining territories. In the southern states of Germany, where Luther's opposition to the Peasants' Revolt had already alienated large numbers from Lutheranism, Calvinism permeated the middle classes. The Treaty of Augsburg, which recognized only the Catholic and Lutheran Churches, prevented the spread of Calvinistic doctrines. In Germany they did not attain toleration until the end of the Thirty Years War.

The Netherlands, due to their proximity to Germany, were naturally exposed to the reform movement. But Charles V tried energetically to stamp out the Lutheran heresy, and he largely succeeded. Yet in the end it was succeeded by another form of Protestantism, for Calvinism was descending from Geneva along the Rhine provinces. In the southern provinces—Spanish

Netherlands—the Catholic Church persisted, but the northern part of the country in its fight for independence from Spain emerged dominantly Calvinistic.

POLITICAL NATURE OF THE ENGLISH REFORMATION

The English Reformation was mainly a political movement clothed with religious phrases. Prior to the Reformation a strong anti-clerical and anti-papal movement had arisen. There had been constant antagonism between the clergy and the people, for it was felt that the clergy formed a state within a state, subject not to English control but to that of Rome.

England had never been one of the strongest pillars of the Catholic Church. From the days of William the Conqueror there had been a dislike of the interference of Rome in English affairs. John Wyclif had fulminated against the interference of the Church in secular affairs. He wished church property to be confiscated, and his ideas on this point had been very well received at the time. After the establishment of Tudor supremacy (1485), English nationalism had grown even stronger and with it the hatred of Rome.

The marital affairs of Henry VIII (1509-1547) brought the issue of England versus the Roman Church to the fore. Henry cared little if anything about religion. At the appearance of Lutheranism he wrote a pamphlet in defense of the Catholic doctrines for which he received the title, Defender of the Faith, from the pope. Later he took the opposite view. His main concern was the consolidation and perpetuation of his rule.

Henry's wife, Catherine of Aragon, was the widow of his younger brother, Arthur. This marriage, although against church law, had been permitted by the pope. Catherine gave birth to many children, but only one, the sickly Mary, survived. Some feared that Catherine had become barren because of the breaking of the church law. Above all, Henry wanted a legitimate male heir in order to insure the continuity of his line. To make matters worse he fell in love with the pretty Anne Boleyn. Soon he turned to the pope, Clement VII, for an annulment of his marriage; but Charles V, the nephew of Catherine, used his influence to prevent Clement from granting the decree.

The king became impatient, especially because Anne was awaiting the birth of a child who, Henry hoped, would be a boy. Henry put a series of acts through Parliament (1529-1534) establishing the Church of England, with the king as its head. The king was divorced from Catherine and soon married Anne who bore him a daughter, Elizabeth.

SUPREMACY OF THE CHURCH OF ENGLAND

The formulation of a religious doctrine for the new church was conditioned by political considerations. At the prospect of an alliance with the German princes, Henry leaned towards Lutheranism. As the prospects faded, his Lutheran feelings did likewise. Toward the end of his reign many Catholic doctrines were restored. However, both Catholics and Protestants were burned for non-conformity to Henry's changing beliefs. Confiscation of monasteries and other church property proceeded all through Henry's reign. The immorality of the clergy had been the excuse for having Parliament pass successive acts confiscating the extensive property of the church. Part of the revenue was devoted to the king's own uses, and the rest was parceled out among the nobles who were most in need of persuasion.

At Henry's death he was succeeded by Edward VI (1547-1553), a son by his third wife, Jane Seymour. Extreme Protestantism flourished for a while, but the early death of the frail king brought Mary (1553-1558) to the throne. Being the daughter of Catherine, she had been brought up a Catholic. In her short reign she incurred the lasting enmity of all England. The Catholic religion was restored and many dissenters were burned. The populace called her "Bloody Mary." Her marriage to the hated Philip II of Spain did not add to her popularity. Mary's efforts to restore Catholicism failed, for she soon died without leaving an heir.

Her successor, Elizabeth (1558-1603), had no other choice but Protestantism. The Catholics regarded Henry's marriage with

QUEEN ELIZABETH OF ENGLAND

Anne Boleyn as void. Hence they looked upon Mary, Queen of Scots, the great-granddaughter of Henry VII, as the legitimate queen. Under Elizabeth the Anglican Church took its final shape. Doctrine was of minor importance to Elizabeth: she was interested in securing conformity and loyalty. The Anglican doctrine, as stated in the Thirty-nine Articles (1583), was most nearly Catholic of all the Protestant creeds.

Elizabeth felt that loyalty to her was synonymous with loyalty to the Church of England. Therefore neither Catholics nor dissenting Protestants were tolerated. A Court of High Com-

QUEEN ELIZABETH BEING CARRIED BY
HER COURTIERS

mission was established to deal with heresy, be it Protestant or Catholic.

Nevertheless, large sections of the English people were not good Anglicans. Within the church a group known as Puritans demanded that Anglicanism be cleansed of its Catholic elements. Outside of the church, Presbyterians, Independents, and other Protestant sects were growing apace. There was also a considerable Catholic minority.

REFORMATION IN SCOTLAND

North of England, in Scotland, events were unfolding rapidly. The Church was in a deplorable condition. The clergy was licentious, turbulent, and much too wealthy for its own good. The Church owned half the wealth of Scotland. The government was in a chaotic condition. The nobles were in a constant state of war, either with the English, or uniting against a weak king or regent.

In 1525 the first Lutheran influence was felt in Scotland. One of the first converts, a noble by the name of Patrick Hamilton, was executed in 1528. The king, James V, attempted to suppress Lutheranism, but he died in 1542, and Cardinal Beaton carried forward the persecution until a few incensed Protestants stopped his activities forever in 1546, by murdering the Cardinal in his castle.

JOHN KNOX OF SCOTLAND

The name which dominates the Scotch Reformation is that of John Knox. Knox had felt the "call" of the Reformation at an early age. Within a short time he was arrested and committed to the galleys. After his release he went to England where his religious convictions became stronger. For a time he was the royal chaplain, but after the accession of "Bloody Mary" he fled to the Continent. Knox soon turned up at Geneva where he was greatly affected by Calvin. From Geneva he became the counselor of the ever growing Scotch Reform party.

At the insistence of the Scotch lords, Knox returned to Scotland where the Protestants already had a pre-eminent position. This fact, together with the support of England, placed power in the hands of the Protestant lords. The return of the fiery Knox fanned the flame. As he thundered against idolatry and popery, the reform movement grew by leaps and bounds.

Mary, Queen of Scots, who had ascended the throne, was compelled to summon a parliament. Here the burghers and small lords assumed control and effected a religious revolution. The new faith was called Presbyterianism, an extreme form of Calvinism and destined to become very influential.

The new faith was accompanied by a new regime, a partly democratic, puritanical theocracy in which the ministers and elders of the church were in control. As in Geneva, the life, manners, and thoughts of the people were subjected to narrow and rigid supervision. In theory, church and state were to work hand in hand. In fact, the "kirk" was the state.

MINOR SECTS—THE RADICAL PROTESTANTS

The Reformation was not only the revolt of Lutheranism and Calvinism against the Catholic Church, but there were also many diverse, opposing factions. It was a thorough religious revolution; a dozen new sects were formed, most of which had an individualistic tendency and failed to co-operate with the leading Protestant faiths.

Most of these minor sects can be classified as radical Protestants. They generally relied on the Scriptures for their beliefs, rejected all those religious usages that were not expressly commanded by the Bible, and usually opposed any form of church organization. What made these radical sects really dangerous, however, was their view of government. They were ardent advocates of a general overthrow of the governments and the establishment of some form of communism or even complete anarchy. It is understandable, therefore, why their members were ruthlessly persecuted by political authorities, as well as by Lutherans, Calvinists, and Catholics.

The Anabaptists were a curious sect, exemplifying the principles of Evangelicalism, a system in which the emotional element predominated. It insisted on an individual, spiritual intimacy with Christ, a relationship which was totally divested of theological doctrine. Evangelicalists believed that the Scriptures, word for word, were divinely inspired. Besides these evangelicalistic principles, Anabaptism believed in baptism for adults, since only the conscious and mature decision of an adult could effect conversion and salvation. The foremost preacher and leader of the Anabaptists was Thomas Münzer. After failing to win Luther's sympathy, he wandered through Germany, preaching political and religious anarchy. He was finally executed after passionately supporting the peasants in their revolt.

A very strange form of Anabaptism existed temporarily in the Westphalian city of Münster. Here a communistic group was organized under John of Leiden, a Dutch tailor. He believed himself to be the successor of King David, and he followed his prototype in everything including the sanction of polygamy. But after a short-lived existence of two years, the city was reoccupied by the Catholics, and "King David's successor" was beheaded.

Anabaptism had many recruits from the lower classes, miners, peasants, and crude craftsmen. It appealed generally to people who wished to live a humble life. There existed several versions of this faith, and among these the tenets of the Mennonites from Holland were prominent. In later times Anabaptists have been called simply Baptists.

Congregationalism did more perhaps than any other faith to cause the creation of numerous sects. Its intrinsic principle is an emphasis on independent "congregations" free from the influence of an institution or even from outsiders. These bodies consisted of lay members who elected their own officers, and who were subject only to the rules of their own congregation. From this tendency toward local freedom there arose various similar sects whose very names indicate their nature: Separatists, Independents, Puritans.

In contrast to the Evangelicalists, there were radical Protestants who rejected the mystical elements of Christianity and sought an intellectual interpretation of religion. These radical groups, which were violently opposed by the Catholic and Protestant Churches, later formed the Unitarian sect.

While most of the radical Protestant sects were comparatively unimportant in the beginning, it is certain that they considerably influenced the further development of Protestantism. The critical tendencies of Unitarians gave rise in the eighteenth century to Deism and the modern "Liberal Christianity" which has become the religious attitude of most Protestants in recent times. Evangelicalism, on the other hand, was instrumental in the development of Puritanism and Methodism in England.

THE CATHOLIC REFORMATION

The great upheaval that was caused by the Protestant Reformation was bound to give rise to a reaction on the part of the Catholic Church. Far from being indifferent, the Church was well aware of the criticism advanced by the rebels, and it made an honest effort to remove the main grounds for discontent. It is difficult to determine whether the Catholic Church would have undergone an inner reform regardless of the Protestant revolt, or whether it reacted to the revolt with a "counter-reformation" to safeguard its existence. In either case, the seriousness of the Protestant revolt certainly gave further impetus to the Catholic reformation. It is significant that the Church possessed so much flexibility of action despite the hardened dogmatism of its teachings. It was just such flexibility as this that has enabled the Catholic Church to overcome all crises and to maintain its position to this day.

The foremost defender of the Catholic Church during the sixteenth century was the former Spanish soldier, Ignatius of Loyola. Realizing the danger that threatened the Church, he resolved to organize an order which would assist in the fight against the rebels. Insisting on absolute obedience, poverty, and chastity, the Jesuits, by educating children and by carrying Catholicism to natives in America, Africa, and Asia, succeeded in winning back

IGNATIUS OF
LOYOLA
Spanish soldier,
founder of the
Jesuit order.

many members. The Jesuits used every possible device to re-establish the authority of the pope; the powers of rulers and traditions of literature, art, and science were enlisted to reinforce the Catholic Church.

Complementary to the aggressive actions of the Jesuits, the Church attempted to fight heresy by reviving an old, but rather ineffective, institution of the thirteenth century, the Inquisition. Adhering rigidly to the "Index," a list containing a series of proscriptions of heretical books, the Inquisition proceeded to punish any possible offenders. It was especially active in Spain and Italy, but as a measure for opposing the Protestants it was decid-edly less effective than other more enlightened methods taken by the Church.

Of great importance in stimulating further reforms was the meeting of the Council of Trent in the middle of the sixteenth century. Although Protestants had been invited to attend, no Protestant was present. The council remedied most of the abuses and clearly defined certain doctrines. All of the principles of the Church, like the sacraments and indulgences, were retained, and Protestantism was completely rejected. This position, while it purified and clarified the Church as an institution, utterly prevented reconciliation with the rebels.

POPE SIXTUS IV
(1471-1484)

A pre-Reformation pope of the famous Italian della Rovere family.
In his pontificate, the Sistine Chapel was built and the Vatican
Library greatly enlarged.

THE GATHERING STORM

THE TREATY OF AUGSBURG in 1555, while it offered
a temporary truce between Catholics and Protestants, contained one vexatious and unsettled issue, the so-called Ecclesiastical Reservation. At the time of the treaty, no agreement
could be reached on this provision, which prohibited further
secularization of church lands. Since land is, after all, of singular
importance because of the wealth that is produced, and since land
was owned and ruled by princes, it is easily conceivable why the
powerful princes were primarily interested in the provisions of
the treaty of Augsburg. For the Catholic princes it had already
meant the loss of a great deal of property; for the Protestant,
"territorial" princes it meant a good possibility of making additional territorial gains. The series of wars which followed more
than half a century after the Augsburg peace was fought by and
in the interest of princes. The Thirty Years War was, therefore,
predominantly a political war.

As a result of the persistent efforts of the Catholic reformation, the Catholic party had succeeded in regaining a large number of territories from the Protestants. In order to retain these
gains and definitely to check any further spread of Protestantism,
the Catholic princes formed a league under the leadership of Duke
Maximilian of Bavaria. Likewise, the Protestants were preparing
for effective opposition by means of the Protestant Union, headed
by the ambitious Frederick, Elector of the Palatinate. But it was

not only an issue involving Catholic and Protestant princes; the danger of Hapsburg absolutism was equally apparent to both parties. Emperor Matthias had made some attempt to centralize Hapsburg power, and there was strong possibility that, being childless, he would be succeeded by the far more ambitious and fanatic Ferdinand of Bohemia.

Because he was a man of iron determination, cool-headed even in the most trying difficulties, and bearing a passionate hatred for anything non-Catholic, the accession of Ferdinand was certain to result in a formidable advance against all Protestant factions. Emperor Matthias had been forced frequently enough, under the pressure of the threatening Turkish peril, and the dangerous Protestant alliances, to make concessions to the latter in regard to the religious and secular provisions of the Augsburg treaty.

By the opening of the sixteenth century there had developed an unbearable tension between all political and religious factions in the Holy Roman Empire. While political greed was the main issue, religious sympathies added new vitality to the alliances, and religious motives furnished a convenient guise for more material ambitions. Sweden's part in the war is a good example of this dual motivation, while the case of France plainly reveals the political considerations, since that country disregarded religious sympathies altogether.

BOHEMIAN PHASE OF THE THIRTY YEARS WAR

In 1618 an event occurred which gave the signal for belligerent action. Bohemian nobles, who feared the election of Ferdinand to the imperial throne, forced their way into a conference of imperial representatives in the castle of Prague, and threw them out of the window into a moat which surrounded it. Following this "defenestration," which was a gross insult to imperial prestige, the Bohemian nobles deposed Ferdinand from the throne of Bohemia and elected the head of the Protestant Union, the Calvinistic Frederick, elector palatine, as the king of Bohemia.

To the great distress of the Bohemian nobles, Matthias I died in the same year and Ferdinand of Bohemia was elected Holy

CASTLE OF EMPEROR CHARLES IV AT PRAGUE
It was here that Bohemian nobles, fearing election of Ferdinand, forced entrance and threw Ferdinand's representatives into the moat.

Roman Emperor. Ferdinand presently proceeded to oust Frederick from the Bohemian throne. Under the command of Count Thurn the Bohemian army staged a revolt in Prague. The Protestant Union joined the Bohemians by sending them the adventurous and hot-headed Count Mansfeld with an army. The new Emperor, Ferdinand II, having now allied himself with the duke of Bavaria, as well as with Spain and the elector of Saxony, was able to inflict a disastrous defeat on the Protestant forces. Frederick lost his Bohemian crown, his lands in the Palatinate were confiscated, and he himself was compelled to seek refuge in Holland. As a consequence of the defeat of Frederick, now called the "Winter King" because of his short-lived kingship, the Catholic armies, with the help of the Spanish, conquered the Palatinate. Protestantism was outlawed in Bohemia, and the Protestant Union was dissolved.

For the Protestants the future looked sinister. The dominance of the Hapsburg crown, with its powerful allies, seemed definitely assured. The Protestants, however, were badly weakened, and lack of mutual agreement made co-operative action impossible. The hopes that were pinned on the Elector Palatine were shattered since his ignominious defeat, and the expected aid from his father-in-law, James I of England, was not forthcoming.

DANISH INTERVENTION

At this point, the Protestant future brightened up temporarily by the intervention of Christian IV of Denmark. Christian was anxious to increase his control over the Baltic Sea, and as duke of Holstein he was opposed to the encroaching authority of the Hapsburgs. Liberally subsidized by the English, and furnished with troops by numerous German princes, he invaded Germany. He was met by the imperial troops under Tilly and the extraordinary general, Albert of Wallenstein. The latter was a Bohemian noble who had reaped an immense fortune out of the confiscated property of rebels. Prompted by boundless ambition for power and wealth, he organized a private army and offered his services to the Emperor. Faced with a new enemy in the person of Christian IV, Ferdinand was only too glad to accept the services of Wallenstein, and appointed him chief commander of the imperial army. The combined forces of Tilly and Wallenstein were able to defeat the Danish king and drive him out of German territory. Hostilities ceased with the signing of the Treaty of Lübeck in 1629, which permitted Christian to keep all of his possessions with the exception of a few German bishoprics.

In the same year, the Catholic party followed up its successes by persuading the Emperor to issue the Edict of Restitution, which provided for the restoration to the Catholic party of all property illegally confiscated by the Protestants since the Treaty of Augsburg in 1555. The Emperor was also persuaded to dismiss the all too powerful General Wallenstein on the grounds that his armies supported themselves by robbing and plundering the German population.

The third phase of the war was characterized by the appearance of a new power on the Protestant side. Gustavus Adolphus, king of Sweden, led by similar political and religious motives as Christian of Denmark, decided to oppose Hapsburg power by aiding the Protestant forces. He was an ambitious monarch who had dreams of extending his influence on the Baltic by a possible acquisition of Pomerania and Prussia, which would raise Sweden to the status of the leading power of northern Europe. He was also convinced that he was the divinely appointed champion of the Protestant cause, just as Ferdinand felt himself to be the ordained protector of the Catholic Church. Gustavus Adolphus landed in Pomerania with a powerful army, the best disciplined and most modern of this time, drove out the imperial forces, and succeeded in gaining the support of the Elector of Saxony and the Elector of Brandenburg. Leading his armies to southern Germany, at the battle of Lützen he was able to defeat the imperial army under the command of Wallenstein, who had been hastily reinstated as commander in chief. At this battle, however, the great protector of Lutheranism in the north was mortally wounded.

Following the death of Gustavus Adolphus, the government of Sweden passed into the hands of the king's loyal adviser and tutor, Oxenstierna, who decided to continue the war with the Hapsburgs. The German princes reaffirmed their support of Sweden in the alliance formed by the League of Heilbronn.

In the succeeding battles no decisive advantage was gained by either side until, in the battle of Nördlingen, the Swedish army was practically destroyed. In the same year, Brandenburg and Saxony withdrew from the war and peace was made with the Emperor at Prague in 1635.

FRENCH INTERVENTION AND END OF THE THIRTY YEARS WAR

France, under the dictatorship of the shrewd Cardinal Richelieu, had given little actual support to the Protestants up to this time. Richelieu, although a Catholic, was moved by other than religious considerations. His main fear was the threatening absolutism and hegemony of the Hapsburg family, and he was determined to oppose them by fair means or foul. Negotiations had already resulted in subsidies for Gustavus Adolphus, and now, after his death, there was strong possibility of Sweden's withdrawal from the war. The ambitious cardinal now openly declared war against the Empire and sent his ablest generals, Condé and Turenne, to reconquer the Palatinate of the Rhine and to oppose the Spanish forces in the Netherlands. In 1636 the war lost much of its meaning and vitality due to the sudden death of Ferdinand II. The new monarch, Ferdinand III, was desirous of peace, and, because of the general exhaustion of most of the participants, negotiations for peace were begun. Finally, after several years of indecision and disagreement, the Peace of Westphalia was signed in 1648.

Under the terms of the Peace of Westphalia, Sweden received as a fief of the Empire, Pomerania and various German cities on the Baltic coast, as well as a few bishoprics and a large sum of money. France was given the important cities of Metz, Verdun, and Toul. Brandenburg was compensated for the loss of Pomerania by the gain of the city of Magdeburg and three other bishoprics in central Germany. In this treaty also, the United Netherlands and Switzerland were finally recognized as independent republics. In general, there was an attempt to return to the status quo before 1618. The religious conflicts were settled in a compromise giving recognition to Lutherans and Calvinists on an equal footing with Catholics. Württemberg, Baden, and the lower Palatinate were permitted to exercise their new religion, while the rebels of Austria and Bohemia were given no additional rights. The ecclesiastical reservation was to be enforced in the future, while all territories secularized before January 1, 1624, were to remain as such.

CLIMAX OF THE REFORMATION

Thus ended the great conflict between Catholics and Protestants, between the Hapsburgs and their enemies, between the old time and the new. Protestantism was able to gain complete recognition, but it was not able to eliminate Catholicism. It is erroneous to think that, with this recognition, the principle of religious freedom and toleration was achieved; after all, the Protestant showed as much intolerance toward Catholicism and other Protestant sects as did the old Catholic Church toward them.

Religious freedom is a very recent achievement, and is only indirectly due to the efforts of Protestantism. It is often believed also, that Protestantism furthered the democratic principle; but this is true only of the Calvinists with the system of self-government in their organization. It is also interesting to note the opinion of some scholars that modern capitalism was in part derived from the Reformation. Here too, the Calvinists may be regarded as largely responsible for the ethics of work and thrift which were advocated in Calvinistic teachings, and which were favorable to the accumulation of capital.

PART II

EMERGENCE OF EUROPEAN NATIONS

CHRISTIAN RECONQUEST OF SPAIN AND PORTUGAL

DURING THE MIDDLE AGES the Moors conquered nearly all of the Iberian peninsula. As time went on, however, a group of Christian feudal principalities managed to establish themselves in the north, while the Moors were continually pushed southward. The Christian states gradually united into a few large political units, so that about 1300 there existed three large Christian kingdoms in the peninsula: Aragon, Castile, and Portugal, in addition to the smaller states of Moorish Granada and Christian Navarre.

Portugal was on the verge of becoming a flourishing nation in the fifteenth century. This alluring prospect was largely the result of the courageous efforts of Portuguese explorers and traders, and the achievements of many capable kings. The discoveries and adventures of the Portuguese sailors will be discussed in a succeeding section. It suffices to mention here that Prince Henry the Navigator is a famous figure in Portuguese history, and that his name indicates the sponsorship of numerous discoveries and explorations. The beginnings of a large Portuguese empire were laid by Prince Henry and his intrepid seamen.

The monarchy in Portugal, like that in many other countries of that day, was absolute. After 1521, the Portuguese Cortes, or parliament, ceased to meet regularly and exerted little political influence.

In 1580 the Portuguese king died and left no immediate heir. Consequently, the Portuguese throne was won by Philip II of Spain, who was a close relative of the deceased Portuguese king. Thus two large colonial empires were united under one head, and for over sixty years Spanish and Portuguese colonial expansion and exploration in the New World went hand in hand.

The history of Spain as a modern state begins with the marriage of Ferdinand of Aragon and Isabella of Castile in 1469, thereby unifying the largest two Christian kingdoms in the Iberian peninsula under one head. After their marriage, Ferdinand and Isabella set out to conquer the rest of the peninsula excepting that part held by Portugal, and in 1492, Granada, the last Moorish stronghold, was captured. The surviving Mohammedans were promised liberty of religion, but this promise was broken and persecutions took place. Finally, in 1610, all the Mohammedan survivors, numbering over half a million, were exiled from Spain into North Africa. This expulsion, as well as the persecution of the Jews, greatly weakened the commerce and industries of the country, which previously had been limited almost solely to these two non-Christian peoples.

NATIONAL CONSOLIDATION

The methods of internal consolidation employed by Ferdinand and Isabella in Spain were much like those used by monarchs of the other rising states of Europe. In order to secure co-operation of the middle class against the ambitions of the nobility, the former were given extensive protection and privileges. Trade and commerce were fostered everywhere.

Also, Isabella and Ferdinand established the infamous Inquisition as a state institution. The Inquisition originated in the attempt of the Church to ferret out all unbelievers such as Jews, heretics, and others. Pope Sixtus IV turned the control of the Inquisition over to the Spanish state in 1478. It soon became a state tribunal, entirely under the control of the sovereign. Nonconformists in religion were regarded as dangerous to the security of the state. It is asserted that between 1401 and 1492, two thousand Jews were burned alive in Andalusia. The methods of the Inquisition were extremely cruel, and no attempts were made to give fair trials. The introduction of the Inquisition into the Spanish Netherlands proved to be a boomerang to the Spanish monarchs.

For a time, however, Spain was destined to become the greatest nation in Europe. Several factors contributed to this phenomenon. In their long struggle with the Moors the Spanish armies gained much experience, and were considered the best and bravest in Europe. Spain was also one of the richest countries in Europe. Wealth flowed in from the West Indies, Mexico, and Peru. The discovery of America had been sponsored by Isabella and Ferdinand, and Spain became a great empire builder. In addition, the Spanish kings by advantageous marriages and clever intrigue were able to add to their territory, power, and glory.

ATTEMPTS TO UNIFY THE HOLY ROMAN EMPIRE

We must now turn our attention to the Holy Roman Empire, which had been gradually decreased in territory and influence. By the fifteenth century the development of independent states, such as France, Spain, and England, had deprived the Emperor of all allegiance from these countries. The Empire from now on was to include primarily the German-speaking countries. Its internal weakness was proverbial; decentralization and confusion were its characteristics. Duchies, baronies, counties, and free cities continually asserted their independence and acknowledged only nominal allegiance to the Emperor. They were involved in continual warfare with one another, and at times even took the field against the Emperor himself. It was only the fear of Slavic and Turkish invasions that gave the Empire some cohesion.

By 1400 it had become the custom of the German princes called Electors, to select a member of the house of the Austrian Hapsburgs as Holy Roman Emperor. One of the Hapsburgs, Maximilian I, Emperor from 1493 to 1519, is known for his military campaigns into Italy, his hostility to France, and his attempt to bring unity to the Empire. He gathered the Diet of German princes at Worms in 1495, and put an end to the pernicious warfare between petty princes and nobles by compelling them to bring their quarrels before a new supreme court, the Imperial Chamber. He also established a regular postal system, and divided the Empire into ten districts for the better maintenance of public order.

A series of significant matrimonial alliances, of great importance to the reigning Austrian family and to Spain, were arranged during this period. The marriage of Maximilian with Mary of Burgundy gave control of the Netherlands to the Hapsburgs. Maximilian's heir was Philip who married Joanna, the daughter of Ferdinand and Isabella of Spain. Philip and Joanna had two sons who became prominent in European politics. The elder of these sons was Charles, who inherited the Austrian possessions from his father and the Spanish possessions from his mother. The younger son was Ferdinand, founder of the German Hapsburgs, who married the sister of the last king of Bohemia and Hungary. This union brought the crowns of those countries to the house of Hapsburg.

After the death of Philip in 1506, Charles became king of Spain and lord of the Netherlands when he was only six years old. In 1519, on the death of his grandfather, Maximilian, Charles inherited the Austrian possessions of the Hapsburgs. The German princes elected Charles as Holy Roman Emperor in 1519. His activities as Emperor were largely determined by events which had been taking place in eastern Europe.

TURKISH THREAT TO EUROPE

In the late Middle Ages, Mongol pressure forced the Turks westward in Asia and finally brought them into Europe. Earlier it was the Seljuk Turks who were warring with the Byzantine emperors in Syria and Asia Minor. Presently the Ottoman Turks took their place, and founded the great Ottoman empire. They made the Black Sea a Turkish lake, and held all the territory on the east and south of the Mediterranean. They ruled at Bagdad, Alexandria, Cairo, Tunis, Tripoli, and Algiers, as well as at Smyrna, and later at Constantinople.

MARY OF BURGUNDY
First wife of Maximilian I.

Between 1350 and 1400 the Turks transferred their military activities to eastern Europe and crossed the Bosporus. The Byzantine emperors, who from the west were harassed by the Slavs, could offer little resistance. By 1400 the Turks had conquered the entire Balkan peninsula except Constantinople. That city fell in 1453 after a long siege by the Turks under Mohammed II.

All Europe became alarmed at the advance of the infidels, as the Turks were called; but, because of internal dissensions, little was done about it.

Sultan Suleiman II (1520-1566) intended to extend his empire still farther. He conquered all of present Rumania and Hungary, and finally laid siege to Vienna in 1529; but here the Turkish avalanche was finally stopped, although the Emperors and the Polish kings failed in several attempts to drive the Turks from Rumania and Hungary.

The Ottoman empire by its nature was not a homogeneous political unit. It was inhabited by hundreds of different peoples, belonging to various races, speaking different languages, and professing different religions. What held this empire together was the military prowess of the Turks and the administrative ability of their sultans. The latter were not always the intolerant tyrants often pictured. Their Christian and Jewish subjects were usually granted religious liberty under special edicts of toleration.

However, the advance of the Turks into Europe was regarded as a great danger by the Western world at that time. It explains why the German princes selected the strongest one among their number as leader—the man who must meet this invader.

CHARLES V AND HIS DIFFICULTIES

The empire of Charles V did not constitute a unified, central state, but it was a group of states, brought together by marriage and inheritance under the House of Hapsburg. This fact made the tasks of Charles V almost overwhelming. Each of the political units under his control had to be ruled according to its own administrative system, its own laws and customs, and in its own language. Conflicting interests had to be reconciled and some sort of unity had to be achieved in order to present a united front to foreign foes. While Charles V thus headed an aggregation of many countries, their lack of unity detracted greatly from the total strength one might have expected them to possess. Charles V had an unusual quota of administrative ability, a quality which enabled him to overcome many seemingly insurmountable obstacles.

Above: FRANCIS I OF FRANCE
Left: CHARLES V OF THE HOLY
ROMAN EMPIRE

Charles was opposed by Francis, both having been rival claimants for the crown of
the Holy Roman Empire.

FRANCIS I, CHARLES V, AND CARDINAL ALESSANDRO FARNESE
ENTERING PARIS
(Fresco by Taddeo and Zuccaro)

During most of his reign, Charles was forced to oppose the ambitious French king, Francis I. France was almost surrounded by Hapsburg territories, a situation which was far from pleasing. Francis and Charles had been rival claimants for the crown of the Holy Roman Empire; but the latter's bribes proved more decisive than those of Francis in the election at Aix-la-Chapelle in 1520. The two monarchs also had designs on territories in other parts of Europe, especially Italy, Flanders, and Navarre. The outcome of these struggles usually favored Charles V, but Francis I and his successors were by no means inclined to renounce their plans to weaken the Hapsburgs.

Charles V was also bothered by many internal problems. He was a devout Catholic, and for both religious and political reasons he watched with alarm the growth of Protestantism and dissension in the various parts of his huge empire. His failure to deal with and to suppress these irresistible religious developments has been dealt with in the discussion of the Reformation.

Although born in the Netherlands, which Charles continued to regard as his native land, he spent most of his time in Spain. The latter country during his reign was easily the predominant nation in Europe, and Charles gained the loyalty of the Spanish by making them feel that he regarded their country as the most important part of the empire. His persecution and extermination of the Moors received hearty approval. Also, at this time, a wonderful colonial expansion was taking place and Spain was building a great empire in the Americas. In his various wars Charles relied greatly on aid from the Iberian peninsula. Without the abundance of gold, resources, and the superior soldiers and ships of Spain, Charles could not have been successful in war.

The people of the Netherlands were personally loyal to Charles, whom they regarded as one of themselves. But the increasing foreign and Spanish influence was greatly resented. They also felt that the growing wealth of the Netherlands, which were heavily taxed, was used chiefly to advance imperial interests rather than for their own benefit. Heresy also grew by leaps and bounds, especially in the north. Lutheran, Anabaptist, and, later, Calvinist doctrines were widely accepted. The persecution of these heretics by Charles V was resented, even by non-Protestants. The Dutch revolt against Spain did not take place, however, until the rule of Charles's son, Philip II of Spain.

CHARLES'S POLICIES IN THE HOLY ROMAN EMPIRE

The attempts of Charles V at reform in the Germanies proved to be a total failure. The German peoples at the time had some vague feeling that they really belonged to one race and nation; but the conflicting interests and ambitions of princes, dukes, kings, and free cities were too great to be overcome by this still hardly conscious feeling of national unity. A German national state was to be achieved much later and by an entirely different process.

At the Diet of Worms in 1521, Charles outlined plans for the political consolidation of the Empire. A Council of Regency was created, representing the interests of twenty-three German princes. This council was intended to bring stability and uniformity to the Empire, so that continuity might be secured in case of the absence or death of the Emperor. The Council, however, found itself powerless to overcome dissension. It had no administrative and judicial branches and no military power to carry out its decisions, which were simply ignored or badly enforced by the various rulers. Many princes had developed Lutheran sympathies. The attempts of the Council to put down two rebellions, one in 1522 and the other, the so-called Peasants' Revolt in 1524, were only partially successful. The German princes themselves stepped in to deal with these rebellions, which clearly showed the growing economic discontent of the time.

THE STRUGGLE WITH THE TURKS

When Charles V became Emperor, the Ottoman empire included what formerly had been the Byzantine empire. During his reign, Ottoman encroachments on Hungary and Bohemia were the order of the day. Charles's brother, Ferdinand, held the throne of these two countries during the Turkish advances. The Moslem danger became so great that Ferdinand was forced to make concessions to the Protestant heretics in his territories. Charles also temporarily had to come to terms with the Protestants in the Empire, in order to give more effective aid to Ferdinand in his struggle with the Turks.

The Turkish siege of Vienna failed in 1529, but their advance into Austria was resumed in 1532. Charles's preoccupation with his other possessions left Ferdinand to carry on the struggle alone. In 1547 he and the Emperor were forced to sign a treaty of peace with Sultan Suleiman the Magnificent, leaving most of Hungary in the possession of the latter. Hungary agreed to pay the sultan an annual tribute of thirty thousand ducats.

RELIGIOUS ISSUE TEMPORARILY SOLVED

Meanwhile, religious strife tore the Empire asunder. Charles at times was able to subdue the various princes, but could not check the spread of the Protestant faith among the German people. In 1552 a revolt of the German princes, aided by Henry II of France, forced the Emperor to compromise. A religious truce was arranged at the Diet of Augsburg in 1555, referred to as the Religious Peace of Augsburg. It was agreed that each German prince was to choose the state religion for his own territory. The religion of each state thus became that of its ruler. The choice lay only between Lutheranism and Catholicism, however; nothing was said about Calvinism. It was decided that the Protestant princes could retain the lands confiscated by them prior to 1552.

Charles V abdicated in 1556, shortly after the Peace of Augsburg. He experienced one more disappointment when the German Electors refused to choose his son Philip as their Emperor. Philip therefore became king of Spain and Italy and lord of the Netherlands, while Ferdinand, by Charles's will, inherited Austria and was elected Emperor of the Holy Roman Empire.

CONSOLIDATION OF ROYAL POWER IN FRANCE

THE BARONS SUBDUED

THE DEVELOPMENT OF FRANCE as a national unit illustrates how the multitudes of feudal fiefs in Europe were consolidated into various larger areas, each with its own language, common culture, common national feeling, and political organization. It answers the questions which no doubt have often arisen in the reader's mind: How did nations arise? How did it happen that the anarchic, feudal arrangement of thousands of more or less independent political units was finally replaced by relatively few and larger units—the European countries as we know them today?

We have already seen how the decline of feudalism was accompanied by such factors as the rise of towns, the growth of trade, and the ascendancy of the middle class. While formerly there had been only the simple rural economy of serfs and nobles, the burghers in the towns now became a powerful influence. Later we shall see how the kings, in order to consolidate their position, used the new middle class as an ally in their struggle against the nobles who were envious of the growing power of the king.

Philip II (1180-1223) was the first king of France who, by a series of successful wars, was able to subdue the recalcitrant barons in his own territory. By conquest and by the inheritance of

LOUIS IX
King of France for more than forty years.

LOUIS XI
One of the most crafty of the Bourbon kings.

Artois he also enlarged the scope of his domain. For more than forty years in the thirteenth century, Louis IX furthered centralization of power in the reigning house. He inaugurated internal reforms and deprived the feudal lords of absolute judicial authority over their serfs by permitting appeal to the royal courts.

The kings now strengthened their position by doing away with the civil and military services of the barons. Civil servants were recruited from the middle class and the groundwork was laid for a faithful royal bureaucracy on which the king could depend in the administration of the country. Mercenary troops and hired fleets replaced the intermittent aid of the undependable military bands formerly supplied by the feudal barons. It is easy to surmise that the latter measure especially added to royal independence and power. Great sums of money were required to support the operations of these royal armies, and it was not strange that the people failed to enjoy the game of hide-and-seek they were compelled to play with tax collectors.

The invention and use of gunpowder and cannons also weakened the position of the barons. Hitherto, it was possible for a feudal lord to wage war or go out on a plundering expedition, and, when danger arose, to retreat into his castle. The mercenary armies of the king, equipped with primitive artillery, were now able to break down the once impregnable castle walls.

To gain the favor and financial support of the middle class, or *bourgeoisie*, Philip IV established the French parliament, or Estates General. Its importance lay in the fact that not only the representatives of the clergy and nobility were summoned, but also that the middle class was asked to send its representatives. The latter were called the "third estate."

The French parliament, however, did not gain the power and prominence of its British counterpart. Under more powerful kings the French Estates General was never able to wring liberties and privileges from the king. The French people never had a Magna Charta. The English people were gradually able to abolish royal absolutism through the growing dependence of the king on Parliament for money. In France royal power, which had served to weld a great people into one nation, and which retained control of its own purse, later became oppressive and led inevitably to one of the greatest social upheavals of all time—the French Revolution.

BURGUNDIAN AMBITIONS

The largest independent fief that challenged the power of kings was the duchy of Burgundy. We have seen how the duke of Burgundy aided the English in their invasion of France during the Hundred Years War by attacking the French from the east. The dukes of Burgundy aspired to a powerful independent kingdom of their own. Already by conquest, inheritance, and marriage they had greatly extended their territories, which for a long time included the entire Netherlands. Finally, Charles the Bold (1467-1477) nearly succeeded in defeating France, but by arousing the ill-will of his warlike neighbors, the Swiss, he soon faced enemies on all sides and was killed in battle. The clever intrigue of Louis XI of France contributed much to this result.

Mary of Burgundy, who succeeded Charles the Bold, was aided in her struggle with France by her husband, Maximilian

of Hapsburg. Upon her death Maximilian was forced to surrender
the duchy of Burgundy to France. The remainder of his holdings,
including the Netherlands, was incorporated into the territories
of the Austrian Hapsburgs.

FAILURE IN ITALY

During the fifteenth century the French kings made a series
of invasions into Italy. Milan and Naples were easily conquered
by Charles VIII and later again by Louis XIII. Few lasting results remained from these invasions. France for a time held the
duchy of Milan, and it was the French invasion which led to the
downfall of the Medici in Florence. The warlike Pope Julius II
had first united with the French in their conquest of Venice.
When he had gained his objectives he made a separate peace with
Venice. By forming the Holy League, composed of the Papacy,
Venice, Spain, as well as the Swiss, Maximilian of Hapsburg, and
Henry VIII of England, Julius soon drove the French from
Italian soil.

Italy, however, was left in a state of disunity, anarchy, and
intrigue. Spain had conquered the kingdom of Naples. The
emergence of Italy as a national state was delayed for three more
centuries.

TRIUMPH OVER CHURCH AND NOBLES

Louis XI (1461-1483) was one of the most crafty of the
Bourbon kings. Under him France was strengthened and more
closely unified. Clerical privileges were curtailed, judicial appeals
to Rome were forbidden, and the rights of the French church
were emphasized. The extinction of the House of Anjou in 1480
added Anjou, Provence, Maine, and Lorraine to the royal domains of Louis XI. Several powerful nobles were executed on
various charges. Internal order was restored and the king thereby
gained the favor of the middle class, which desired peace and
security for its trading activities. The *bourgeoisie* were given
further privileges, such as the election of their own magistrates.

SAVONAROLA
Great monk preacher who welcomed the ad-
vent and rule of Charles VIII in Florence.

Industry and trade were greatly encouraged, and with Louis XI the medieval system in France almost came to an end.

His son Charles VIII (1483-1498) was able to suppress a serious rebellion led by the duke of Orleans and Brittany. The marriage of the king with Anne, the duchess of Brittany, in 1491 added this last great feudal territory to his dominions. The boundaries of France at the end of the fifteenth century were thus very much like those of the France we know today.

RIVALRY BETWEEN FRANCE AND SPAIN

Francis I, king of France during the first half of the sixteenth century, is of importance to world-history because of his struggles with Charles V, emperor of the Holy Roman Empire, king of Spain and Austria, and lord of the Netherlands, for the leadership in European affairs. From this time also dates the role of England as the preserver of the balance of power in Europe. The early diplomatic attempts of England under Henry VIII to preserve the *status quo*, or prevailing conditions, in Europe were not as successful as they were to be in later English history.

The territories of Charles V almost surrounded those of France. To the south lay Spain, to the east lay the Holy Roman Empire, and the Netherlands bordered on the north. Francis did not enjoy seeing Hapsburg territory wherever he looked, but there were other reasons for enmity with Charles V. Francis had been a candidate for the imperial crown, and there were certain provinces in the Netherlands which he desired, while both monarchs hoped to extend their power in Italy. Here Francis controlled the duchy of Milan, and Charles V, as king of Spain, ruled the kingdom of Naples. It was in Italy that most of the fighting took place.

The allied forces of the emperor and Pope Leo X drove the French from Milanese territory, and established the power of Charles V in northern Italy. Francis himself was taken to Spain as a captive. He obtained his freedom in 1526 by the Treaty of Madrid, in which he renounced his claims to Milan, Genoa, and Naples. But on his return to France he promptly repudiated the cession as having been dictated by force.

Soon the people of Italy and the pope, tired of foreign interference, turned in vain against their would-be liberators. The Emperor's troops crossed the Alps, and in 1527 took place the infamous sack of Rome by German and Spanish troops. The Emperor's conquest of Italy was completed in 1530 and he became virtual master of all Italy.

At the Peace of Cambrai in 1529, Francis was forced to pay a large indemnity and again to renounce his claims to Italy. Charles, crowned "king of Italy" and Emperor by Pope Clement VII at Bologna, was the last ruler to hold both titles.

HENRY IV AND THE DUKE OF SULLY

As we have seen in a previous section, the internal history of France during the sixteenth century was characterized by bloody religious conflict. In the latter part of the century political and religious motives became mixed in the civil struggle, which was not always beneficial to the Protestant cause. Henry IV, who ascended the throne in 1589, increased his political power by insti-

HENRY IV OF FRANCE

tuting religious reforms. Although the religious problem was of great importance, Henry's most difficult tasks were to restore prosperity to a country devastated and disordered by civil war, and to restore the prestige of the monarchy. He began a series of political and economic reforms which were continued in part by his successors and which made France the greatest and strongest nation in Europe.

Henry IV, like most French kings, lived a life of personal pleasure and extravagance; and, like his successors, he knew how to select capable civil servants. The most noted of these was his chief adviser and minister, the duke of Sully. The latter strictly controlled the landed gentry and provincial governors. He fostered agriculture, which he believed to be the foundation of the

MARGARET, WIFE OF HENRY IV OF FRANCE

nation's prosperity. A beginning was made with the building of roads and canals, which until then had scarcely existed. France soon had the best roads in Europe. Commerce was stimulated thereby, but the political significance of a good system of highways should not be forgotten. It enabled the kings to move their troops swiftly and economically.

Sully's contribution to the financial administration of France is of importance. Within ten years the national debt was reduced eighty-five per cent. Between 1596 and 1609 the revenue was more than doubled; still later the treasury showed a large surplus, the arsenals were prepared for war, and the fleet was well equipped. This new emphasis on national efficiency and capable administration was something new in the history of Europe. It

RICHELIEU, CARDINAL AND STATESMAN
Actual ruler of France for twenty years during the reign of Louis XIII, Richelieu laid the
foundation for the power and influence exercised by Louis XIV.

was a factor of primary importance in the building of the new national state. It aided the king in consolidating his power, both internally and externally.

RICHELIEU—CARDINAL AND STATESMAN

When Henry IV was assassinated in1610, Louis XIII ascended the throne. During his reign the Estates General, or national parliament, was summoned for the last time before the French Revolution. Its powers were so limited that it exercised little real authority. The centuries before the Revolution in France were characterized by absolute royal power with little or no popular control.

France was actually ruled by Cardinal Richelieu, one of the greatest of modern statesmen, diplomats, and administrators, for nearly twenty years during the reign of Louis XIII. He was a capable and resolute ruler, unscrupulous as to means and clear-headed about his aims. He crushed all plots against his power and overcame the resistance of the nobles. The Huguenots, suppressed primarily for political reasons, were finally mastered in the capture of their chief stronghold, La Rochelle, in 1629. The final outcome of the Thirty Years War was greatly influenced by his policy and his success. France at his death in 1642 succeeded Spain as the foremost nation in Europe. Richelieu thus laid the foundations, both at home and abroad, for the power and influence exercised by Louis XIV.

MAZARIN AND THE FRONDE

THE REIGN OF LOUIS XIV (1643-1715) ushered in a period of warfare which continued, with intervals of peace, from about 1650 to 1815. These wars centered largely around the struggle of France and Great Britain for colonial supremacy, and the desire of France to become the foremost power on the European continent. These struggles far exceeded previous wars in importance if we judge by the number of combatants engaged, the power and resources of the belligerents, the skill of the commanders, and the interest attached to the chief battles fought on land and sea.

Louis XIV was but five years of age at the death of his father, Louis XIII, and the regency was held by his mother Anne. Fortunately, the young king was aided in his early years by the capable advice of his chief minister, Mazarin. The latter was a political and diplomatic pupil of the great Richelieu. It was he who continued Richelieu's policy of interference in the Thirty Years War, and gained Alsace for France by the Treaty of Westphalia in 1648. He also succeeded in defeating the Hapsburg king of Spain, and by the Treaty of the Pyrenees France gained Roussillon and a part of the Spanish Netherlands.

LOUIS XIV OF FRANCE
His court "became a symbol for sparkling
fountains, beautiful women and conspicuous
luxury."

A civil uprising, called the Fronde, occupied the attention of
Mazarin from 1648 to 1652. It was the last effort on the part of
the nobility to regain their lost authority. They were joined by
some groups of the middle class, which had become alarmed at
the rise of royal absolutism. Mazarin had abolished the weak Paris
parlement, or supreme court, and this action had been a cause for
alarm. In addition to its judicial powers, the *parlement* had obtained the right to "register" the royal decrees: it formerly
promulgated the king's orders as laws to the country. At times
the *parlement* had shown a desire to refuse to promulgate these
decrees if in its view they did not promote the welfare of the
country.

The *parlement* defied the young king and his minister in 1648,
and claimed that its consent was necessary to any kind of taxation.
The mob in the street supported these demands by active street
fighting. For the moment Mazarin had to give in; but, once the
troops were recalled from Germany, he annulled his concession
and deprived the *parlement* of all its political and financial powers.
The nobility's power was broken, and except for minor uprisings royal absolutism went unchallenged until the final reckon-
ing—the French Revolution.

"MASTER OF KINGCRAFT"

Louis personally assumed direction of state affairs when Mazarin died in 1661. At once he showed himself a master of his position. Macaulay describes him as "a consummate master of kingcraft—of all the arts which most advantageously display the merits of a prince, and best hide his defects." At all times he was in full command of the situation. Never did a European sovereign demand and receive a submission so closely resembling that given to an oriental sultan. He wielded despotic power. Although he seldom employed force in internal affairs, he always kept it in the background. Louis, like James I of England, thoroughly believed in the divine and absolute right of kings. But unlike James he did not have to deal with deep-rooted traditions of popular representation and liberty which greatly modified the Stuart's claim to absolutism.

Louis XIV, though somewhat pompous, was dignified and graceful in his manners. He promoted French culture, art, and the sciences. His name is closely associated with those of Corneille, Racine, and Molière. The court at Versailles became a symbol for sparkling fountains, beautiful women, and conspicuous luxury.

COLBERT AND LOUVOIS

Louis possessed a remarkable talent for choosing as ministers, diplomats, administrators, and generals, capable men from all ranks of life who were the ablest of their day. Foremost in this distinguished company was Colbert, the financial adviser and administrator. He somewhat lightened the financial burden of the peasants by substituting general taxes for their special burdens. He encouraged agriculture, manufacture, and commerce, and developed France by the building of roads and canals. The Languedoc Canal, which joins the Mediterranean and the Atlantic, was constructed by him. Under his guidance France for the first time emerged as a great naval power, and various colonies were

Courtesy German Railroads Information Office

THE MIGHTY ZUGSPITZE IN THE BAVARIAN ALPS
"It was the ambition of Louis to extend the frontiers of France to the Alps, the
Pyrenees, and the Rhine."

acquired. Louvois was Louis' great war minister. Under his supervision France evolved the efficient military machine which Louis
used to keep Europe in turmoil for nearly fifty years.

DUTCH OPPOSITION TO THE GRAND MONARCH

It was the ambition of Louis to extend the frontiers of France
to the Alps, the Pyrenees, and the Rhine, and ultimately to gain
European predominance through the annexation, by alliance with
the House of Bourbon, of all the Spanish dominions. No sacrifices
of blood and resources by the French people were considered too
large to achieve these grand designs. Little respect was shown
either to obligations of public faith or to foreign treaties. Wars
were begun whenever opportunity presented itself.

When the French king's father-in-law, Philip IV of Spain,
died in 1665, Louis claimed the Spanish Netherlands, and in 1667
Turenne marched into Flanders at the head of fifty thousand
French troops. The Flemish fortresses were soon conquered, and
so was the territory called Franche-Comté. Holland and England
now became alarmed and feared a disturbance of the balance of
power in Europe. Under the leadership of the capable Dutch
statesman, Jan de Witt, the famous Triple Alliance was formed
between England, Holland, and Sweden. This combination was
too much for Louis, and in the Treaty of Aix-la-Chapelle he was
forced to give up Franche-Comté, but retained the fortresses of
Flanders.

Bent on revenge, Louis bought the neutrality of England by
the secret Treaty of Dover with Charles II. A great French army
under Condé and Turenne poured into Holland. Louis accompanied this army in person. He was opposed by the young and
apparently feeble William of Orange, who afterward became
William III of England. The French soon overran most of Holland
and all seemed lost for the Dutch cause. But the French forces
were driven from much of the country when William ordered the
dykes to be cut, and so turned Holland into a sea out of which
Amsterdam stood up like a vast fortress.

William, by capable statesmanship, formed a new coalition against the French, composed of the Emperor, the Elector of Brandenburg, and the Spanish Netherlands. De Ruyter fought effectively on the sea against combined French and English fleets. In the end the French were forced to leave the Netherlands, and the Rhine countries became the new battlefields. The outcome of the war was indecisive and the Peace of Nimwegen in 1678 left France in possession of many of the Flanders fortresses and, in addition, of Franche-Comté.

Louis did not disband his army, however. His troops took part in numerous wars and campaigns. More territory was gained for France in the Rhineland, including the city of Strassburg. Louis aided Austria in its struggle against the Turks, and in order to weaken Spain he worked to sustain the independence of Portugal. Quarrels with the pope were settled in Louis' favor and he made his influence felt in Italy.

BALANCE OF POWER RESTORED

In 1686, French aggression again led William of Orange to rouse Europe against Louis, by forming the League of Augsburg which included the Emperor, several German princes, Sweden, Spain, and the Netherlands. In retaliation the French invaded Germany, devastated the Rhenish Palatinate, and sacked Mannheim and Heidelberg.

Three years later, William of Orange, now king of England, succeeded in forming the "Grand Alliance" by adding England to the League of Augsburg. The French fleet was defeated at La Hogue when it was about to transport James II and a French army into England to regain the throne for the House of Stuart. The French armies won many brilliant victories, but William never permitted the French to take full advantage of them. The wars were costly to France, which could not forever stand the strain on its men and resources. But with the Peace of Ryswick in 1697, the French king's acquisitions in Spain and Flanders were restored, and Alsace and Strassburg remained in his possession.

WAR OF THE SPANISH SUCCESSION

Louis' desire for power and territory, however, was not yet satisfied. It now drew France into the War of the Spanish Succession which ended less fortunately for her, practically bringing to a close the period of French dominance in Europe. In his will in 1700, Charles II of Spain had left all his dominions to Philip of Anjou, grandson of Louis. The latter exultantly exclaimed: "There are no longer any Pyrenees!" This indicated that he intended to unite France and Spain under one crown. But the Emperor Leopold claimed the Spanish throne for his son; and England and Holland, to maintain the balance of power, opposed this latest piece of French diplomacy.

The "Grand Alliance" was instantly reorganized by William III, whose death in 1702 was a great blow to the Dutch and English. Louis recognized James Stuart as William's successor. In the naval engagement which opened the war, the allies were able to defeat the French and Spanish fleets. It was at this time that the fortress of Gibraltar fell to Sir George Rooke, an acquisition which was never relinquished by England.

On land Louis was not as successful as in his previous wars. The French people had sacrificed much and were exhausted. Louis was driven out of Italy by the Emperor, and the combined forces of the Dutch and English under Marlborough defeated the French in Flanders. In 1704, Marlborough and Eugene of Austria defeated the French at Blenheim.

TREATY OF UTRECHT

The war was concluded in 1713 with the Treaty of Utrecht. The Dutch Republic received security by gaining the right to occupy a series of fortresses along the French frontier. Savoy and Prussia also received more territory. The Spanish Netherlands (modern Belgium) were turned over to the Emperor and thus became the Austrian Netherlands. Philip V, however, retained the crown of Spain, with the stipulation that the crowns of Spain and France were to be kept separate, a decision which settled the original matter in dispute.

From the viewpoint of international diplomacy the treaty marks an important epoch in European history. While Spain had been predominant in the sixteenth century, and the Dutch had been the foremost nation in Europe during the early part of the seventeenth, in the latter half of that age France had been decidedly the foremost nation of the world. France, upon the death of Louis XIV in 1715, entered upon a period of decline and internal weakness. The primary role in Europe was now assumed by Great Britain.

TRIUMPH OF MERCANTILISM

Since the record of early modern European history is marked by wars, fought on a greater scale than ever before, the reader may well wonder what type of economic organization made such costly ventures possible. The simple feudal economy never could have supported the extensive and intensive military operations of this period, which involved expensive army equipment and naval vessels, and tens of thousands of trained soldiers instead of the thousands in the temporary feudal levies.

A new system of economic production and distribution arose. The beginnings of modern capitalism occurred at this time, replacing the simple feudal and handicraft economy. The new national states fostered these beginnings. This early form of state-supported and state-regulated capitalism is called mercantilism. France, better than any other European country at the time, illustrates mercantilism as an instrument of national and royal policy. In Spain, Holland, and England mercantilism was more closely related to colonial expansion, and therefore will be discussed again in the treatment of that subject.

CAPITALISTIC PRODUCTION

Hobson, the English economist, defines capitalism "as the organization of business upon a large scale by an employer or company of employers possessing an accumulated stock of wealth wherewith to acquire raw materials and tools, and hire labor, so

A BUSINESS DISTRICT IN MODERN BRUSSELS
Brussels early became an important commercial center, as well as a
stronghold of craft guilds.

as to produce an increased quantity of wealth which shall constitute a profit." Production in feudal times was much simpler in
its operation than the new capitalism. Agricultural products were
produced co-operatively on large estates and consumed locally,
and no attempts were made to accumulate large savings. The same
was true of the manufacturing of goods, in which the craft guild
played the important role.

At the beginning of the sixteenth century a noticeable change
took place. Landlords began to rent their lands to tenants instead
of exacting services from serfs. On the lands managed by the owners themselves, hired laborers replaced the serfs. The craft guilds
were gradually superseded by manufacturers who hired labor and
produced goods for a large market. To fill the need for capital,
modern banking emerged.

The new economic order, as compared with the old, is characterized by the free flow and mobility of labor and capital, thus
making large scale production possible; by a desire to make a

profit; by the production for a large market and unknown con-
sumers; by the rise of the middle class, or employer group, which
regards itself as socially superior to the workers it employs; and
by the splitting up of ownership into stocks or shares, making
possible the concentration of capital from various sources in single
large-scale enterprises.

The new national states soon took a hand in stimulating and
regulating capitalism. The idea became prevalent that a country
in order to be wealthy and powerful should have in its possession
a large supply of money, and large stocks of silver and gold. This
was one of the central ideas of mercantilism. Colbert, minister
of Louis XIV, stated, "I believe . . . it is only the abundance of
money in a state that determines its greatness and power." As a
result of this widely-held view, national policy was aimed at
securing and keeping as much gold and silver as possible within
the national domain. Spanish and Portuguese ships and colonies
were raided by the Dutch, French, and English in a mad scramble
for the possession of precious metals.

TARIFFS, REGULATIONS, MONOPOLIES

King Henry IV in 1603 forbade the exportation of gold and
silver from France. Heavy duties were laid on the importation of
manufactured goods, and the export of raw materials, such as
wool, was forbidden. A complete system of protective tariffs was
gradually developed, which in France, reaching its height under
Colbert, was called Colbertism. Internal tariff boundaries on the
other hand were eliminated, thus making the country one great
economic unit.

Another aspect of mercantilism was the giving of economic
privileges by the king to individuals or companies. These often
took the form of monopolies. Outstanding examples were the
great trading companies of France, England, and Holland, which
were given monopolies in certain geographical areas. The British
East India Company was one of the greatest of these companies.

Regulation of economic life in its minutest detail was the order
of the day and often took ridiculous forms. In France the size of

weaving tools was prescribed and the use of certain colors and
kinds of dyes forbidden. An elaborate system of bounties and
premiums was organized to stimulate capitalistic enterprise and
exports. Colbert alone handed out five and a half million francs
in bounties.

The prestige and power of the state was greatly increased by
this emphasis on a national economy. The new merchant and
manufacturing class looked to the king for help and support.
Local thought and feeling were supplanted by a national outlook.
Thus feudal localism and the ambitions of the nobility were gradually eliminated and supplanted by royal absolutism. Royal revenues increased greatly. The annual income of the French kings
increased from ten million livres in 1600, to nearly five hundred
million livres a hundred years later.

However, in the growth of royal power and the process of
state unification, the wishes of the common people and working
classes were not consulted. The mass of people lived in ignorance
and misery, had few privileges and liberties. They were required
to make great sacrifices to support royal wars, royal court life and
extravagance, and royal bureaucracy, which became more oppressive and exploitive as time went on. Eventually royal power was
destroyed, but the national state remained as the permanent
political unit in the world.

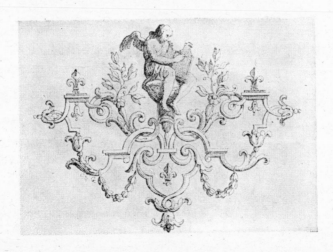

THOMAS CRANMER, ARCHBISHOP OF CANTERBURY
Author of the Book of Common Prayer and leader of the
English Reformation.

TWO CENTURIES OF ENGLISH
DEVELOPMENT

HENRY VII—FIRST OF THE TUDORS

WHILE THE KINGS OF FRANCE were consolidating their power and attempting to become the masters of Europe, England was passing through a series of crises. During the period from 1485 to 1713, the Reformation swept over England; significant constitutional changes occurred; the sea power of Spain was humbled; an English empire was built abroad; and England challenged France for supremacy in the international arena.

The Wars of the Roses, waged between the houses of Lancaster and York for control of the crown, so weakened and exhausted the English nobility that it became easy for a strong king to assert his authority. The people generally were tired of continual civil war and wanted someone who would be a king for all of England. This national feeling was strengthened by the policies of Henry VII who, in 1485, became the first Tudor king after defeating the treacherous Richard III in the battle of Bosworth.

By his marriage to Elizabeth of York shortly after coming to the throne, Henry united the White and Red Roses and embarked upon a long and peaceful reign. He carefully limited the power and number of the nobles, and encouraged the rising middle class by fostering commerce and business. He governed efficiently, and levied his taxes lightly upon the mass of the people. By the end of Henry's quarter-century reign the new line of

HENRY VII, FIRST OF THE TUDORS
(Portrait by an unknown Flemish artist)

monarchs had become firmly established. He had averted war, checked rival claimants to the throne, and left to his son a more united nation and increased royal power.

HENRY VIII AND THE BREAK WITH ROME

Henry VIII, one of the most colorful of English kings, succeeded his father in 1509. Young, handsome, and intelligent, he was already popular. The first part of Henry's reign was featured by the brilliant if not lasting diplomatic ventures of his great adviser, Cardinal Wolsey. The cardinal, by taking advantage of the rivalry between Emperor Charles V and the French king, gave England the balance of power; but no lasting gains were obtained, and the result of his policy was that Charles obtained control of the papacy just before Henry wanted the pope to annul his marriage to Catherine of Aragon, the Emperor's aunt.

When Henry had reigned twenty years without having a son, he convinced himself that his marriage to his brother's widow was unlawful. This, with a passion for young Anne Boleyn, drove him to press the pope for a divorce. The pope, influenced by Charles V, refused, and Henry began the separation of the English

ANNE OF CLEVES, QUEEN OF ENGLAND
Fourth wife of Henry VIII.

church from Rome. The process was completed by the Acts of Annates, Appeals, and Supremacy, which set up a national church with the king at its head.

Desire for Anne Boleyn and a son to succeed him was not the most important cause of Henry's break with Rome. Deeper causes, long rooted in English history, were at work; and the break was really the religious aspect of the growth of nationalism and independent spirit in England. People did not want the Church to be ruled by a foreign head, and the Renaissance, by fostering the spread of knowledge, made some laymen grope for a religion more personal and not dominated by the clergy.

Henry rudely put down those who refused to see in him the supreme head of the Church, and in 1536 began to seize and abolish the monasteries. The great wealth of these religious homes Henry took for himself; he also rewarded private families friendly to the Crown. The king, however, departed but little from traditional Catholic doctrine, and maintained many of the ceremonies of the old church.

By the end of Henry's reign England had moved far toward a permanent national unity. The king had advanced the work, not only by aiding the formation of a state church, but also by maintaining the absolute sovereignty of the Crown in Parliament. He consolidated England's boundaries, began to reorganize Ireland, and incorporated Wales into the English state.

RISING DISCONTENT

Edward VI, who came to the throne in 1547, was the son of Henry VIII by Jane Seymour, the third of his six wives. Since Edward was but ten years old at his accession, his uncle, Edward Seymour, was named Protector, and made duke of Somerset. Even in his youth the king was learned and religious, and like his uncle, was markedly Protestant. Their haste in pressing advanced Reformation ideas upon the country led to a minor revolt; but this was put down, and the religious changes continued. Images in the churches were done away with, Henry's six articles of faith repealed, and a new service-book, the Book of Common Prayer, was compiled and ordered to be used in the churches.

Left: TITLE PAGE OF THE BOOK OF COMMON PRAYER (1549)

Right: TITLE PAGE OF THE BOOK OF MARTYRS By John Fox (1563)

Somerset was faced, however, with increasing social and religious resentment throughout the nation. Competition was beginning to be substituted for custom as the dominant economic principle, and land was coming to be regarded as a source of money. With the amassing of large estates and the change from corn-growing to sheep-grazing, small tenants were evicted; there was more profit in large-scale wool-growing than in small-scale farming. Thousands of countrymen became hired laborers or were thrown out of work. This new vagrant class began to drift to the cities and seaports, there to aid in the growth of industries and shipping.

MARY, SPAIN, AND CATHOLICISM

The end of the Somerset regime came in 1552. John Dudley, earl of Warwick, excited the nation against the Protector, and the latter was deposed and executed. Dudley, created duke of Northumberland, now became Protector. Learning that Edward was not likely to live long, he defied the will of Henry VIII by persuading Edward to name Lady Jane Grey, the Protector's daughter-in-law, as the next ruler. But with Edward's death in 1553, the country reacted against the extreme Protestantism of his reign. Nobles and commoners joined to bring Mary, Catholic daughter of Henry VIII, to the throne, and Lady Jane Grey's career as queen lasted but nine days. It was with almost universal joy that she was deposed and Mary named Queen of England.

Mary soon lost her initial popularity. By putting England under the influence of Spain, whose king she married, and by restoring the authority of the pope, she alienated English national spirit. Those who advocated Protestantism and England's independence of the papacy, were severely persecuted, hundreds being burned at the stake. In aiding Spain, Mary lost Calais by warring with France, and offended the spirit of expansion in English nationalism by prohibiting Englishmen from competing with the Spanish in the New World. The news of Mary's death, in 1558, was received joyously by the nation. Henceforth, it would be impossible for any ruler to subjugate England to Spain or to renew the influence of Rome in English religion.

GOOD QUEEN BESS

With the accession of Elizabeth, Mary's Protestant half-sister, England was to enter upon one of the most glorious periods of her history, a period in which her ardent nationalism was to start the country on a career of growing influence in European affairs. Elizabeth opened her long reign by restoring England's independence. All connection with the papacy was abolished, and the state church set up once more. Typically English, the queen stood for compromise in religious affairs. Although the Catholic connection was severed, she offended the early Puritans by retaining some Catholic practices. Elizabeth, however, showed marked Protestant tendencies. She drew the fire of Catholic Europe by helping to expel the French from Scotland, and showed her independence of Spain by aiding the Dutch against Philip II, her brother-in-law. Subtle and wise in her diplomacy, Elizabeth, aided by such gifted advisers as Cecil and Walsingham, started England on a rapid road to success in rivalry with other nations.

Two factors entered into England's rise: the genuine national feelings of the people, and an aptitude for seafaring. Aiding in the rise of nationalism was the flexibility of English character and society. The people readily adapted themselves to changes. The growth of the middle class was stimulated by the fact that there was no rigid line between it and the nobility. Younger sons of noble families often went into trade and business, and commoners frequently rose to the rank of the nobility. Justices of the peace, heavily relied upon by the Tudors, were often descended from successful city men who had established themselves in the country. Elizabeth herself was the great-great-granddaughter of a London mayor. All in all, one of the important factors in England's rise to power was the fact that the government was responsive to the commercial classes, important in the expansion of any nation. There never existed in England that scorn of commerce which was characteristic of the Continental rulers and nobility.

Likewise, the English readily took to the sea, and the pope's prohibition of English expansion in the New World had the effect of arousing the strongly Protestant feeling of English seamen, as had Mary's refusal to allow them to compete with Spanish colonizers. The English sailors, therefore, began to prey on Spanish and Portuguese shipping and colonies. When Elizabeth came to the throne, this became a national sport, and such sea-dogs as Drake and Hawkins became the terror of the Spanish colonies and shipping-lanes.

MARY, QUEEN OF SCOTS

STRUGGLE WITH SPAIN

The depredations of these gay, devil-may-care English sailors widened the already broad rift between England and Spain. Philip had never given up his hopes of making England Catholic, even after Mary's death. In 1569 the northern English earls had risen in favor of Mary, Queen of Scots, a Catholic, but had been easily suppressed by Cecil, one of Elizabeth's ministers. This defeat and the pope's excommunication of Elizabeth in 1570 shattered the Catholic party, and the majority of Catholics accepted the state religion; but a number fled to foreign courts, there to conspire with Spain to recover England for Catholicism.

Gradually the two countries drifted apart, although a truce existed for several years. But there could not be compromise between Spanish and English desires in the New World, and between Protestant English nationalism and Spain's desire to reconquer England for the Catholic Church. The Spanish acquisition of Portugal, the assassination of William of Orange, Dutch Protestant leader of the revolt against Spain, and Spanish victories in the Netherlands led Elizabeth to act. She aided the Dutch, executed

Above: SIR FRANCIS DRAKE
He helped destroy Spanish sea-power.

Right: SIR WALTER RALEIGH
English explorer and author.

PLAZA ISABELLA II, CADIZ

the Queen of Scots, sent Drake to raid the Spanish West Indies in 1585, and destroyed Philip's fleet at Cadiz in 1587.

Philip finally retaliated in 1588 with the Spanish Armada. Under the delusion that the majority of the English people would rise against Elizabeth if given the chance, he sent an immense fleet to aid them. But England arose as one man to repel the invader. Her prowess on the sea served her in good stead, and English seamanship and gunnery, plus the effects of a Channel storm, forever destroyed Spanish hopes of conquest. Her continuance of the war was merely based on the hope of getting guarantees against English interference in the New World. To this end, Philip incited the Irish to revolt, but England easily suppressed them, and embarked upon the first real conquest of Ireland.

GOLDEN AGE OF ENGLAND

Elizabeth's reign was one in which all fields of English endeavor began to express the national feelings of the people.

Particularly after the defeat of the Armada, when the fear of foreign intervention had passed, English nationalism began to express itself in many new ways. Spenser, Sidney, Shakespeare, and Marlowe developed a truly great English literature, relatively free from foreign influences and models.

In domestic politics Parliament, after years of being overshadowed by the Tudor rulers, began to assert itself. The old alliance of Crown and Parliament against the Church and foreign interference was being changed. More democratic ideas of government in church and state led Parliament to challenge the Crown's right to establish monopolies, to levy indirect taxes without its consent, and to imprison subjects arbitrarily. Now that the nation was strong and independent, the people, too, no longer favored a powerful monarchy. Gradually the nation began to demand more self-government, even before Elizabeth's death in 1603 ended the sway of the Tudor family. England was now truly a national state.

KINGS BY DIVINE RIGHT

James I, who now ascended the throne, was the first of the Stuart family of kings. He was the son of Mary, Queen of Scots, and had long been king of Scotland. James, who was a political theorist, ardently believed in the divine right of kings, and forgot that heredity had not been the only means of succession. Parliament lost no time in telling him that it would not let him have the power that Elizabeth had wielded. James's stubbornness and the belief that he was using selfishly the authority that had been wielded by the Tudors for the good of the nation, widened the breach between the king and Parliament. There was no desire for democracy, but a general feeling that parliamentary legislation should be supreme.

The disputes over religion, Parliament's rights, and foreign affairs made the House of Commons reluctant to levy taxes for James's treasury. In 1606 the king levied additional customs duties; they were legal, but increased James's unpopularity. Various other levies, and arbitrary interference with the decisions

HOUSES OF PARLIAMENT, LONDON

of the judges, enlivened the closing years of his reign, and maintained the breach between king and Parliament.

With the accession of Charles I, son of James, in 1625, the
dispute over taxation came to a head when the sturdy country
gentlemen and merchants of the House of Commons refused to
vote certain lifetime grants to the king. Charles claimed that
Parliament had lost the right to refuse them. He levied them on
his own authority, and demanded a forced loan from part of the
people. When five knights refused to pay it they were sent to
prison. In retaliation, Parliament passed the Petition of Right in
1628, protesting against such forced loans, imprisonment without
due process of law, billeting of soldiers in private homes, and
martial law in time of peace.

In 1629 the quarrel between king and Parliament broke out
again over Charles's right to levy certain duties. In anger he dissolved Parliament, and for eleven years ruled without one. During this time he obtained money by reviving old forms of taxation,
which he levied on his own authority. Those who were provoked
to resist, suffered prison for their pains. But by 1639 Charles had
tapped dry these tax sources, and needed sums which only Parliament could raise.

TOWER OF LONDON AND LOWER BRIDGE

RELIGIOUS DIFFICULTIES

Another important factor was creating discord between the king and part of his people. The growing strength of the Puritans, despite the opposition of James and Charles, led them to dare to join those who stood against the illegal political acts of the king. James had frowned upon Puritanism, and Charles's adviser, Archbishop Laud, was following a steady policy of forcing everyone to conform to the practices of the state church. But Puritan sentiment grew, for punishment could not alter men's consciences. Thousands of the Puritans, who stood for high personal morality and the elimination of certain practices from the established church, went to America; but the vast majority remained to add religious discontent to the grievances against Charles.

In 1638 Charles attempted to pattern the Scottish church after the English state church, but the Scotch revolted and set up Presbyterianism. Charles went to war to enforce his will, but needed Parliament to levy taxes to pay his expenses. Called in

1639, Parliament was dissolved because it refused to give the king any money unless he consented to redress their grievances. But Charles still needed money, and in 1640 called the Long Parliament, which realized that it was now master of the king. It demanded that a Parliament be called every three years at least, and that the king choose ministers whom Parliament approved. To show how insistent it was upon the responsibility of the king's advisers to Parliament, Stafford and Laud, two of Charles's chief ministers, were executed.

CHARLES I, KING OF ENGLAND
For eleven years he ruled without a Parliament, but in 1640
Parliament again became the ruling power.

THE ROUNDHEAD REVOLUTION

When Parliament, leaning toward Presbyterianism, began to attack the state church, Charles fled to Oxford, set up the royal flag, and gathered his supporters about him. With this began the civil war. The Royalists were successful at first, but eventually Oliver Cromwell led his hard-fighting, deeply religious Roundheads to victory in the battles of Marston Moor and Naseby, and in 1646 the king surrendered himself. The Roundheads were Independents, that is, they stood for religious tolerance, and Charles tried to regain his authority by playing them against the Presbyterians, who were for a state church. But Charles's crafty plan fell through and led to a second civil war, his execution in 1649, and the abolition of the monarchy and the House of Lords.

Cromwell had now crushed Catholic Ireland and Presbyterian Scotland, and turned to the problem of governing England. Religious tolerance was established, but his new Commonwealth

CROMWELL LISTENING TO A RECITAL BY MILTON
Cromwell's Roundheads eventually gained control of England, and Charles I was executed.

government soon became a military despotism. Cromwell himself was practically a monarch, with the title of Protector. In 1657 he attempted to re-establish a Parliament, but his death the following year threw the country into anarchy, which ended by the recall in 1660 of Charles II. Curiously enough, divided internally though England was during the Commonwealth Period, she presented a united front in foreign affairs. Cromwell was really the founder of the modern English navy, and his captains swept the seas clear of Spanish and Dutch ships. During this period England began her long dominance in the Mediterranean. Foreign nations were compelled to recognize the Protector and English trade began to expand rapidly.

THE RESTORATION

Charles II, handsome, able, unscrupulous, and popular, returned to England and entered upon his reign with one main objective: to avoid having to "set out on his travels again." He had two secondary hopes: to secure the Crown from outside control, and to emancipate Catholics from their position of restricted political power. But he could not do both, for he needed the help of the established church to increase the power of the Crown, and the church was not willing to relax the decrees against Roman Catholics.

Charles first was led by his chief adviser, Clarendon, to support the church; but in 1667 he replaced his veteran aide by the "Cabal," no member of which was a good Anglican churchman. With its aid he issued his "Proclamation of Indulgence" for Roman Catholics and Dissenters and tried to secure help against Parliament by signing a secret agreement, the Treaty of Dover, with Louis XIV of France. In 1672 Charles plunged the nation into war with the Dutch in return for subsidies from France. The war was not entirely unpopular, since England had twice warred with the Dutch over trade during the previous decade; but the discovery of the secret treaty made the nation reluctant to fight their fellow-Protestants. The church led resistance against the now unpopular war, and Charles saw the danger of a new period of exile, so he disbanded the Cabal and permitted the passage of the Test Act which put the Catholics in a worse position than before.

Convinced of the failure of his Catholic policy, Charles discarded it, and began to concentrate on making the Crown independent of Parliament. But the nation was still alarmed over the Catholic danger. The opposition party, who came to be called Whigs, took advantage of a fictitious "Popish Plot" to strike hard at the Tories, who upheld the king. Panic followed, but after a period of disorder, during which the Habeas Corpus Act was passed, Charles turned the national reaction to his own advantage. The Whig leaders were silenced, Tories put in control, and for the last four years of his reign Charles ruled as an absolute monarch, without Parliament, but with the support of the English church and the Tory party.

THE GLORIOUS REVOLUTION

Charles was succeeded, in 1685, by his brother, James II, an avowed Catholic. Things looked well for James at the beginning of his reign, despite two rebellions against him. These were suppressed without much difficulty. He had a Tory Parliament, and by the nation he was respected for his honesty. Unwisely, however, James deviated from his brother's later policy and began to revive the earlier Roman Catholic program, thereby cutting off the important support of the church. Laws were suspended and dispensed with, Catholics placed in the army, the universities, and the privy council, and a large standing army was raised. In attempting to secure his control of municipal governments, he met the opposition of seven bishops whom he prosecuted for seditious libel. This was the last straw. Men of all parties invited the Protestant William III, king of the Netherlands and husband of James's daughter, Mary, to replace James on the throne. James fled at the deliverer's approach; unlike his father, Charles I, he had no group to aid him in his hour of trial.

The peaceful change of rulers, called the "Glorious Revolution," was culminated by a series of acts which established the

"SPAYNE AND ROME DEFEATED"
A noted and influential caricature circulated during the Puritan period.

firm basis of the modern English nation. By the Act of Succession, William and Mary were conjoined as co-rulers, James was excluded from the throne, no Catholic was henceforth to rule England, and Parliament firmly established itself as the deciding voice in regulating the succession.

KING SUBORDINATED TO PARLIAMENT

The Bill of Rights established political liberty by declaring unconstitutional James's arbitrary acts of royal power—the suspension of laws by the royal prerogative, levying of taxes without parliamentary consent, the maintenance of a standing army in time of peace, interference with justice, the exaction of excessive bail, and the denial of the right of petition. It further upheld freedom of debate in Parliament, freedom of elections, and freedom of petition. Religious toleration, freedom of speech, and freedom of the press were guaranteed by other acts.

William III, intent on his wars with Louis XIV, gave Parliament an opportunity to establish itself in its new position. Political

CARICATURE OF LOUIS XIV. BY THACKERAY
"Majesty," Thackeray said, "is made out of the wig, the high-heeled shoes, and cloak. . . .
Thus do barbers and cobblers make the gods that we worship."

parties came into active existence as the Whigs and Tories, descendants of the old groups of the time of Charles II, scrambled for influence in the government. William preferred the Whigs because they favored his war policy, but the country frequently selected Tories. Internal developments were of little interest to William III, although in 1691 he suppressed an uprising in Ireland led by the former king, James II. At the time of his death, he was still ardently defending Holland and England against the aggressive policy of Louis XIV.

ANNE AND ENGLISH SUPREMACY

Anne, a daughter of James II, succeeded William III in 1702. At this time England was deeply involved in the War of the Spanish Succession, and a ministry from all parties was formed to secure united parliamentary support. But the country was saved from its danger by the military genius of the duke of Marlborough. By a series of victories initiated by the smashing defeat of the French and Bavarians at Blenheim, the duke destroyed both the armies and prestige of Louis XIV and raised England to a commanding position in European politics.

At home, the wing of the Tory party which favored peace split with the war-favoring minority, and the latter became purely Whig in 1708. Two years later, however, the cabinet fell, and was replaced by one exclusively Tory. Anne, a quiet woman of average intelligence, acquiesced in this growth of the responsibility of ministers to Parliament. The Tory majority forced the withdrawal of England from the war in 1711, but so potent had been Marlborough's earlier victories that at the peace settlement England emerged as the dominant power of the world. By the Peace of Utrecht, in 1713, she secured favorable trade rights from Spain and Portugal, and was given a large part of Canada.

With the signing of the treaties which made up the Peace of Utrecht, England completed a significant step in her development as a nation. Disorganized and weakened by the Wars of the Roses in 1485, she had been united internally by the Tudors. Under the Stuarts occurred the transition from a strong monarchy to a limited one, in which Parliament, representative of the whole nation, constituted the fundamental power.

England was now fully prepared to take the position of the world's leading power. Not even a change of dynasty in 1714, when Anne, last of the Stuarts, died, could alter her status. The relative flexibility of her social system, the advanced degree of freedom existing within her borders, and the sensational growth of English commerce were to maintain the position attained in 1713.

STATUE OF ROLAND, LEGENDARY HERO OF THE
FRANKS, IN HALLE

By the treaty of Westphalia, Halle, former member of the
Hanseatic League, came into the possession of Brandenburg.

PRUSSIA AS A NATIONAL STATE

DECLINE OF THE EMPIRE

THE INTERNAL WEAKNESS of the Holy Roman Empire during the sixteenth century has been discussed. As a result of the Thirty Years War (1618-1648) which left the population decimated and impoverished, this weakness became more accentuated in the next century. Over three hundred separate political units existed at the time. Causes contributing to this result were: the mutual jealousies among the various rulers; the inability of the Emperor to establish his power absolutely, and at the expense of the lesser princes, as had been done in other countries; the conflict of authority between the emperors and the popes; and the religious struggles and dissensions within the Empire.

Although the Holy Roman Empire was little more than an aggregation of petty, quarreling states, a centralizing force made itself felt in the Germanies during the seventeenth century. The agent of this force was the small but dynamic principality of Brandenburg, later called Prussia, which grew in power and extent until Germany emerged as a strong national state in the nineteenth century.

INCREASING IMPORTANCE OF BRANDENBURG

An event of great importance in later German history occurred in 1415. In that year the Emperor vested the House of Hohenzollern with the electorate of the border province called Brandenburg. Until that time the Hohenzollerns had been an un-

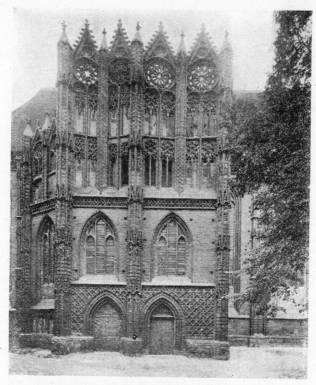

CHURCH OF ST. KATHARINE, BRANDENBURG

important family in southern Germany, but they shifted their residence to the north when they became members of the German Electoral College.

The Hohenzollerns accepted Lutheranism in the sixteenth century, and so were able to strengthen their position by the seizure of all the church lands, and by freeing themselves of all papal and religious restrictions on their political power. Soon Prussia was recognized as the leading Protestant state of Germany, just as Austria in the south was recognized as the principal Catholic state.

The Thirty Years War played havoc in the Brandenburg territories; but for various reasons Brandenburg benefited from this struggle. As a result of matrimonial arrangements, the duchy of Cleves and the duchy of East Prussia were acquired. The latter was located near the Baltic and north of Poland. At the end of the war still other territories were gained and imperial influence over this region greatly decreased. Though nominally still a vassal of the Emperor, in fact, the Hohenzollerns were becoming independent.

THE GREAT ELECTOR AND HIS SUCCESSORS

Frederick William (1640-1688), also known as the Great Elector, has a historical reputation which extends far beyond the borders of Germany. He realized that vigorous measures were necessary in order to rehabilitate his country, which had been laid waste by war and which was poor in natural resources. A firm believer in absolutist government, he was an extremely capable administrator. Previous to his accession to power, various parts of the Great Elector's realm possessed their own separate political institutions. There were three different diets or parliaments, armies, and administrations. After a severe struggle with various vested interests, Frederick William succeeded in unifying the various military units into one national army, in bringing all financial administration under his personal control, and in depriving the diets of their political power. The new state was to be characterized by highly centralized, efficient administration and royal absolutism.

Frederick also greatly improved the internal economy of Brandenburg. Industry and agriculture were aided, and several marshes were drained. The Frederick William Canal, joining the Oder and Elbe rivers, was built under his direction. With the revocation of the Edict of Nantes by Louis XIV in 1685, nearly twenty thousand Huguenots fled to Brandenburg. They were highly industrious and taught their trade skills to the Germans. Berlin, the capital, in a short time grew from a town of eight thousand inhabitants to a city of twenty thousand.

The Great Elector was also successful in foreign affairs. At the Treaty of Westphalia, by skilful diplomacy, he obtained important territories. He used the war between Sweden and Poland (1655-1660) to his advantage. Later he defeated the Swedes and thereby established the reputation of his army in Europe.

The son of the Great Elector, Frederick III, did not exhibit the same capacity for administration. He was more extravagant and somewhat frivolous, showing a strange contrast to his father. His interest in the arts, sciences, and learning was great, however. Under his patronage the University of Halle was founded and so were the Academy of Arts and Academy of Sciences at Berlin.

By bargaining with the Emperor, Frederick III obtained the latter's consent to change his title from the simple "Elector of Brandenburg" to "King of Prussia." This consent was purchased by the sending of eight thousand troops to aid the Emperor in the War of the Spanish Succession. The title of king of Prussia had considerable prestige and gave Prussia a new vantage point on the chessboard of European diplomacy.

KING FREDERICK WILLIAM

Under the rule of King Frederick William I (1713-1740), Prussia rose to the rank of a first-rate power in Europe. In every respect this king displayed the same characteristics of austerity and efficiency as his grandfather, the Elector Frederick William. He realized that his country was poor in resources and his methods were designed to make up for this deficiency. By rigid economies and by the introduction of a scientific system of budgeting, the treasury was soon well filled. His army became the best trained and best equipped in Europe, which gave much weight to his position in continental affairs. He was the first king in Europe to make free, elementary education compulsory for the people.

Frederick William I was able to carry government to previously unattained heights of efficiency and responsibility. He made a distinct contribution to the art of government by introducing merit as the basis for selection of government officials. Positions were nearly all given to recruits of the middle class, in sharp contrast with the usual practice of the day when sons of the nobility were usually placed in government service.

The new class of officials was industrious, incorruptible, and took great pride in its position. Its loyalty to state and king went unquestioned. Many aims were secured at once by these methods.

On the one hand, government was made efficient and financial resources were released for military purposes and internal improvements. On the other hand, the development of a professional group of government officials, recruited from the middle class and absolutely loyal to the king, completely broke all power of the nobility. Prussian history does not record strong resistance by the aristocracy to royal authority.

Frederick II, known to history as Frederick the Great, ascended the throne when his father died in 1740. The new king was greatly tempted to employ the fully trained and well-equipped army his father left him. Since his foreign diplomacy and wars have much to do with Austria of that time, it is well to retrace our steps and discuss shortly the historical developments within that country.

AUSTRIA AFTER CHARLES V

From the thirteenth century, the electors usually chose as Emperor the head of the House of Hapsburg. This powerful family had ruled Austria and the neighboring provinces since 1268. The rule of this latter region was hereditary and the title "Archduke of Austria" was kept distinct and separate from that of "Emperor of the Holy Roman Empire," bestowed by election, even though the same individual usually held both titles. His power as Emperor was not great, especially after the Thirty Years War, but in his own hereditary domain of Austria an opposite trend appeared. Here royal power was consolidated and Hapsburg rule became absolute. The territories of Austria were also expanded. Ferdinand I, brother of Charles V, also became king of Bohemia and Hungary by marriage, and the succeeding Hapsburgs retained these thrones. They ruled over a combination of various races and peoples, and the Austrian empire lacked internal cohesion. Revolts often took place, especially on the outskirts of Hungary, where the Croats, Rumanians, and the Slovaks often were a cause of disturbance. A revolt of the Czechs of Bohemia against Ferdinand II inaugurated the Thirty Years War.

TURKS ADVANCE AGAIN

In the seventeenth century the Hapsburgs once more had to deal with the Turks who, bent on conquest, again conquered all of Hungary, and the legions of Mohammed IV soon appeared before the walls of Vienna. Leopold I (1658-1705), the ruling Hapsburg at the time, found himself in a desperate situation. At the critical moment the brave king of Poland, John III, came to his rescue, defeated the Turks, and saved Vienna. The pope also became aroused and issued a call to all of Christendom to drive back the infidel. What has been called the Last Crusade was organized, and the combined resources and men of Austria, Poland, Venice, and Papal States, Russia, and even France, after a long struggle, drove back the Turk. Most of the fruits of this religious fervor were reaped by Austria, which regained all of Hungary and the territories north of the Danube when the Treaty of Karlowitz was signed in 1699.

The fortunes of Austria in the War of the Spanish Succession have been discussed. At the treaty of Utrecht in 1713, the Belgian Netherlands, the duchy of Milan, and the kingdom of the two Sicilies came under the rule of the Hapsburgs. Thus Austria, though lacking internal unity, grew in territory and prestige. From now on its history becomes the story of rivalry with rising Prussia for the predominant position among the German peoples.

Charles VI (1711-1740) of Austria had no sons or brothers, and long custom dictated that only male heirs could inherit the throne. The break-up of the Austrian domain seemed imminent. But in a document, since called the Pragmatic Sanction, Charles declared that, in the absence of a male heir, a female heir might inherit the throne. During his reign he succeeded in obtaining assent to this new ruling, not only from his own dominions, but also from the great foreign powers of Europe, including France, Great Britain, Russia, and even Prussia. When Charles died in 1740, his only daughter, Maria Theresa, came to the throne of a large domain, which, however, was financially poor and equipped with only a small army. That same year Frederick II became king of Prussia.

FREDERICK THE
GREAT, KING OF
PRUSSIA

FREDERICK THE GREAT AND HIS ROLE ON THE CONTINENT

Frederick II came to the throne at the age of twenty-eight. Because of his interest in art and science he had been harshly treated by his father, who had a thorough contempt for learning. Frederick also forsook the orthodox religion of his father and became an adherent of the rationalism prevalent in his day. His intellectual activities as an enlightened despot will be described elsewhere.

Upon his accession to power, Frederick immediately disregarded the Prussian promise given to Charles VI, concerning the Pragmatic Sanction. The internally weak Austrian Empire seemed a fair prey to his ambitions. At once he disputed Maria's right to her throne, and made agreements with France and Bavaria for the spoliation of Austria. The Elector of Bavaria was to be made Holy Roman Emperor, France desired the Austrian Netherlands, and Frederick wanted to add Silesia to his realm. The latter was a rich country and inhabited chiefly by Germans.

Frederick promptly seized Silesia, while Bavaria and France attacked Austria from the west. Maria fled to Hungary, but soon the Magyars, Austrians, and Bohemians rallied to her banner. There ensued a long war, called the War of the Austrian Succes-

MARIA THERESA, ARCHDUCHESS OF AUSTRIA

sion. Spain and England also joined, but on opposite sides. England, because of her rivalry with France, sent money and troops to defend the Netherlands against France and Hanover against Prussia. Spain, which was then ruled by a Bourbon relative of the French king, aided France and Prussia in order to regain the possessions in Italy which had been lost at the Treaty of Utrecht in 1713. Holland, fearing French aggression in the Netherlands, also joined England and Austria.

FREDERICK VICTORIOUS

The fortunes of war wavered and numerous bloody battles were fought. Maria Theresa, however, was unable to dislodge

MADAME DE POMPADOUR
Mistress of Louis XV.

Frederick from Silesia, and at the Treaty of Dresden, in 1745, she was forced to cede this territory to Prussia. A general peace was made at Aix-la-Chapelle in 1748, which left the map of Europe as it had been before the war, except for Silesia. Maria was recognized as the legitimate ruler of the Austrian domains. Thus ended the first phase of the struggle between Prussia and Austria for supremacy in the Germanies.

Frederick was well aware that the Peace of Dresden was only a truce. The jealousy of Austria had been strongly aroused by Prussian success, and Maria Theresa was brooding over the loss of Silesia. Frederick used the following eleven years of peace to inaugurate internal improvements of Silesian resources, and to maintain his splendid army in the highest state of efficiency. There were other European powers which regarded Prussia with envy, and Maria, preparing for revenge, had no difficulty in finding allies. Both the Russian Tsarina Elizabeth and Madame de Pompadour, the mistress of Louis XV, had been greatly offended by Frederick's sarcastic poetry, and this resentment was a factor in leading both Russia and France to come to Austria's aid. France was offered the Austrian Netherlands as a reward for its help.

Britain, meanwhile, interested in the breakdown of French colonial power, supported Prussia. Thus a complete realignment of forces took place in Europe. This shift of forces preceding the Seven Years War is officially called the "Diplomatic Revolution."

THE SEVEN YEARS WAR

Frederick the Great, supported by British gold, was now completely surrounded by enemies. In the final analysis it was his military genius which saved Prussia from complete extinction. In 1756 he invaded Saxony, which sided with Austria, and held it during the entire period of the war. The Austrians suffered a series of severe defeats at his hands. But Frederick failed to capture Prague and was forced to fall back into his own country to meet invading French and Russian armies. With a small force he completely defeated the French, then suddenly turned upon and defeated the Austrians gathered in Silesia at the battle of Leuthen in 1757. Napoleon later extolled this battle as a masterpiece of tactical skill.

Frederick's resources, however, were small compared to the combined forces of his enemies. Only British money saved him from complete financial ruin. His armies were shattered and his country had too small a population to fill the ranks again. Russian troops from the east overran the country, and twice Berlin was captured. The death of Pitt in England also meant disaster, since his successor made peace with France.

By a stroke of luck, Prussia's fortunes changed suddenly with the death of Tsarina Elizabeth of Russia. The new Russian Tsar, Peter III, was a friend and personal admirer of Frederick the Great. The former's wife, later known as Tsarina Catherine II, was a German princess, who knew Frederick well. The Russian troops were ordered to desert Austria and to side with Frederick. Silesia was regained. A combination of luck and military genius had saved Prussia from utter destruction. The Seven Years War finally came to an end with the Treaty of Hubertsburg in 1763. Maria Theresa failed in her reconquest of Silesia, and Prussia emerged as a leading power in Europe. The predominance of Great Britain over France was secured by victories at sea and abroad.

FIRST PARTITION OF POLAND

Frederick the Great's ambitions were not yet satisfied. He was fully aware of Catherine the Great's designs upon Poland, and so he made an alliance with her in order to share in the booty. In 1772 the first partition of Poland took place. Prussia obtained West Prussia, thereby connecting Brandenburg and East Prussia, which formerly had been separated by Polish territory. Catherine II annexed the lands east of the Düna and Dnieper rivers. Maria Theresa, though verbally professing her opposition to the shady transaction, annexed Galicia. Of her, Frederick said: "She wept, but kept on taking." Poland lost one fourth of its territory.

Prussia definitely became the leader of the northern Protestant princes and gradually weakened Austria's influence. When Austria claimed part of Bavaria in 1778, during a dispute as to the succession of its elector, Frederick frustrated Austrian designs by diplomatic maneuvering and threats of force. As Austria's sun was slowly setting, Prussia rose in power and influence. In the nineteenth century this development became more clearly evident, but, for the present, Austria was still a world power, whose wish must be given full consideration in any continental affair.

FREDERICK'S INTERNAL POLICY

The efforts and capacities of Frederick the Great, however, were not entirely directed toward war and destruction. He spent considerable energy on the internal development of the country. He loved his people much and styled himself "their first servant." Every day he worked hard from morning till night and expected his officials to do the same. During his reign, canals and roads were constructed, over fifteen hundred square miles of marsh and wasteland were redeemed, and even new villages were built to attract settlers from all Europe. His economic policy was mercantilistic in the attempts to keep money and wealth within the borders of the country. Taxes were heavy, but the people felt their money was well spent.

Frederick was a great king in many ways. In addition to political achievements, his intellectual and artistic pursuits must be mentioned. His writings fill over thirty volumes. In religious tolerance he was far advanced for the age. It is safe to say that he may be characterized as the most remarkable enlightened despot in history.

RUSSIA BECOMES A EUROPEAN POWER

RISE OF MUSCOVY

BEFORE AND DURING THE MIDDLE AGES, what we now know as Russia was occupied by numerous tribes of Slavic peoples. They were subjected to attacks of the Mongolian tribes and the Tatars from the east, to the influence of Byzantine culture from the south, and to the pressure of Scandinavia from the west. By the ninth century, a group of eastern Slavs formed a small state called Kiev. This civilization, however, was broken up by more Mongolian raids two hundred years later. Although the Slavs continued to found additional settlements in the north, they were disorganized until the fifteenth century because of these oriental invasions, Scandinavian interference, and internal disagreements.

During this time the grand duchy of Muscovy grew in importance, and one of its rulers, Ivan the Great (1462-1505), took the first steps toward making Russia a great nation. One of his most outstanding acts was to end the Tatar control of the Russians. Moreover, through the influence of his wife, Sophia Paleologus, niece of the last Byzantine emperor, he assumed the position of successor to the Byzantine emperors and ruler of Russia, instead of Muscovy only.

His grandson, Ivan IV, (1533-1584) called the Terrible because of his cruelty, further extended Russian power. He assumed the title of Tsar of all Russia, and during his reign the Russian church, which was Greek Orthodox, was freed from the control of the bishops at Constantinople.

During the next two centuries, some progress was made in expansion. The Slavic peoples migrated and settled along the many rivers of Russia. Many dangers were encountered, and bands of bold Cossacks were organized to act both as a spearhead of the expansion and as a military guard for the new settlements. These Cossacks were to be important in later Russian history. The Russians also expanded into Asia, settling in many places now included in Siberia. But Russia did not develop rapidly as a strong national state. Its predominantly agricultural organization, its large territory with poor communication and transportation, and its lack of outlets to the western seas combined to prevent the rise of a national spirit. Long contact with Byzantine and oriental culture made it difficult to introduce Western customs.

Furthermore, the Russian people suffered a lack of good rulers. With the death of Ivan the Terrible, the old Rurik line of rulers came to an end, and the succeeding struggle for the throne caused this period to be known as the "Troublous Times." Not only did the Russians themselves disagree, but Sweden, Poland, and the Ottoman Empire, profiting from the confusion, acquired territory and power at Muscovy's expense. Finally in 1613, a national assembly of nobles met to elect a tsar, and chose Michael Romanov who was distantly connected with the family of the Ivans. His government gradually restored order and stopped the incursion of the militant neighbors.

RUSSIA FACES WEST

It was Michael's grandson, Peter the Great, who first made Russia an important nation. Peter began ruling with his imbecile brother Ivan in 1682, but in 1696 Ivan died, leaving Peter sole ruler. The young tsar was intensely interested in mechanical things and in all phases of the culture of Western Europe. He was determined to westernize Russia as well as to increase her power. To do this he needed both a knowledge of Western affairs and outlets to the Western world.

PETER THE GREAT OF RUSSIA

In a war against the Turks, Peter captured the port of Azov, but could make no further progress without European support. Therefore, he traveled through continental Europe and England. Although he failed to get support, since Europe at that time was about to go to war over the Spanish succession, he acquired much information and sent many experts and workmen back to Russia. These foreigners were to be used only until such time as native Russians were able and willing to assume their duties.

While Peter was abroad, he learned that the *streltsi*, the royal military guard, had revolted. He hurried back to Russia, mercilessly annihilated the *streltsi*, and began the reorganization of the

country. An autocrat by nature, he was convinced by his observation of European governments, particularly that of Louis XIV,
that absolutism was the best form of rule.

One of his first projects was to replace the rebellious *streltsi*
by a powerful and well-disciplined army formed on the Prussian
model and completely subordinate to his will. He next obtained
control over the Church, which might otherwise have opposed
him. By transferring the power of the Moscow patriarch to a
body called the Holy Synod, whose members he himself selected,
Peter made himself supreme in ecclesiastical affairs. He realized
the importance of the church in the lives of the people, who
retained the Orthodox faith wherever they went; therefore, he
rigorously persecuted all nonconformers.

Another of Peter's accomplishments was the centralization of
government. By abolishing the existing local governments and
dividing the country into districts, with his army officers in
charge, he increased royal power. These officers ruthlessly extracted money from the peasants, thus providing the funds needed
for his reforms. He also made the Duma, or nobles' council, practically powerless by transferring their work to himself and his
personally chosen aides.

SOCIAL AND ECONOMIC CHANGES

The rigid class system, which existed into the twentieth century, was largely the result of Peter's work. He raised many of
his supporters to the rank of nobles, simultaneously rewarding
them and weakening the power of the old nobility who were not
his enthusiastic admirers. At the same time the lower classes were
further regimented, and the institution of serfdom was extended
and more firmly established.

Peter's attempts to improve agriculture were only partially
successful; but he did succeed to some degree in promoting trades
and industries which Russia so woefully lacked. So thorough was
his attempt to westernize Russia that he even forced the people
to wear Western dress, the men to shave their beards, and the
women to emerge from their traditional seclusion. As might be

expected, many of these changes affected the upper class only, while the lower classes lived much as before. More momentous was the construction of his new capital, called St. Petersburg, which was built upon land reclaimed from the marshes. Symbolically it was known as "Peter's Window into Europe."

SUPREMACY OVER SWEDEN

Peter's foreign policy was to gain territory and to win satisfactory outlets to the seas. The Ottoman Empire, to the south, and Sweden, to the west, were to feel the force of these Russian ambitions.

Since the days of Gustavus Adolphus, Sweden had been regarded as the leader of northern Europe; so vast was her territory around the Baltic Sea. The opposition of France, Denmark, Brandenburg, and Poland failed, and the treaties in 1660 confirmed Sweden's holdings. However, her strength was less than it seemed, because her borders included many nationalities so restless that an armed force was needed to keep them in subjection. Further weakness was caused by the belligerent disposition of the Swedish rulers whose wars exhausted the wealth, man-power, and enthusiasm of the nation.

When Charles XII, only fifteen years old, came to the Swedish throne in 1697, his foreign rivals saw an opportunity to strike and to divide his possessions among them. Prussia refused to take advantage of the king's youth, but Saxony, Russia, and Denmark formed an alliance and prepared to fight what is known as the Great Northern War. To their surprise, Charles, who loved a fight as much as his predecessors, caught them unprepared and defeated them. He then turned south, defeated the Poles, and forced them to dethrone their king, Augustus, and accept his candidate, Stanislaus Leszczynski. Charles was not satisfied with these victories, and, while he delayed making peace in hope of getting more than the allies offered, Peter the Great reorganized his army, renewed the war, and overwhelmed the Swedish at Poltava (1709). Charles then sought Turkish aid against Russia, which Peter prevented by returning the port of Azov to the

Ottoman Empire. Charles still persisted in his opposition, and Great Britain, Hanover, and Prussia joined the coalition against him.

Not until his death in 1718 was peace restored. By the treaties of Stockholm in 1719 and 1720, Sweden lost nearly all of her German holdings to Hanover and Prussia. Poland was allowed to re-establish Augustus as king. The next year, by the Treaty of Nystad, Russia took from Sweden the Baltic provinces of Latvia and Esthonia and other territories as well. Peter had acquired his opening to the Baltic and became a leader of Europe.

CATHERINE EXTENDS RUSSIA

The immediate successors of Peter were an undistinguished lot who did little to change the status of Russia; but, with the accession of Catherine the Great, Russia made another great advance. She was a German princess, and her marriage to Tsar Peter III of Russia had been arranged by Frederick the Great, who thereby increased his influence in the Russian capital. In 1762 Catherine disposed of her half-mad husband, and from then on ruled alone for thirty-four years. Desiring to appear an enlightened despot, concerned only with the welfare of her people, she made some pretenses in that direction, such as encouraging learning among the upper classes, corresponding with the French philosophers, and showing interest in science.

At heart, however, Catherine was an autocrat of the first order. Dominating, passionate, and utterly without moral scruples, she opposed real enlightenment because it would decrease her power. She was undisturbed by the sufferings of the masses and made the central government stronger than ever. By transferring church property to state control, she put the church entirely at her mercy.

However grim a picture her internal policy presents, her foreign activities did add to the glory of Russia.

CATHERINE THE GREAT OF RUSSIA

WAR AGAINST THE TURKS

One part of her program was directed south against the Ottoman Empire, for she realized its weakness and degeneracy. In Turkey, the government's corruption and inefficiency were revealed by the fact that buying and selling all offices from the lowest to the highest was an established practice. Confusion increased, because the many nationalities included in the empire required a powerful army if order were to be maintained; this the Turks lacked, for corruption had also demoralized the army. Discipline was lax, and equipment and tactics were behind the times. It was indeed an excellent time for Catherine to intervene.

The opportunity came in 1768 when a border incident caused war with the Turks. The French, wishing to see Russia weakened, encouraged Turkey, but the inferiority of the Ottomans was quickly revealed in battle, and Russia recaptured the port of Azov, which Peter had won and lost. The Russians went on to greater victories, conquering most of the Rumanian section, and threatening to go farther south into the Balkans.

Finally, in 1774, peace was made. By the Treaty of Kuchuk Kainarji, Russia received the port of Azov and surrounding country; the Turks retained the Rumanian provinces, on condition that the government be reformed; and Russia obtained free navigation in Ottoman waters for her merchant ships and was recognized as protector of certain Christian churches in Constantinople.

By a treaty in 1792 Russian territory was further extended at Turkey's expense. The practical results of these treaties were that Russia now had an outlet to the southern waters and thereby to western Europe, better opportunities to develop her commerce, and the possibility of future intervention and expansion on the pretext of protecting the Christians in the Balkans and in Constantinople.

POLAND FALLS BEFORE RUSSIA'S ADVANCE

Catherine's expansion was also directed westward against Poland, and she had intervened there even before she embarked on the war against Turkey. Here again was a tempting field of activity, for throughout the eighteenth century Poland had been torn by dissension and weakness. The kingdom was a conglomeration of Poles (who predominated), Lithuanians, Latvians, Ukrainians, Cossacks, and Germans. Of these, the first three groups were fairly well united, and in the seventeenth century co-operated in opposing the Swedes in the Baltic and helping Austria against the Turks, thereby acquiring territory. The others, however, were distinctly minority groups, whose eyes turned toward Russia and Germany. Worse still, these many nationalities were of several religions. The majority—Poles and

Lithuanians—were Catholics; the Germans were Lutherans; the various Russians were Greek Orthodox; and there were many Jews. The confusion was increased by class difference between the group of selfish, bickering nobles and the mass of mistreated, under-privileged peasants.

Only a strong government could control and remedy such a situation, and, like Turkey, Poland had none. One weakness was the choice of king by election, which caused serious quarrels and enabled the noble electors to collect immense bribes from the candidates. In 1733, this problem led to the War of the Polish Election. Stanislaus Leszczynski, who had been the candidate of Charles XII for the throne, was now supported by his son-in-law, Louis XV. Austria and Russia favored Augustus, the Elector of Saxony, and only a five years' war settled the problem. France was defeated, Augustus III ascended the throne, and most important, Poland was further weakened.

Not only was the kingship weak, but legislative action was practically impossible because, by the freedom of veto, the opposition of one member of the Diet could defeat any proposal.

The incident which actually afforded an opportunity for Russian intervention was the death of Augustus III in 1763. Catherine had her favorite, Stanislaus Poniatowski, made king, theoretically independent, but actually at her command. Frederick the Great and Maria Theresa co-operated with Catherine to prevent the now aroused Polish people from making any governmental reforms which would strengthen Poland. Finally in 1772 the three rulers united in the first partition of Poland, which has already been noted.

This wholesale robbery aroused even the hitherto indifferent Polish nobles, but, because of the losses of the first partition, Poland was far too weak to make any progress. It was merely a matter of time until fresh depredations would be made. Although Frederick and Maria Theresa died in the eighties, their successors were willing to carry on the evil work. In 1793 and 1795, therefore, they joined Catherine in the second and third partitions of Poland. The Poles under the valiant Kosciuszko resisted desperately, but they were easily defeated by their powerful enemies. King Stanislaus II resigned and moved to Russia, and Poland ceased to be.

By the partitions of Poland, Catherine had extended Russia's boundaries westward until they adjoined Austria and Prussia. By Catherine's effective, if unethical, methods, Russia had become an important part of western Europe.

KOSCIUSZKO, POLISH LEADER

PART III

EXPANSION OF THE EUROPEAN WORLD

AN ALL-WATER ROUTE TO INDIA

EUROPE LOOKS BEYOND

SINCE THE BEGINNING OF recorded history, civilization has been moving westward. As the peoples of the Tigris and Euphrates valleys reached the height of their cultures, they lived to see their western neighbors of the "fertile crescent" region adopt their civilization and adapt it to the new and different requirements of their environment. Later the Greeks took the torch of civilization, then the Romans. Each time culture traveled, some of its characteristics were retained; but the acquirement of the new frontier caused changes and variations in the old order. This influence of the frontier has been one of the most important factors in the development of civilization.

This process of movement and change was about to make its most spectacular westward leap at the opening of the modern era. At the same time that kings were centralizing their power and modern nations were making their appearance, Europe was looking beyond its borders.

Part of this enlarged point of view was a result of the Crusades. Knights, on returning from the Holy Land, brought with them strange tales of stranger lands. They aroused interest and curiosity about what existed beyond the knowledge of those who stayed at home. Their awakened imagination demanded more information of the East.

The returning Crusaders brought with them something of even greater importance—spices! The value of this eastern product was obvious to a Europe which had no refrigeration, and was accustomed to food of uncertain age. With this oriental luxury, dining became more enjoyable; in fact, so accustomed did the noble and middle-class families become to these condiments that, lacking spices, the food formerly eaten without question became almost inedible. Spices from the East had become necessities.

IMPORTANCE OF THE RENAISSANCE

Two centuries earlier this interest in the East and the demand for an eastern product would have gone largely unsatisfied. Now, however, there were those who were ready to meet the need. This was a result of the great change, known as the Renaissance, which had swept over southern Europe by the middle of the fifteenth century.

No longer were the most intelligent and best educated minds restricted to supernatural matters. An interest in things worldly was no longer condemned. The attitude of the Church toward business and commerce was relaxed, as can be seen in the Catholic theologians' arguments that the taking of interest on money loaned was no longer a sin, and in the beginnings of the Medici banking facilities in Italy. Throughout Europe trade was awakening and commerce was developing under a crude capitalistic system. This commercial revolution, which has been described in a previous section, was part of the general awakening which was affecting every phase of European life.

The Renaissance, however, did not change the attitude of Europe merely toward trade and commerce. The new interest in history, literature, and the humanities seemed to increase the thirst for knowledge of things beyond the limited confines of the European world. An appreciative audience was found by travelers and merchants who told of their visits to India, China, or Japan.

MARCO POLO

The most famous of the men who recounted what had been seen in the East was Marco Polo. This merchant of Venice and his uncles, Nicolo and Maffeo, after several years of trading in the Near East, traveled entirely across the continent of Asia until they reached the magnificent court of the Tatar emperor, Kublai Khan, in Pekin, China. Graciously received, they were soon enjoying positions of honor in the government. Marco, especially, became a favorite and was entrusted with numerous missions throughout the kingdom. Wherever Marco went, he was tremendously impressed by the splendor and riches of the Orient. In comparison with thirteenth-century Europe, Asia was a promised land of untold wealth. For seventeen years Marco lived in the East, returning to Europe by sailing along the Chinese, Malayan, and Indian coasts, and then traveling overland to the Mediterranean. Shortly thereafter he was captured in a naval encounter by sailors of Genoa, which was engaged in one of the almost continuous series of wars between Italian city-states. Thrown into prison, Marco Polo wrote his memoirs (1298).

Europeans who read his surprisingly accurate account were almost unable to comprehend the picture. To the circumscribed European at the end of the thirteenth century, the tales were unbelievable; Marco Polo must have exaggerated. But, even if only a small proportion of his story were true, the Far East was nevertheless a rich region worth struggling to reach. For the next two hundred years Europe sought to learn more about this most fascinating land.

NEW INVENTIONS

Great inventions and discoveries in the field of science made it possible to spread information about lands beyond Europe. To Johann Gutenberg of Mainz is usually given the credit for the invention, about 1447, of printing by means of movable type although the use of movable initial letters, certainly a forerunner of the invention, was in use previously. This epoch-making invention's effect on the spread of knowledge can hardly be over-

PAGE FROM THE GUTENBERG BIBLE

The most famous example of Gutenberg's printing is the Forty-two-Line Bible, of which a number of copies are in existence. The book consists of nearly 1300 pages about twelve by sixteen inches in size, highly decorated.

emphasized. Information regarding discoveries or explorations would henceforth be rapidly diffused over broad areas. As each new seeker of knowledge set out, he had at hand the combined information gained by all of his predecessors.

About the same time more accurate maps and charts were introduced. Earlier, the compass and astrolabe had come into use. These new aids permitted the navigator to make longer voyages. No more must the mariner hug the coast and follow each irregularity of the shoreline. Finally the invention of the telescope, though it occurred much later (1609), freed the sailor from much of the uncertainty of sea travel.

TRADE ROUTES OF VENICE AND GENOA

The first European traders to profit as a result of the demand for products of the East were those of the Italian city-states. Making their way through the Mediterranean to Asia, these Italians were met by Arab traders, who had carried goods from such centers as Calicut and Malacca. These products were then distributed in Europe by the Italians themselves or passed on to merchants from the countries of northern Europe. The Asiatic routes were either over land, across deserts and mountains, or else by a long sea-route around the eastern and southern coasts, then through the Red Sea or Persian Gulf, and finally by land to the cities of the Black and Mediterranean seas.

Either by land or by sea, this means of transporting goods was uncertain and very expensive. Not only was the route long, and the mountains, deserts, and seas dangerous, but the threat of bandits and pirates was always present.

In spite of the tremendous risks involved, Venice, Genoa, and the other Italian cities profited because of their geographical position. The position of Italy made it the logical center of Mediterranean shipping, and trade bound for the German rivers of northern Europe found it convenient to use Venice or Genoa as southern terminals. It was partly an accident of geography that gave Italy a virtual monopoly of intercontinental trade.

This monopoly depended upon two conditions: the eastern end of the Mediterranean, the gateway to the Orient, must remain open; and this gateway must be the only one into Asia. The Portuguese and the Ottoman Turks threatened to remove these requirements for monopoly. Portuguese navigators, directed by Prince Henry, began cautiously to advance along the unknown African coast in an attempt to find an all-water route to India. If they succeeded, not only would transportation costs be lowered significantly, but also the bulk of the trade from the Orient would avoid the Mediterranean and Italy entirely by following the Atlantic coast to the northern European market.

The idea that the Turks closed the trade routes, and so caused the discovery of America and the all-water route to India, persists in spite of revelations which modify that interpretation. Traders from Italian city-states enjoyed favored positions in important Near Eastern cities. Their privileges were threatened by the expansion of the Ottoman Turks, and considerable friction resulted. Mohammed II began in 1452 to levy tariff duties, or tribute, on trading vessels passing through the Bosporous. Constantinople fell in 1453, and ten years later the Turks and the Venetians began a war which lasted until 1479. During this period there were clashes in Syria, Asia Minor, Greece, and the Mediterranean islands. By 1500, Genoa as well as Venice lost important colonies in the Near East.

The northern trade route from the Orient was threatened by warfare between the Tatars and the Turks; but Damascus, Beirut, Aleppo, and Alexandria grew in importance while the middle and northern routes were practically closed. The Turks continued their advance. Damascus fell in 1516, and in the following year Cairo was added to the Ottoman possessions. So it was that by 1520 the old routes between Orient and Occident were under Ottoman control.

PRINCE HENRY THE NAVIGATOR

Significant events were happening in the West while the Ottoman Turks were successfully challenging Italian preëminence in the Near East. Prince Henry, a younger son of King John I of

Portugal, was directing the Portuguese search for an all-water route to India. The Navigator, as he is known to history, had taken part in the conquest of Ceuta and was inspired with the hope of finding the rumored kingdom of Prester John. Henry possessed an independent income and was keenly interested in geography and navigation. The astronomical laboratory which he built on the promontory of Sagres in southwestern Portugal, became the gathering place of those daring navigators who were advancing down the African coast. As these voyages continued, Henry apparently lost much of his desire to effect an alliance with Prester John to attack the Ottomans from the rear, and concentrated his attention on discovery.

Trained in the school conducted at the laboratory, financed by the prince, encouraged and aided by new charts and maps, daring mariners made important progress. The Madeira Islands were reached by 1420, and then in time the whole western coast of Africa became known to Europeans. Cape Verde was reached in 1445, the mouth of the Gambia River in 1455, and, when Henry died in 1462, his navigators had advanced to a point within twelve degrees of the equator.

Tracing the African coastline was only one of the contributions made by Prince Henry and his associates. An even more important result was the training given to navigators and the development of navigation. It can be said that the science of navigation originated with Prince Henry, since it scarcely existed before his day. A large number of the early explorers and discoverers of the New World were trained by Henry, and they all profited from his efforts.

DOWN AND AROUND AFRICA

Moreover, the attempts to encircle Africa did not die with the prince. Portuguese captains continued their efforts. When Cape Palmas was discovered and it was found that the coast bent eastward, there was great rejoicing. Now the sea-route to India had been found! The southern coast of Africa had been reached! Hopes were dashed the following year when they discovered that, after twelve hundred miles, the coast again swung southward. The slow, progressive, stage-by-stage following of the coastline had to be continued. In 1471 the equator was crossed, and thereafter progress was more rapid.

In 1486, Días encountered a storm off the coast and for thirteen days was blown southward, out of sight of shore. When he saw land again, he found he was two hundred miles east of the southern tip of Africa. Upon his return, Días named this point the Cape of Storms; but soon afterward King John II changed the name to Cape of Good Hope, because it gave promise of a sea-route to India and great profits.

Both of these hopes were realized in 1498 when Vasco da Gama reached India and on his return brought back a cargo worth sixty times the cost of his expedition. This discovery of a sea-route to India was the finishing blow to Italian trade supremacy. The Asiatic land-routes were almost wholly discarded and the Atlantic superseded the Mediterranean as the center of European sea trade. World economic leadership moved westward from Italy to Portugal and her neighbor in the Iberian peninsula, Spain.

THE SEARCH FOR "EL DORADO"

COLUMBUS

THE ENTERPRISING Spanish monarchs, having expelled the Moors from Spain, were free to turn their attention to the pleas of Columbus, a Genoese seafarer, who had lived for several years in the Madeira Islands. Here he listened eagerly to his fellow sailors discussing stories and legends of the uncharted lands to the west. He had early accepted the views of the new scientific school: that the world was spherical in shape and that but a short stretch of water lay between western Europe and the Orient. He was fired with the desire to be the first to find a western route to the rich spice markets.

Repeated discouragement and failure met his efforts to gain royal aid in both Portugal and England. Queen Isabella of Spain, however, was finally won over by his enthusiasm and persistence. Thus, but for the short-sightedness of John II of Portugal and Henry VII of England, those countries might have had the honor of discovering the new world.

Three tiny ships, scantily outfitted and reluctantly manned by inexperienced crews, set sail from Palos on August 3, 1492. It is not hard to imagine the wild delight and genuine relief of Columbus and his frightened men when, after ten weeks of weary and monotonous voyaging, they came in sight of land (October 12, 1492). This was probably the island known today as Watling Island in the Bahama group. The natives found there were called "Indians" by Columbus, because he believed he had reached the Indies.

Courtesy Chicago Historical Society

THE LANDING OF COLUMBUS

CHRISTOPHER COLUMBUS
(From the painting by del Piombo, in the
Metropolitan Museum)

After sailing along the coast of Cuba and exploring the island of Haiti in a fruitless search for gold and spices, Columbus left for Spain with two vessels of the fleet. The wreckage of the third, which ran aground on the shores of the island of Haiti, was used to construct a fort for the forty-four Spaniards who remained and founded the first colony in the New World.

Columbus was received by Ferdinand and Isabella with great honor and was granted the titles of admiral, and viceroy of all the lands he had discovered. He made three other western voyages, in which he touched various islands of the Caribbean, the northern coast of South America, and what is now British Honduras. He died in 1506, probably not knowing that instead of discovering a new route to the Indies, he had found a New World.

It is indeed fitting that Americans formally honor the great discoverer on Columbus Day (October 12) each year. No other individual has contributed more to the physical and mental expansion of the modern world. Europe and Asia were no longer to mark the limits of man's imagination and experience. Now a world horizon was the only boundary to his thoughts and dreams.

EARLY NORSE DISCOVERIES

There is fairly valid evidence to show that Leif Ericsson discovered America in the year 1000, and gave the name Vinland to the region he visited. No permanent results came from this discovery, and so far as the European world is concerned, Columbus was the discoverer of America. Although Columbus made one of the greatest discoveries in history, the New World was named for Americus Vespucius. Without any basis of fact, Vespucius claimed to have made a voyage to the New World before Columbus' voyage of 1498, and geographers called the new lands America.

Spain and Portugal divided the newly discovered lands between them by the Treaty of Tordesillas in 1494. This treaty took the place of the papal bull of 1493, and gave to Portugal those areas which lay east of a line drawn 370 leagues west of the Cape Verde Islands, while Spain was to have those areas which lay west of the line.

AMERICUS VESPUCIUS
(By an unknown 16th century master)

MAGELLAN

Various Spanish expeditions between 1493 and about 1530, traced the American coastline from what became New England to the Straits of Magellan. Greatest of all these explorers was Magellan, a native of Portugal who entered Spanish service.

On September 10, 1519, Magellan's little fleet of five vessels and some 250 men set sail from Spain. Only one of the five was to complete the first voyage around the world. After spending the winter on the shores of Patagonia in southern Argentina, quelling innumerable mutinies among his crew, and suffering terrible physical hardships, Magellan reached the Philippine Islands early in the spring of 1521. Here he lost his life in a native uprising. In spite of the loss of leader, vessels, and crew, one ship of the original fleet, the *Victoria*, persevered and cast anchor in Seville on September 8, 1522, just three years after it had left Spain.

This voyage, supplemented by earlier ones, gave the Spaniards a limited idea, at least, of the Atlantic coastline of the New World and definitely proved that the Spice Islands could be reached by sailing west. Spanish interest in the lucrative spice trade was reawakened, and stately galleons soon appeared in the regions visited by Magellan and his companions.

CORTÉS—GREATEST OF THE CONQUISTADORES

Balboa, a bankrupt stowaway on an expedition to Central America, led an expedition across the Isthmus of Panama in 1513 and discovered the Pacific Ocean, which he called the South Sea. Unfortunately, Balboa was executed by the treacherous Pedrarius Dávila, the governor who was sent by Charles V to take charge of affairs on the Isthmus.

Great as were the achievements of Balboa, another explorer was to surpass them within a few years. This man was Hernando Cortés, who possessed remarkable military and executive ability. After distinguishing himself in the conquest of Cuba, Cortés won greater glory in Mexico. The governor of Cuba gave him command of an expedition to Mexico in 1519, a command which Cortés retained in spite of later efforts to remove him. Equipped with eleven vessels, four hundred soldiers, two hundred Indians, thirty-two horses, and ten cannon, Cortés set out for the mainland and disembarked at what is now Vera Cruz.

In Mexico he found the Aztecs, a powerful and highly civilized people who had migrated from the north early in the fourteenth century. They had quickly conquered the natives and set up a harsh rule over them. The subjugated tribes saw in Cortés and his army a way to avenge themselves and were eager to join forces against their hated rulers. Montezuma, the Aztec king, feared that these white strangers were the supernatural beings for whom his subject people had been waiting to free them from oppression. He hastened to send gifts to the Spaniards rather than to attack them. Cortés, fired with the zeal of conquest, proceeded on his way to the Aztec capital, Mexico City, or Tenochtitlán, as it was then called.

The magnificence of this city, with its great stone buildings and its vast stores of precious metals, exceeded even the most extravagant hopes of Cortés and his followers. The daring Spanish leader immediately strengthened his position by seizing the person of Montezuma and assuming virtual charge of the government. His successful conquest, however, was interrupted by a recall ex-

SOUTH AMERICA IN 1700

pedition sent out by Velásquez, governor of Cuba. Cortés ignored the governor's command, defeated his forces, and incorporated them into his own troops.

Upon returning to the Aztec capital, the Spanish conqueror found the city and countryside in a state of insurrection. He released Montezuma, hoping that his influence would quiet the frenzied condition of the Aztecs. This stratagem was of no avail, for the native ruler was fatally wounded by one of his own race when he urged obedience to the Spaniards.

Attacked by Indian hordes, Cortés' army suffered severely, losing most of its horses, cannon, and treasure, although a few soldiers survived and escaped to friendly nearby tribes. Sufficient reinforcements arrived from Cuba late in 1520, however, so that by the summer of the next year, Cortés recaptured Mexico City and proceeded to consolidate the conquest of the rest of Mexico. Not content with this, he organized new expeditions to explore the territory south of Mexico, and to voyage along the Pacific coast in an attempt to find a strait through the continent.

CONQUEST OF THE INCAS

Similar activity was going on in South America with Panama as a base. The most spectacular of these expeditions and conquests was that of Pizarro in Peru, which parallels the earlier Mexican conquest in many instances. The natives of Peru, the Incas, were as far advanced in government and civilization as the Aztecs in Mexico. By conquest and amalgamation, the Inca empire had acquired great wealth and political efficiency.

Pizarro, the Spanish conqueror of Peru, was of humble origin. His was a striking military character, with tremendous capacity for work, and indomitable perseverance. Though less brilliant and attractive than Cortés, Pizarro gained the confidence and obedience of his subordinates. Associated with him were an adventurous soldier named Almagro and a renegade priest known as De Luque. This priest had gained a considerable fortune and served as financier of the Pizarro expeditions.

Black Star Photo
A GREAT STRUCTURE IN YUCATAN
Showing the survival of culture found there by Spanish explorers.

After several perilous attempts, Pizarro sailed for Peru in January 1531, with an army of less than two hundred men, and twenty-seven horses. He established his headquarters near the present Tumbez. Here he learned of civil war caused by the jealousy of two Inca brothers, Huascar and Atahualpa. The latter had succeeded in establishing his authority in Cuzco, and like Montezuma, was inclined to believe the white intruders were supernatural beings and sought to placate them with gifts.

The Spaniards, in the meantime, moved into the interior toward Caxamarca, which they found deserted. Outside the city, Atahualpa and the Inca army of forty thousand drew up ready to annihilate the tiny Spanish force. Pizarro stationed his forces in strategic positions, seized the Inca, and slaughtered great numbers of the over-confident natives. Atahualpa hoped to secure his release by assembling a dazzling store of treasure; but the Spaniards took the treasure and then executed the Inca because of his complicity in the death of Huascar.

PANAMA CITY: THE FAMOUS FLAT ARCH
This piece of Spanish-American architecture is 300 years old.

Pizarro entered Cuzco in November, 1533, and began to consolidate his victories. Details of government, allotment of lands and Indian laborers, management of mines, and the organization of new expeditions occupied the efforts of Pizarro for the next few years. Civil wars and rebellion disturbed the peace of Peru until the Pizarros and the Almagros were eliminated, but the conquest of South America continued.

EXTENSION OF SPANISH CONTROL

Tales of mines of fabulous wealth, rich cities, and incredible buried treasure kept these eager conquerors in constant search of "El Dorado." Hostile natives, swamps, rivers, pathless mountains, deserts, disease, and jealousy did not daunt them. Always just beyond, they expected to find the veritable pot of gold. Although Cortés and Pizarro present the most fascinating and picturesque figures among them, many others in a lesser degree carried on similar conquests in Ecuador, Colombia, the Amazon basin, and Chile.

Spanish conquest of the central portion of the continent, now occupied largely by Argentina and Paraguay, began with the expedition of Mendoza to the Plata basin in 1536. An early attempt to found Buenos Aires failed, but control over the great river system which converges into the estuary known as La Plata, was secured after 1537. In that year a fort was built at the site of Asunción, now the capital of Paraguay. Martínez de Irala governed Asunción with more than usual skill, and sent exploring expeditions into the Gran Chaco west of the Paraguay River. Buenos Aires was finally founded in 1580 by Garay; but by that time the western portion of modern Argentina was being settled from Chile and Peru.

SPANISH CONQUESTS NORTH OF THE GULF AND THE RÍO GRANDE

Spanish efforts in the New World were by no means confined to Mexico and South America during the era of the *conquistadores*. Florida, the northern Gulf coast, and the great southwest were traversed by Spanish forces before 1550.

The first Spanish adventurer to visit what is now the United States, was Juan Ponce de León who sought in vain for the Fountain of Youth in Florida. Many attempts to colonize Florida failed. An expedition led by Narvaez in 1528 was almost completely destroyed. Hernando de Soto landed at Tampa Bay in 1539 with more than five hundred men. For three years De Soto led his men through the wilderness in an irregular march which crossed most of what is now the southern part of the United States east of the Mississippi River. De Soto himself was buried in the Mississippi when he died in 1542, and the remnants of the expedition returned to Mexico.

Francisco Vásquez de Coronado led another expedition into the great southwest while De Soto was on his odyssey. Coronado was seeking the Seven Cities of Cibola, supposedly rich in gold and other treasures. The exploration took Coronado as far as

Courtesy Chamber of Commerce, St. Augustine, Florida
OLD COQUINA CITY GATES
Once the only entrance to St. Augustine.

modern Kansas, but no wealthy cities were found. A party from this expedition discovered the Grand Canyon of the Colorado and added much to knowledge of the regions visited.

In the same year that Coronado returned to Mexico, 1542, explorations were made by sea northward along the California coast by Cabrillo and Ferrelo. Sixty years later Vizcaíno sailed along the same route.

Successful Spanish colonies were established by 1609 at two points in what is now the United States. The first was that of St. Augustine, Florida, which Menéndez de Avilés founded in 1565 to defeat French efforts to gain a foothold. The second was Santa Fe, New Mexico, which Juan de Oñate placed on a permanent basis between 1598 and 1609.

Spain was less successful in her colonizing efforts in continental North America than in the southern continent. This situation is partially explained by the wide area over which Spanish efforts were scattered, and by the small population of Spain itself.

Then, too, the northern wilderness was far less attractive than the more southern regions where Indian tribes were usually more docile, and where there were rich civilizations to conquer.

POLITICAL ADMINISTRATION IN SPANISH COLONIES

The whole Spanish colonial policy was dictated by royal authority. The Spanish possessions in the New World were considered as belonging personally to the sovereigns of Castile. With the rapid growth of colonial territory, it was necessary in 1524 to organize a special advisory committee. This royal body, the Council of the Indies, was the final legislative and judicial authority of Spanish America. It organized territorial units, and filled political and religious offices.

At first the king had allowed private adventurers to organize and subsidize their own expeditions, and rule and dispose of the territory they had conquered, with certain royal restrictions. It was found, however, that frequently the "conqueror" was tempted to ignore superior authority. Thus the king decided to send a royal appointee, known as a viceroy, to represent him personally in the New World. The territory over which he had charge was known as a viceroyalty.

The *audiencia*, in reality an administrative court system, grew up as a check on the viceroy. This body acted as the supreme judicial authority in the colonies, and had original jurisdiction over matters concerning the crown and the Indians. It came to act in a supervisory capacity over trade and finance, as well as over general preservation of law and order.

In the colonial towns, some degree of self-government manifested itself. The function of the *cabildo*, or municipal council, was similar to that of the New England town meeting. The tendency in Spanish America, however, was away from municipal democratic political organization, due largely to royal hostility and local corruption. Spain made an effort to maintain an honest and efficient colonial administration, which resulted in a system of checks on all officials. The viceroy was watched by the *audi-*

encia, which in turn was spied upon by the lower officials. Later on, a *residencia,* or royal visitor, was sent over to look into the conduct of all the officials, large and small, in a given political unit.

Since corruption, however, was a chronic malady in Spanish America, the wonder is not that the governmental structure finally weakened, but that it survived as long as it did.

ECONOMIC ORGANIZATION IN SOUTH AMERICA

The economic life of the Spanish colonies was also closely supervised by government officials. Spain, as well as the other nations, held mercantilist views of commerce. The welfare of the state, so the theory proposed, required a full treasury of gold, a large consuming and producing population, and an extensive merchant marine. A favorable balance of trade must be always maintained; therefore, exports must exceed imports so that specie might come into the country. To accomplish this, raw materials must be brought in, manufactured, exported, and sold.

Colonies, it was held, should furnish raw materials and markets for the mother country, but must not be competitors. It was the policy of each European state to monopolize and control the trade of its colonies.

As early as 1503, Spain organized the *Casa de Contratación* or House of Trade, for the purpose of controlling colonial commerce. Certain ports, such as Seville in Spain and Vera Cruz and Porto Bello in America, were opened for colonial trade. To protect and supervise this commerce, a fleet system was established. Land commerce in America had to be carried on by pack trains and river boats, while wholesale and retail trade was conducted in markets and fairs, the most famous of which was held in Porto Bello in Panama.

In spite of her efforts, Spain was not able to maintain her trade monopoly, for Dutch, English, and French freebooters and pirates captured her treasure fleets, and smuggled great quantities of goods into Spanish colonial ports.

The labor supply in Spanish America came largely from the native population. The first "conquerors" were given the right to the labor of the Indians living within their royal grant. This plan was known as the *encomienda* system and aimed to protect and civilize the native, as well as to exploit him. Among those who early opposed this virtual enslavement of the Indian population was Father Las Casas. He used his influence against the continuance of this system, but, strange to say, favored Negro slavery in its place.

The principal occupations in Spanish America were agriculture and stock-raising, although mining attracted the attention of the more adventurous and was heavily subsidized by the home government.

SOCIAL LIFE IN THE SPANISH COLONIES

Spanish American civilization became a composite of Spanish and native culture, based on a fairly rigid caste system. Most of the high political offices were held by native born Spaniards, while next in the social scale were the Creoles, who were American born. Below them came the *mestizo*, half Spanish and half Indian, who made up the larger part of the army. The two lowest classes, the Indians and the Negroes, had no social or political privileges and were held in slavery by the other groups.

Education was by no means neglected, but it too was based on the caste system. Only the sons of government officials, wealthy merchants, and professional men attended the colonial universities. In fact, the scholarship of the universities of Mexico and Lima, established by royal decree in 1553, was recognized by contemporary European institutions of higher learning. Many of the clergy were devotees of intellectual pursuits, and books were written on historical, ethnological, and popular subjects.

Instruction and curriculum in the universities, as well as in the mission school, were supervised closely by the Church. Only the most elementary educational institutions were opened to the *mestizos*.

The influence of the Church, however, was perhaps felt most in the frontier Indian mission, where the *encomienda* system failed or proved unprofitable. Members of the Jesuit, Dominican, and Franciscan orders were especially zealous in carrying Christianity

and European civilization to the frontier natives. The aim of
these missionaries was not only to gain religious converts, but to
give industrial training.

Each mission had its grain fields, ranges, vegetable gardens,
orchards, and vineyards, which were cared for by the Indians. The
men were given instruction in carpentry and wine-making,
while the native women learned spinning, weaving, sewing, and
cooking. The intention was to train the natives to support themselves, and eventually to give them the mission lands and transfer
their religious care to the parish priest.

By continuing this process, the Spanish missionaries gradually
carried Christianity north of the Río Grande into Texas, and by
1776 they had gone as far north as the present San Francisco.

Courtesy San Diego-California Club
MISSION SAN DIEGO DE ALCALA
Founded by Fra Junípero Serra in 1769, this was the first mission established in
California under supervision of Franciscan padres.

Courtesy Field Museum of Natural History

HEROIC PERUVIAN SCULPTURE

Prominent among these zealous *padres* were Kino and Serra who planted missions in the southwest and in California.

Frequently military posts, *presidios*, were found necessary to protect the mission outposts. Thus the *padre* and the soldier became the two civilizing forces on the frontier. In spite of these military and religious efforts, however, the Spaniards were unable to gain more than a feeble political hold on what is now southwestern United States.

Whatever the shortcomings of the Spanish treatment of the native population, it does not compare unfavorably with that of other European powers. Spain aimed at racial, religious, and cultural assimilation rather than annihilation as England did. This practice resulted in a large population of mixed blood and the removal of racial antipathies. Today there are in Spanish America relatively few families of pure European blood.

CONTRIBUTIONS OF SPAIN TO THE AMERICAS

Historians in the past have unjustly minimized Spanish contributions to the Americas. The "conquerors" bore not only the sword, but also Christianity to the New World. They brought with them such plants as the citrus fruits, sugar and cotton; and such animals as cattle, sheep, horses, and mules.

From Mexico to Chile, the Spanish language and institutions are still dominant. Some of the United States have Spanish names, namely, California, Florida, Colorado, and Nevada. Innumerable rivers, mountains, towns, and cities north of the Río Grande bear Spanish names, while the southwestern Indian tribes in the United States still speak Spanish in preference to English. In many of the cities in the same region, there is a Spanish quarter in which life goes on much as it has done for generations past. Spanish architecture is still popular, and today in Florida and the southwestern states one may visit interesting old missions and government buildings erected by the early Spaniards.

The southern and western festival, rodeo, and mission plays are carried over from colonial days. Even the American cowboy has inherited his trade, his horse, his outfit, vocabulary, and methods from his earlier Spanish prototype. Bells in numerous belfries of mission churches and cathedrals from Florida to California bear the Spanish royal coat of arms; while land surveys in many of the southwestern states still rest on early Spanish grants, whose original records are now in Mexico City or Madrid. In fact, the literature, history, and life of this whole region of the United States is distinctly colored by its early background. Thus in spite of the fact that Spain was eventually pushed out of the limits of the United States, she has left us a rich heritage.

Her greatest contribution, however, was made to the present Latin-American nations. Today the Spanish blood, language, religion, and culture are the dominant forces in the republics to the south. This once-proud European country no longer controls the political destiny of any area of the New World, but she still wields immeasurable influence in her gift of Hispanic civilization.

FRENCH VOYAGEURS AND JESUITS
IN THE WILDERNESS

EARLY EXPLORATIONS AND SETTLEMENTS

EARLY IN THE SIXTEENTH CENTURY, France began
to contest the exclusive claim of Spain and Portugal to the
New World. Her ambitious young monarch, Francis I,
actively encouraged exploration. Verrazano, a Florentine, was
the first explorer authorized to sail to America under the French
flag. He was to seek a northwestern route to the Orient. Although
the voyage failed in this objective, Verrazano sailed along the
North American coast from Cape Fear to Newfoundland. To
the St. Lawrence area, he gave the significant name of New
France. Cartier's three voyages (1534-1541) continued these explorations. He established French territorial claims to Newfoundland, the gulf area of the St. Lawrence River, and sailed as far
inland as the present Montreal.

The first attempt at a permanent French settlement in North
America was made by Ribaut on Port Royal Sound in the Carolinas in 1562. Composed entirely of men, ill-adapted to an agricultural life, and surrounded by hostile Indians, the colony was
soon abandoned. Two years later, the Huguenot, Laudonnière,
led an expedition to the St. Johns River in Florida. Here the
active opposition of the Spaniards prevented a permanent settlement.

A FRENCH VOYAGEUR
(From an old drawing)

FRENCH IN CANADA

French fishermen had long been among those Europeans who frequented the Newfoundland fisheries. Except for this contact, France for over fifty years after Cartier turned her back on the New World and consolidated her position on the Continent. There were several attempts at settlement in the early seventeenth century. The first was made on the island of St. Croix in 1604. The severe winter nearly destroyed the colony, and the survivors removed across the Bay of Fundy, locating at Port Royal, the present site of Annapolis, Nova Scotia.

The founding of Quebec by the intrepid Champlain in 1608, marked the beginning of the active French regime in Canada. His earlier experiences in the Caribbean area had fitted him for strenuous explorations in the north. He coasted along the New England shore to below Cape Cod. Later he explored the interior south of Quebec, discovering the lake that now bears his name. Champlain's most important exploring expeditions, however, were those which took him on fur-trading ventures and on elusive quests for a northwest passage. He ascended the Ottawa River in

SAMUEL DE CHAMPLAIN
Founder of Quebec and discoverer of Lake
Champlain.

1613 and reached the shores of Lake Huron two years later. Nicolet, his agent, entered the Lake Michigan area in 1634. Shortly thereafter, the explorer-traders, Radisson and Groseilliers, entered the region west and north of Lake Superior.

Champlain, with his vision of empire, found the French court indifferent to his plans. His settlement at Quebec seemed feeble when compared with the thriving English colonies, but by 1650 it was the center from which all French activities in North America radiated. The "city on the rock" was also the center of the Jesuit missionary operations. This religious order proved invaluable to France in winning Indian allies and exploring the interior. Unfortunately for the French, their friendship for the Algonquins, dating from Champlain's aid to them in 1609, had won the implacable hatred of the Iroquois. This hostility was to drive the latter into an alliance with the British that continuously threatened the French fur trade. In venting their enmity, the Iroquois made no distinction between adventurers and missionaries. Martyrdom came to Father Jean de Brébeuf and many of his contemporaries during these years.

GOVERNORS OF NEW FRANCE

After a period of inactivity, New France became a royal province in 1663. Among the new personnel sent out to administer the government, were men whose names were to rank with Champlain's. Authority in the colony was vested in three officials: governor, bishop, and *intendant*. Bishop and governor repeated overseas the familiar European struggle between civil and religious groups for supremacy. The *intendant* was often left to execute the actual tasks of government. The first of these, Jean Talon, was appointed in 1665. He directed the administration of justice and audited financial and military records. He took advantage of his wide supervisory power and sent agents into the interior. The expansion of agriculture, fishing, and the production of naval stores, were encouraged.

Among the colonial governors, the Count de Frontenac was perhaps the greatest figure. He possessed unusual insight into the ultimate importance of the interior in relation to the impending Anglo-French duel. Frontenac planned a chain of forts to extend southwestward along the Great Lakes and Mississippi. He appreciated the importance of Indian allies, and whooped and danced around camp fires with the Indian braves when good policy demanded it. Bitter quarrels with the bishop and the *intendant* brought about his recall in 1682. Seven years later he was reappointed to secure New France against English attack.

FRANCE IN THE CARIBBEAN

While interest in Canada had lagged, France sought tropical islands. She was no more immune to the lure of the Caribbean than were the other nations. Her belated entrance into competition with the English, Dutch, and Spanish put her at some disadvantage, but by 1664 France held fourteen of the lesser islands. The early trading companies had sold out to proprietors who were prospering on the sugar business, made possible by a plantation and slave economy. When Colbert became finance minister in 1662, he sent agents to curtail these private powers and to reestablish royal authority. Two years later, Louis XIV chartered the West India Company, granting it a forty-year monopoly of trade and colonization. Despite royal patronage, the company could not defend its holdings against England and Holland, and dissolved in 1664.

FRENCH IN THE MISSISSIPPI VALLEY

Several of the early Jesuits had ventured to the Great Lakes and entered some of their tributaries. French influence on the Mississippi, which began with Marquette and Joliet in 1673, was extended by one of the greatest of explorers. This man was La Salle, member of a wealthy bourgeois family, who bore a royal patent to build forts and engage in the fur trade. He was fortunate to

LA SALLE, EXPLORER AND DREAMER OF EMPIRE

have the complete sympathy and aid of Governor Frontenac. Together they worked out a plan of action based on their mutual interest in the building of a French empire in North America.

La Salle and his faithful lieutenant, Tonty, made several expeditions into the Upper Lakes region. On one occasion, La Salle returned to Fort Frontenac for supplies, leaving Tonty at Fort St. Louis in Illinois. An Iroquois attack forced him to retire to Green Bay, where La Salle later found him. Meanwhile, Father Hennepin explored the upper Mississippi area and, though captured by the Sioux, was rescued by Duluth, or Du Lhut, cousin of Tonty. In February, 1682, La Salle and Tonty were launched on their greatest exploit. Floating down the Mississippi they reached the Gulf on April 9, and took possession of the entire valley for their king.

THE FRANCO-SPANISH FRONTIER

With the French entrance upon the Gulf of Mexico, a Franco-Spanish frontier was formed. In 1684, La Salle returned from France to plant a colony at the mouth of the Mississippi. Insufficient geographical knowledge and faulty navigation caused the expedition to land at a lonely spot on the Texas coast. Spanish ships, like so many vultures, were dispatched at once from Vera Cruz to destroy the trespassers. Five expeditions sailed and returned, however, without having sighted them.

Throughout a weary three years, La Salle and his party tried to find the Mississippi, his original goal. It finally became evident that their only hope was to attempt to reach Canada overland. A small group, led by La Salle, undertook this journey in 1687. The daring leader, unfortunately, was assassinated by mutineers while they were still in Texas. Only a handful lived to reach Canada.

Spain had a dual reason for awakening to the necessity of defending the northern Gulf coast in the late seventeenth century. The English had firmly entrenched themselves in Carolina and were expanding westward through trade connections. The French, also, were becoming a menace in the Mississippi Valley. To meet this competition, Spanish officials decided on the occupation of Pensacola Bay. An expedition left Mexico in October, 1698, only a few days before a French fleet sailed from Europe, bound for the same destination.

The French government had bestowed La Salle's patent upon Iberville, distinguished in French service in the Hudson's Bay region. He put in at Pensacola for supplies. Beneath the elaborate exchange of Latin courtesies between the commanders, it was obvious that Spain had made good her claim. Iberville went on to the Bay of Biloxi, and from that port proceeded to re-discover the Mississippi River.

The French were anxious to prevent the Gulf from becoming a Spanish lake, and knew the miserable state of the Pensacola settlement. In turn, the Spanish were aware that the French Gulf colonies were intended ultimately to serve as bases for the conquest of the Mexican mines. The *entente* of the two royal houses in Europe, however, prevented open hostilities and kept unblemished the veneer of diplomacy and courtesy.

MOBILE BAY SETTLEMENT

Iberville moved his colony to a site on the Mobile River in 1702. When he returned to France, Bienville, his brother, replaced him. Under the latter's leadership, Mobile was founded in 1710, New Orleans in 1718, and numerous French posts appeared on the Red and Arkansas Rivers. At the same time, Alarcón, the Spanish governor, established San Antonio across the narrowing frontier.

Under the cloak of exploration, plans were made to extend the French forts northward to cut into the trade with the prairie tribes and open a route to Mexico. Along what is now the Canadian-American frontier, the La Vérendrye family penetrated beyond Lake Superior to Lake Winnipeg in 1733. A few years later they reached to the Missouri River and the Black Hills.

Frequent clashes occurred on the Louisiana-Texas frontier. It was evident that, despite orders from Europe, there were many New World issues which could be settled only in the areas concerned. The long period of Franco-Spanish rivalry in the Gulf region ended with Spain's alliance with France in 1761 against the

Courtesy New Orleans Chamber of Commerce

HEART OF OLD NEW ORLEANS
Showing the Cabildo, St. Louis Cathedral, Presbytery and Pontalba Apartment, with Jackson Square in the foreground.

traditional English enemy. Spain was rewarded for its support by the cession of that part of Louisiana which lay west of the Mississippi. The problem of frontier maintenance now was vastly increased. For France, after 1763, the bitter struggle with England and Spain for the domination of the New World was a phase of the past. The wonder is not that France, like Spain, lost her colonial possessions, but that she held them as long as she did.

FRENCH RULE IN AMERICA

The primary interest of France in her North American possessions lay in the development of fisheries and the fur trade. France, in common with the European economic policy of the seventeenth and eighteenth centuries, had built her colonial system upon the mercantilist theory. The increase of revenue was the goal of colonial administration and conditioned the methods of government. French overseas control soon came to be synonymous with trade monopoly and close unity of Church and state. Paternalism pervaded every phase of society—from the royal governor to the half-savage *coureur-de-bois*. Private enterprise and individualism were completely smothered under such a system. Domination and supervision were the watchwords of every official, no matter how petty his rank.

Colonists did not come to New France with their families or with plans for permanent homes, as they did in the English provinces. Without the transplantation of ordinary family and municipal life, there was no demand for local political institutions. A sparse population spread over a huge wilderness area from Quebec to New Orleans. Tiny trading posts and missions, well-armed forts, and diminutive villages dotted the lakes and rivers of the French western empire.

Missions were established at Cahokia and Kaskaskia in "the Illinois" by 1700. Fort Chartres and Prairie du Rocher, in the same area, were founded in the next four decades. Fort Detroit, built in 1701, was essential for the defense of the western water highways against the Iroquois; while Fort Vincennes, on the Wabash River, founded in 1732, became an important interior post. Fur trading and agriculture were the chief pursuits of these western settlements. A large quantity of produce was exported, to both Detroit and the French West Indies. The agricultural production of all New France, however, was insufficient for its own needs.

It was hoped that these settlements could hold and develop the rich fur-bearing region. The constant concern of French officials was defense against the Indians, the English, and, in the lower Mississippi Valley, the Spanish. New France was then, generally speaking, more of an outpost than a colony.

COMPANY OF NEW FRANCE

The right to exploit French possessions and establish the necessary civil, religious, and military jurisdiction was granted by the king to companies or individuals. To these proprietors the fur trade was the great attraction, and the founding of permanent settlements lagged. In 1627, monopolistic powers were assigned to the Company of New France, patronized by Cardinal Richelieu. Continental entanglements, financial difficulties, and the constant hostility of the English and Iroquois were sufficient to cause its failure.

An organization of merchants in New France now took over the Company's privileges and obligations. In 1647, the king allowed the new proprietors to set up the Council of Quebec. This consisted of the Jesuit superior and the commandant of the troops at Montreal, in association with the governor. Two citizens were added to that body the next year, but it bore no likeness to the representative institutions in Virginia or New England.

New France became a royal province in 1663. Slow economic development and a quarreling officialdom were the reasons for the cancellation of the company's charter. A Sovereign Council of Quebec was created by the Crown and remained a vital arm of the government until the end of the French regime. This body consisted of the governor, bishop, *intendant*, and certain councilors, the number being increased several times. The Council administered and enforced the laws, served as a court of appeal, and regulated trade.

The governor, as the representative of the Crown, acted as official head of the Council. His conduct, in turn, was checked by the *intendant* who had charge of expenditures, and exercised some judicial powers. This system of divided administrative responsibility resulted in bitter conflict and inefficient control.

THE CHURCH IN NEW FRANCE

After the early period of courageous missionary efforts, the Church became an influential temporal as well as spiritual enterprise. François de Laval became the first bishop of the diocese of Quebec in 1658, and exercised ecclesiastical jurisdiction over all of New France. He used his influence in the Council to uphold the Church and to fight the liquor traffic with the Indians. His interest in education led to the establishment of an academy in Quebec, which later became Laval University.

The Church controlled about one-fourth of the lands granted for settlement and was the greatest single landholder. The parish

JACQUES CARTIER MEMORIAL
The village of Gaspé, Quebec, is shown in the background.

was the unit for the administration of justice and the levying of the militia, as well as the basis for the social life of the community. The clergy had complete control over education, and censored the reading material which came into the colony. To the influence of the Church is due much of the picturesque charm and color of the Quebec of today.

LANDHOLDING IN NEW FRANCE

The landholding policy of New France was a system already growing antiquated in France when it was introduced into the New World. The custom of granting land titles and certain privileges and responsibilities to prominent persons was known as the *"seigneurial system."* In this feudal hierarchy, the *seigneur* guaranteed military aid to the Crown, in return for large grants, usually along the St. Lawrence River. His feudal tenants, or *habitants*, occupied the subdivisions of the estate, rendering to the lord certain services and dues, such as produce and labor, at stated intervals. The *seigneuries*, large and small, were always apportioned in the form of long narrow strips, with river frontage to solve the important problems of transportation and communication. With a *habitant* house on each strip, the general impression was of a continuous line of buildings as one went down the St. Lawrence.

SOCIAL LIFE IN NEW FRANCE

The social cleavage between the lord and *habitant* was slight. Frequently the former spent the winter in Quebec, but during the summer months might be found in the field with his tenants. As a group, the latter lived a happy, carefree existence, and left political and economic problems to their officials in Quebec. Social life was relatively simple in the country communities, with the curé, the *seigneur*, and the two counselors of the parish taking the lead in their activities. Quebec and Montreal had some small degree of winter court life, but it was very informal and crude.

This feudal system, however, gradually fell into decay as the

Courtesy Canadian National Railways

CHATEAU DE RAMAZAY, MONTREAL

habitants deserted to become trappers. These *coureurs-de-bois* soon forgot their European heritage as they ranged the forests, often living as members of Indian tribes. This life not only furnished adventure, but also great returns on illicit trade. In fact, the commerce in furs was the only really profitable occupation of the colony, since industry was neglected and primitive agricultural methods produced insignificant results.

At the close of the French regime in 1763, the population of New France numbered only 65,000. Most of the people lived along the banks of the St. Lawrence, and but a few thousand were scattered throughout the Middle West. This population, spaced so thinly over such a vast area, could be only an outpost of French power, but it was a serious barrier to English expansion from the tidewater region east of the Alleghenies.

FRENCH CONTRIBUTIONS TO NEW WORLD

We are apt to conclude that French influence in America ended with their defeat by England in 1763. However, visitors in the province of Quebec today are amazed at the amount of French atmosphere and culture still in existence. This is not surprising, when one realizes that at least eighty per cent of the population is of French extraction. Beautiful churches, wayside shrines, lovely old châteaux, dog carts, and thatched roofs, all testify to an earlier French civilization. The names of innumerable rivers, lakes, villages, and cities throughout the eastern half of the North American continent bear witness to the exploring zeal of the French *voyageur*. Perhaps the most charming bit of New France left in the United States is in the city of New Orleans, where French colonial architecture, customs, and traditions still remain as living evidence of a delightful Old World existence.

ENGLISH COLONIES IN THE NEW WORLD

ENGLISH SEA-DOGS

ENGLISH ACTIVITY in the New World parallels that of France. It took a century of guerrilla warfare on the sea with Spain before England made definite steps to compete with the discoverers of America for its possession. The claim of the British Lion to the Western Hemisphere was based on the voyages of the Cabots, in particular that of John Cabot in 1497. These voyages extended along the coast of North America from about Cape Breton Island to South Carolina. Not only did these voyages furnish England a claim to America, but they laid out an immediately used route to the Newfoundland fisheries. For these great services, the thrifty Henry VII gave Cabot the sum of ten pounds sterling and a promise of a pension of twenty pounds annually.

During the next century, the efforts of England in America were motivated almost entirely by the desire to injure Spain in her colonial empire "for the glory of God and King." Hawkins, one of the most relentless enemies of Catholic Spain, urged his Protestant seamen to read their Bible and sing hymns in the intervals between attacks on Spanish treasure ships. He saw nothing irreligious, moreover, in kidnaping Negroes in Africa and selling them as slaves in the Spanish possessions.

Hawkins' most noted associate in "singeing the Spanish beard" was Francis Drake. He fearlessly preyed upon the Spanish ships conveying American gold and silver to the mother country. He even attacked the Spaniards in their own colonial ports, once sacking Panama, and climaxing his career by sailing through the

Straits of Magellan and capturing the surprised Spanish treasure ships in the harbors of Peru. Then, realizing that the Spaniards would be lying in wait for him on his eastward return, he turned his prow westward and continued around the world (1577).

Other English, as well as French and Dutch, "sea-dogs" made their headquarters in the many islands of the West Indies and on the northern coast of South America. From here they inflicted stinging blows on the Spaniards who regarded them as pirates. For almost three hundred years they made this region, known as "The Spanish Main," a fearsome place indeed.

NORTHWEST PASSAGE

To the north, other English captains were considering America as a barrier which must be penetrated before the more attractive India and China could be reached. Among those who searched for a northwest passage to Asia were Frobisher, who explored Labrador, Baffin Bay, and Frobisher Bay (1576); Davis, who explored the same region (1585); Hudson, who discovered the bay bearing his name (1610); and Baffin (1615-1616). Davis also discovered the Falkland Islands, east of the Straits of Magellan.

Hakluyt is also important in the story of early English exploration. His contribution consisted of collecting and publishing accounts of these voyages, thus popularizing the new geographical knowledge.

EARLY COLONIZERS

England's first attempt to colonize America occurred in 1578, when Sir Humphrey Gilbert was given a charter which assigned land in Newfoundland to him. The group of settlers who went with him found this region unsuitable for colonization and returned to England. Gilbert died in a storm on the return voyage and efforts at colonizing were carried on by his half-brother, Raleigh, who made several attempts to found colonies along the Virginia and Carolina coast. None of these was permanent. Because England was so completely involved in fighting the Spanish Armada in 1588, no supplies were sent, nor any communications maintained with the settlements. When in 1591 an English ship finally did arrive on the Virginian coast, not a single trace could be found of the settlers except the single word "Croatoan" cut in the bark of a tree. Croatoan was the name of a friendly Indian tribe. No more has ever been learned about the fate of this "Lost Colony of Roanoke." Perhaps the settlers were killed by Indians or Spaniards, absorbed by an Indian tribe, or possibly they attempted to move their settlement and were lost at sea. Among those who disappeared was Virginia Dare, the first white child born in English America.

REASONS FOR COLONIZATION

The question arises as to why English colonization took place. Why was it that, within a period of seventy-five years (1607-1682), twelve English colonies were planted on the American continent? The general motives for expansion, found whenever peoples engage in such a movement, are curiosity, hope for trade, religious zeal, discontent with home conditions, desire to lessen the surplus home population, patriotism, and the military need to forestall rivals and to seize strategic points. Almost all of these reasons can be found behind English colonization.

In 1485, Henry VII, a Tudor, became king of England. He needed support in order to keep his throne and turned for aid to the middle class. Although prices were rising as a result of the inflation caused by the great imports of gold from America, Henry VII and his successors favored the merchant class by setting maximum wage regulations. Thus, with prices rising, wages were held static. Workers had to resort to charity as a necessary supplement to their meager incomes.

Until the middle of the sixteenth century the main, in fact the only, source of charity was the monasteries. These, however, were abolished about 1546 by Henry VIII as part of the English Reformation and because confiscation of their lands enriched the purse of the king. Thus the English poor were deprived of charity from the monasteries. Soon beggars infested the streets of cities, and the countryside was filled with those who had been driven to banditry by hunger.

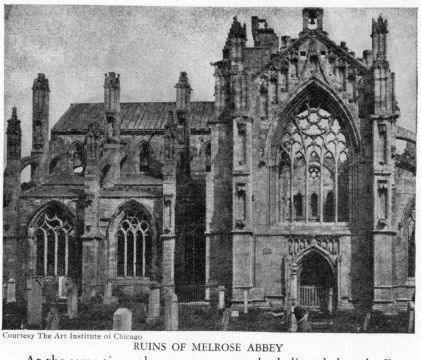

Courtesy The Art Institute of Chicago
RUINS OF MELROSE ABBEY

At the same time, there were many who believed that the English Reformation had not gone far enough. These Dissenters, as they were called, were divided into two groups, the Puritans and the Separatists. The former sought to purify the Established Church, and the latter wished to separate entirely from it. These, together with Catholics, were persecuted by the English government which sought to establish conformity.

With the accession of the first Tudor, Henry VII, in 1485, national patriotism in England grew rapidly. This spirit culminated in the reign of Elizabeth when the feeling of national pride was expressed in almost every field—literature, finance, commerce, and colonization. With this patriotism was combined an intense hatred for Spain. This attitude was exemplified in the actions of Drake, Hawkins, and other "sea-dogs" on the Atlantic, while Shakespeare is generally thought of as expressing the greatest example of English nationalism in literature.

America, in the sixteenth century, was a magic word in Europe. Knowledge of the New World was scant and superficial.

It was generally thought that gold and silver could be found throughout the continent; it was hoped that almonds, silk, and other tropical products could be grown in the Carolinas; and most early settlers spent much time exploring and searching for a passage through the land barrier for a route to India.

PROMOTERS OF ENGLISH COLONIES

These religious, political, and economic conditions all helped to encourage colonization. Individuals were willing to leave their homes and settle in the wilderness to avoid religious or political persecution, and to escape the hard times in England. They hoped to better themselves economically, and were lured on by the bait of free land. Many others, adventurers at heart, went to America imbued with a wanderlust spirit.

Since most of these malcontents had little or no money, their colonization of America would have been impossible if groups in England had not been willing to finance their transportation and underwrite the colonial enterprises during the first years. Several such groups could be found. There were the idealists who thought of America as a model place to try out Utopian schemes and social experiments. There were patriotic groups who hoped to hurt Spain, to establish English trade colonies and develop a mercantile organization, to provide a place for the supposedly surplus population of England, and to relieve England of undesirables. There were religious sects who were determined that the persecuted of their faith should have a place of refuge. Finally, there were groups of merchants who anticipated individual profit in trade resulting from colonial markets. These merchants were willing to invest sums of money in planting colonies if a monopoly of the resulting trade could be assured them and if their personal liability for losses could be limited in some manner.

A model for such a company was the joint-stock trading company. Several of these companies had received charters giving them monopoly rights to all trade in a specified region, to the exclusion of other Englishmen. In 1553, the Muscovy Company had been organized to trade with Russia and to find a northeast passage to China. The Baltic and Turkey Companies were chartered in 1579 and 1581, respectively. In 1600, the great East India Company was organized. Profits were unbelievable; dividends to the amount of 600 per cent per year, in the case of this company, were paid. Hope for such returns led to the formation of similar trade companies, which colonized Virginia, Massachusetts, and Delaware.

THE LANDED PROPRIETORS

During the feudal ages, favorites of the king, or those who had contributed something to the crown or nation, were often given vast tracts of land to be held in fief under the ruler. In the seventeenth century, a practice reminiscent of this earlier age developed. A proprietor or group of proprietors might receive from the king a charter that gave full economic and political control over a region. Usually these proprietors hoped for economic gain through the rental or sale of land and through customs duties. Penn advertised throughout Germany the liberal terms under which he would dispose of his lands in Pennsylvania. Lord Baltimore, John Mason, William Berkeley, and James, Duke of York, attempted to get purchasers for their land in Maryland, New Hampshire, New Jersey and New York, respectively. Eight men who helped Charles II gain the English throne were given a charter granting them the Carolinas. In the next century a board of trustees, headed by James Oglethorpe, was granted Georgia. Sometimes the hope of gain was tempered by a desire to create a place for the religiously persecuted, as in the case of Penn and Baltimore, or by humanitarian interests, as in the case of Oglethorpe.

Some of the settlers of Massachusetts were stockholders of the trading company and took their charter with them to America. Connecticut and Rhode Island were settled in part by malcontents from Massachusetts. They secured charters from the English king and kept them in America. These provinces, which thus held their own charters, were known as corporate colonies.

Another method of securing colonies in America was by conquest. The Dutch conquered the Swedish settlements in Delaware in 1655, as part of the expanding of Dutch influence from

New York. In 1664, an English fleet sailed into New York harbor and at one stroke the three colonies of New York, New Jersey, and Delaware were obtained for England.

VIRGINIA

Virginia was the first permanent English colony in America. It was established by the London Company, one of the trading companies described above. The first settlers were considered as employees rather than as genuine colonists. The early years were tragic. Between one-half and two-thirds of each group of settlers died within a year after leaving England. Disease, hostile Indians, and lack of initiative played their parts in hindering the growth of the colony. John Smith's term as governor and his edict, "He who does not work shall not eat," started the colony on a more prosperous path.

Courtesy Norfolk Advertising Bureau

OLD ST. PAUL'S CHURCH IN NORFOLK
Only building left standing in the city after the English bombardment, January 1, 1776.

About 1617 the discovery of an improved method of curing tobacco accelerated the growth and prosperity of the colony. The English government revoked the charter of the company in 1624, and Virginia came directly under the control of the British crown. Tobacco made the colony fairly prosperous, but, since that became the only crop raised, general prosperity depended almost entirely on the price of the leaf in London.

NEW ENGLAND

A religious group which opposed the rituals of the established church of England sailed from Plymouth in 1620 on the little ship *Mayflower*. After a stormy voyage these "Pilgrims" landed at the tip of Cape Cod. An exploring group was sent to find a suitable place for settlement. On December 21, 1620, the site of Plymouth was selected. The plan of working and sharing in common was tried here at first and proved to be as unsuccessful as it had been at Jamestown.

While the *Mayflower* had been anchored off Cape Cod, the Pilgrim fathers drew up a compact agreeing to draft fair and just laws and to live up to them. The Mayflower Compact, as this agreement came to be called, was the first instrument of government devised in America. It swore allegiance to James I and provided for the setting up of governmental machinery.

About ten years later, a trading company was organized to settle the region around modern Boston. These colonists were Puritans who took their charters with them from England. Within a short time thousands of Puritans migrated from England to America. The soil of New England was not suited to the production of a commercial crop like tobacco. Instead, farms developed around a great many small towns. Besides the raising of food crops, commerce and manufacturing were soon begun. Although most of the colonists had left England because of opposition to the Established Church, in Massachusetts a Puritan state church was soon established and the enjoyment of political rights was dependent upon church membership.

MASSACHUSETTS LIBERALS SEEK SHELTER

General dissatisfaction in Massachusetts led to the establishment of separate colonies by discontented people. Thomas Hooker, in 1636, led a group southwestward to the vicinity of the valley of the Connecticut River. These colonists were impelled by economic and personal as well as by religious reasons. In 1662 the king gave them a charter, which incorporated the New Haven settlements made earlier under John Davenport.

Another group of radical opponents of the Puritan church settled in Rhode Island under the leadership of Roger Williams and Anne Hutchinson. Peaceful relations were maintained with the Indians. Here a colony started without a church establishment, tithes, or compulsory church attendance. Rhode Island, with its fugitives, exiles, and strong individualists, became the most democratic colony in America.

Other groups went north and northeastward from Massachusetts, mainly for economic reasons, and settled in New Hampshire and Maine. As was also true in regard to the other settlements, Massachusetts attempted to retain political control over these northern colonies. She was successful in regard to Maine, but New Hampshire was set up finally as a separate colony. Both regions had originally been given by charter to Gorges and Mason. Their colonies failed and for forty years Massachusetts governed these regions. New Hampshire was established as a royal colony, directly under the control of the king, in 1680.

THE CAROLINAS

While Massachusetts was thus expanding, the same process was taking place in Virginia. To the west and south, frontier settlements grew up. Those to the south, on the Albemarle River, were an especially unorthodox group of malcontents and individualistic colonists. In 1663, when Charles II decided to reward eight of those who helped him gain his throne by giving them land in America, these settlements were included in the grant.

The settlers had left Virginia because they had objected to what they considered excessive governmental regulation. When

ST. PHILIP'S CHURCH, CHARLESTON, S. C.

The first St. Philip's was erected of wood in 1681-82. The second was opened on Easter Sunday, 1723, burned in 1835, and the third first used for service in 1838. St. Philip's is known as the "Westminster of the South."

[228]

the proprietors attempted to install a theoretical type of feudal government, under a novel constitution drawn by John Locke, they were loud in their complaints. So much opposition was encountered by the governors in this northern section of the grant that the plan was never put into effect.

The first and main settlement made by the proprietors was at Charlestown, which had one of the finest harbors south of Baltimore. Charlestown progressed rapidly, especially after 1685 when groups of French Protestants began to arrive. In that year, Louis XIV revoked the Edict of Nantes, which for almost one hundred years had given the Protestants political, social, and religious rights. These Huguenots included members of the sturdy middle class in France, and made ideal colonists. Charlestown and the surrounding region prospered rapidly, and by 1685 it had a population of 2,500.

Although the backers of this colony hoped to raise tropical products such as silks and spices, a fair degree of prosperity resulted from the production of rice and indigo. The Carolinas were divided into North and South Carolina after the failure of attempts to establish a single government over the colony. Large plantations and something of an aristocratic population developed in the southern portion, while the farms of North Carolina remained relatively small and the population retained its large element of independent, quarrelsome, individualistic frontiersmen. It is not surprising that North Carolina was soon referred to as a "Valley of Humility between two peaks of Arrogance." Even today, this phrase describes the relative position and attitudes of Virginia and South Carolina toward their mutual neighbor, North Carolina.

MARYLAND—A CATHOLIC REFUGE

The Carolinas were not the first of the proprietary colonies. As early as 1632, Cecilius Calvert, Lord Baltimore, received a charter granting him a strip of land to the north of Virginia and awarding him full political and economic rights. His father, George Calvert, had long sought such a grant.

George Calvert's main motive was the founding of a large family estate in America. A secondary consideration was his desire to establish a refuge for fellow Catholics who had been persecuted for nearly a hundred years in England. His son, however, who sent out the colonists to Maryland, was impelled primarily by the religious motive; but he also was too good a business man to refuse Protestants who were willing to buy or lease land. In fact, seventy-five per cent of the first group were Protestants, and this proportion was maintained and even increased during the colonial period.

Perhaps in fear lest the English government be offended, no attempt was made to grant specific rights to Catholics. Instead, a general toleration act was passed which gave political rights to all Christians except Quakers and Unitarians. Tobacco and wheat became the chief products of the colony. It was not a lack of prosperity, but the proprietor's attempts to collect quit-rents, or small annual payments for land, which caused most of the discontent. These fees amounted to only a penny per acre or even less, but they caused constant grumbling.

PENNSYLVANIA—AN EXPERIMENT IN BROTHERLY LOVE

To the north was another proprietary colony which belonged to William Penn. This most interesting individual, although a Quaker, was able to remain on friendly and even intimate terms with Puritan leaders of Parliament, Anglican Charles II and Catholic James II. In 1681, he was given the territory north of Maryland in consideration of the royal debts due him.

Penn's primary intention was to found a colony for the persecuted Quakers, of whom ten thousand had been imprisoned and many of whom had died from cruel treatment in England. His hopes were realized, and immigration began on a grand scale. Within three years Philadelphia was the largest town in the colonies, with over four hundred houses. More than eight thousand colonists lived within the limits of Penn's grant. To the English population were added many Dutch and Germans who had responded to Penn's attractive advertisements. Germantown, near Philadelphia, and the large German and Dutch elements on the Susquehanna River even today are reminders that Penn used modern real-estate methods in advertising his lands.

The story of friendship between Quakers and the Indians has been told many times. Although there was much quarreling between the governor and the assembly, and about the collection of quit-rents, the colony made the most rapid progress of any in America.

THE SWEDISH AND THE DUTCH

In the middle portion of the Atlantic seaboard two other nations had attempted to set up colonies. One of these, the Swedish colony, was captured by the Dutch. The Dutch colonies in turn submitted to the English. The Dutch colony in North America was purely a commercial venture. In 1621 a branch of the Dutch East India Company was chartered for the purpose of exploiting the New World, as the parent company was successfully doing in the East. Earlier, a fort and trading post had been erected at Albany, one hundred and thirty-five miles up the Hudson River, which was a splendid gateway to the region of the Iroquois fur trade. Two settlements were made in 1623, one on the site of Camden, New Jersey, and the other at Albany. Three years later, Peter Minuit bought the island of Manhattan from the Indians for goods valued at twenty-five dollars. The third fort and most important settlement were located here.

THE PATROONS

The colony was based almost entirely on the fur trade, and the company attempted to lessen the cost of colonizing by awarding huge tracts of land to patroons, who contracted to bring over a number of tenants. To avoid the complexities of government, the company gave these patroons full political as well as economic control over their tenants. As a result, the internal history of the colony is replete with complaints and remonstrances.

In spite of this, the colonists prospered and expanded in every direction. Eastward they reached the Connecticut River, where they came into contact with the English. Southward they spread over New Jersey until they came in contact with the Swedes in Delaware.

New Sweden had been founded by the South Company of Sweden in 1638, when Fort Christina was built near the present site of Wilmington, Delaware. Although twelve expeditions were sent during the years in which Sweden maintained control, slight progress was made and by 1653 the population was only two hundred. With little effort the Dutch seized the colony in 1655, and New Sweden was erased from the map.

To the north the Dutch held Albany, which became the greatest fur-trade center of the world. One single shipment from here in 1626 consisted of 7,246 beaver skins, almost a thousand otter skins and $25,000 worth of other furs. Soon all Europe was wearing beaver hats. New Netherlands became increasingly prosperous. This prosperity, however, proved her undoing, for England saw in it the threat to her colonies of New England and Maryland as well as the enrichment of her commercial rival. In 1664 an English fleet sailed into the magnificent harbor of New Amsterdam, and old peg-legged Peter Stuyvesant could only fume and storm before hauling down the Dutch flag. Ten years later the Dutch regained the colony for a period of fifteen months, after which it was held by the English until the American Revolution.

ORGANIZING THE MIDDLE COLONIES

New York became the proprietary colony under the Duke of York, and, when he inherited the throne in 1685 as James II, it automatically became a royal colony. Fur trading was the main interest of the inhabitants, and the commercial advantages of New York's geographical position were not utilized until later although its strategic location was early recognized.

New Jersey was included in the grant made to York, but he gave it to two friends. After several transfers the western half

GOVERNOR STUYVESANT DESTROYING THE SUMMONS TO SURRENDER
(From the painting by Powell)

came into the possession of Penn, and the eastern half was purchased by a syndicate of Quakers headed by Penn. In 1685, an attempt was made to unite New Jersey to New York under Governor Edmund Andros, but the Glorious Revolution of 1688 resulted in the restoration of the two Jerseys to their proprietors, who in 1702 surrendered their patents, and the single royal colony of New Jersey was formed.

Possession of Delaware was long disputed by Penn and York. Penn felt his colony must have control of one shore of the Delaware to the sea if the interests of Pennsylvania were to be protected. York granted him the territory in 1682 and Delaware and Pennsylvania were united, although separate assemblies were set up a short while later and Delaware was thought of as a separate colony.

GEORGIA—A HAVEN OF THE OPPRESSED

The last colony to be established by England on the North American continent was Georgia (1733). Several motives were behind the settling of this region. The English government wished to protect its Carolina settlements from Indian depredations encouraged by the Spaniard to the south. There was also the desire to forestall the Spanish occupation of the territory between South Carolina and Florida. Thus, James Oglethorpe, a philanthropist, found the government receptive when he advanced a plan to found a place of refuge for Protestants persecuted in Catholic countries, as well as for Englishmen in jail because of debt.

The character of the settlers and the military purpose of the colony led the organizers to provide for strict political regulations. The settlers were given no voice in their government, and slavery, intoxicants, and large landed estates were prohibited. These restraints, as well as fear of the nearby Spaniards, held back the growth of the colony until after it became a royal province in 1750, when the restrictions were removed.

THE DEVELOPMENT OF THE
ENGLISH COLONIES

LANDHOLDING IN THE ENGLISH COLONIES

UP TO THIS POINT the development of the English colonies during the seventeenth century has been noted. Each of the colonies had to be considered individually, since the motives for settlement, the methods of colonization, and the early experiences were so diverse. However, by 1700 all but one of the thirteen colonies had been settled and these twelve had progressed to the point at which definite patterns can be seen in the various fields of development, such as industry, commerce, government, education, and labor. Thus it is possible and logical to discuss the colonies during the eighteenth century topically rather than geographically.

Since the beginning of history, free land has been a magnet which has drawn civilized people toward new frontiers. In the case of America, the hope of becoming a landowner was one of the most important influences causing the European to cross the Atlantic.

In New England, the township was the unit of landholding. The town proprietors usually assigned to each settler a small farm as well as a town lot. It was held in fee simple and generally divided among all the male heirs when the owner died. Thus small farms, rather than large estates, were typical in the New England colonies.

In the South, the culture of single commercial crops using slave labor led to the development of plantations. It became the practice to hold large areas and cultivate only a part each year. This system was followed because tobacco so exhausted the soil. In general, the system of primogeniture, or the passing of estates to the eldest son, was retained. Quit-rents were supposed to be collected but in reality evasion was the rule rather than the exception.

Since the middle colonies were largely proprietary, a feudal system of land ownership was attempted, although the usual feudal obligations were often translated into terms of quit-rent. On the whole, farms were a little larger than in New England and smaller than in the South. Both forms of inheritance, primogeniture and division among male heirs, were in use.

In the eighteenth century, the fertile lands on the edge of the settlements attracted two types of individuals, the pioneers who wished to settle the land and put it under the plow, and the speculators who wished to hold it for an advance in value. Some individuals secured immense tracts in the West and consequently were hated and despised by the settlers, many of whom were squatters.

LABOR

It was difficult to keep servants and laborers when there was so much cheap land; consequently, forced labor appeared in different forms. The earliest type was the indentured servant or bondsman who was under contract to work for a trading company, colony, or individual for a specified number of years. Many of these servants bonded themselves willingly in return for passage and the promise of land after the period of service, which usually amounted to about seven years.

Others, however, were "shanghaied" by kidnapers in English ports, or were sentenced to indenture service by English courts for misdemeanors and crimes, as well as for religious and political offences. In the colonies, where only fifty per cent of the English were able to pay their own transportation, these servants could

Courtesy Chamber of Commerce, St. Augustine, Florida

OLD SLAVE MARKET IN ST. AUGUSTINE

hope to reach the highest social strata after becoming free. They were particularly numerous in the Middle Colonies, although a few also were to be found in the South.

Slave labor was widely used in the southern colonies, because tobacco and rice could be cultivated by an untrained, servile labor force. In 1619 slaves were introduced into Virginia, and, after the English merchants won an important share of the slave trade, a steady stream of Negroes came into the colonies.

THE PRODUCTS OF THE COLONIES

The main occupation in all the colonies was farming. Commercial crops of tobacco, rice, and indigo came from the South, which also raised a little grain and some fruits. The Middle Colonies were referred to as the "breadbasket" provinces because of their large crops of wheat, corn, and other grains. Other foodstuffs from this section included cattle, sheep, swine, fruits, and vegetables, which were also produced on the small New England farms.

Fishing, commerce, and shipbuilding were important in New England, and were limited mainly to that region. A basic export of the northern colonies was fish, and 10,000 men with about 360 vessels earned nearly $2,000,000 annually in the third quarter of the eighteenth century. New England ships could be found throughout the world, and her mariners played an increasingly important role in international commerce.

The fur trade was most important in New York and the Middle Colonies. However, in the eighteenth century there were indications of a decline there, while Augusta in Georgia was doing a thriving business.

Naval stores—pitch, tar, and turpentine—for the British navy were obtained in the forests of the Carolinas, while the trees of Maine furnished masts. Lumber, staves, and other wood products were exported from almost all the colonies.

MANUFACTURING

Colonial manufactures were discouraged by England, since it was feared that they would compete with English products, a situation contrary to the mercantile theory which guided English policy. Statesmen and merchants in England wanted the colonies to supply raw materials for home industries, and at the same time to be markets for manufactured goods. Regulations designed to place restrictions on colonial trade and manufactures met with only partial success. Smuggling became a customary practice for the evasion of trade regulations; but natural conditions, combined with English regulations, prevented the development of manufacturing to important proportions.

Domestic production and small-scale handicraft industries did develop in the colonies. Some iron and textile manufacturing was carried on widely, and paper and glass were produced in the Middle Colonies. The southern plantations attempted, with only partial success, to make themselves entirely self-sufficient. The distillation of rum became one of the chief manufacturing industries in New England, and became an integral part of the triangular trade. This last term was used to describe the shipping of molasses from the sugar plantations of the West Indies to the distilleries of New England, whence it went as rum to Africa for the purchase of slaves. Negroes were sold in the West Indies in exchange for molasses, which was taken to New England and the process repeated.

RELIGION AND EDUCATION

In all the colonies, except Rhode Island and Pennsylvania, there were established churches at one time or another. Massachusetts and Connecticut supported the Congregational Church, while the Anglican Church was established in the other colonies. During the colonial period, however, the definite trend was toward toleration. Maryland, Rhode Island, and Pennsylvania

CHRIST CHURCH, ALEXANDRIA, VIRGINIA

George Washington rented Pew No. 5 on the day the church was formally delivered to the vestry, February 27, 1773. Washington was then a member of the vestry.

all passed toleration acts, but in the other colonies dissenters encountered many barriers. Of these, the Quakers, perhaps, had the greatest difficulties, although the Baptists, Presbyterians, Methodists, and other lesser sects suffered some political discrimination.

With the exception of a period of religious fervor, known as the "Great Awakening," religion tended to play a progressively smaller part in the lives of the colonists as the century progressed.

Education was early made a part of the colonial life in New England. The ideal of an elementary school in every town was set up in Massachusetts in 1647. Those towns of fifty households which failed to provide schools were subject to fines. There were some public schools in the Middle Colonies; but here, as was the case almost entirely in the South, education depended upon religious and other private agencies. Few schools developed in the South, with its large plantations, great distances, and small centers of population. Perhaps half the population in the South was illiterate in the eighteenth century, in spite of the efforts of private tutors.

By the time of the Revolution there were nine colleges, eight religious and one private. There were Harvard (1636); William and Mary (1693); Yale (1701); College of New Jersey, now Princeton (1746); Benjamin Franklin's Philadelphia Academy, now University of Pennsylvania (1751); King's College, now Columbia (1754); Brown (1764); Rutgers (1766); and Dartmouth (1769). In addition, many wealthy Southerners sent their sons to English universities.

EARLY AMERICAN CULTURE

In studying various peoples, we have noted that every movement of population is accompanied by its culture which becomes adopted to the new environment. By the time of the American Revolution it was clear that a transformation had taken place in the European civilization which had been transplanted to the New World. The result was a new culture distinctly American.

MASSACHUSETTS HALL
Oldest building of Harvard College, founded in 1636.

This culture was represented by more than fifty newspapers, large private libraries, many subscription libraries, and several learned groups. The American Philosophical Society, of which Franklin was the most prominent member, was a leading intellectual group. As yet, there was little of American painting, music, drama, or architecture, although such artists as Gilbert Stuart, John Singleton Copley, Benjamin West, and Charles Wilson Peale, gained both European and American renown.

COLONIAL GOVERNMENT

While the government of the individual colonies varied from time to time, as well as from one colony to another, three definite types of colonial government developed. When the Revolution began, Connecticut and Rhode Island were corporate colonies while Pennsylvania, Delaware, and Maryland remained proprietary. The remaining eight colonies were royal. In all the colonies there were legislative assemblies chosen by the people, but property and religious qualifications usually limited the suffrage; so the assemblies were less representative than might be supposed.

Sitting as an upper house was a council appointed by proprietor, royal governor, or king, or elected by the people. Usually, by the time of the Revolution, the members of this group were colonists, but this was by no means a requirement.

The governor in Pennsylvania, Delaware, and Maryland, was appointed by the proprietor with the approval of the king. Governors of royal colonies were appointed directly by the king, and in all colonies they exercised a veto power over all laws passed by their colonial legislatures. In addition, all colonial laws were subject to the approval of the proprietor and the king. Moreover, since the Privy Council had the right to hear appeals from provincial courts, it had a final right to declare colonial laws inconsistent with the laws of England, and hence null and void. The appointment of colonial judges was usually in the hands of the governor. The Crown appointed all customs collectors and the judges of the admiralty courts.

Local government varied greatly from colony to colony. In New England, the township was the unit of local government. Here the democratic town meeting developed a type of American political philosophy that was to influence materially the cause of the Revolution. The unity of government in the South was the county, patterned on the shire of England. Its chief officer was the justice of the peace, who, with other officers, was appointed by the colonial assembly and governor. People in the southern colonies had little voice in local government when compared with the New England colonists.

AMERICA'S ENGLISH HERITAGE

In spite of the fact that the colonies were somewhat "Americanized" by the time of the Revolution, it must be kept in mind that they had built their culture on English foundations, adapted to life in the wilderness of a new world. This English heritage furnished the strongest common bond among the colonies and was a prominent factor in the movements for union and in the final creation of a single nation out of thirteen separate and distinct colonies.

This English influence enveloped all the colonies, for the largest single group of the colonists had come from England. They formed only fifty per cent of the population, it is true, but the other half of the people represented such diverse nationalities and divided interests that English predominance was emphasized.

In the seventeenth and eighteenth centuries about 300,000 Scotch-Irish came to America. Most of them settled along the Susquehanna in Pennsylvania and in the back-country of the middle colonies. About 200,000 Germans, seeking a haven from war and oppression, had settled on the frontiers from New York to the Carolinas by 1775. In addition there were German groups around Philadelphia and New York. A few Welsh, Scots, and Irish were scattered throughout the Atlantic seaboard by 1763. French Huguenots were numerous in the Carolinas and in the back-country of Pennsylvania and Virginia. There were a few Swiss settlements in several colonies.

Except among the French Huguenots in South Carolina and the Germans on the Susquehanna in Pennsylvania, who were in more or less compact, isolated groups, the English language was generally spoken. Only in the latter section were there newspapers in a language other than English.

The literature of the colonies was the literature of England. The authors read in the colonies were English authors, and the books were, for the most part, printed in England. The colonial historical heroes, in general, were Englishmen who had "singed the beard" of the Spaniard or had fought the French or the Indian.

The government of the English colonies was copied after that of the mother-country. The jury system, the organization of country courts, the legal processes, and the general court-procedure rules were all used in this country with few changes or modifications.

The whole concept of the rights of man and the personal, civil, and political rights which had developed in England from the time of Magna Charta were taken over by the colonials who considered these rights as inalienable. In fact, the very ideas of the American Declaration of Independence are in large part the ideas of the English philosopher and political scientist, John ·Locke.

The American colonies were illustrative of the frontier theory of civilization. English culture had crossed the ocean, but it had been modified so as to produce an Anglo-American civilization.

EUROPE IN SEARCH OF SPICE, LAND, AND SOULS

PORTUGUESE PIONEERS

WHILE SUCH LATINS as Vespucius and Columbus were being impeded by the American continent in their attempt to reach the East Indies, Vasco da Gama pushed around the tip of Africa and on to Calicut. Subsequent expansion by the Portuguese fully justified the title which Pope Alexander VI bestowed on the king of Portugal: "Lord of the navigation, conquests and trade of Ethiopia, Arabia, Persia, and India." In 1505 Almeida was commissioned as the first Portuguese viceroy of India; his successor, Alfonso d'Albuquerque, had been in office only a year when Goa, on the west coast, was captured and made the base of Portuguese operations (1510).

Portuguese expansion was not satiated, however, and control over Malacca was established in the same year. Portuguese merchants enjoyed a monopoly of the India trade during the sixteenth century. Their administration succeeded easily at first because the Indian states were quailing before the thrusts of the Moguls—an Indo-Scythian people. The purpose and organization of Portuguese jurisdiction was to exploit rather than to develop. However this may justify criticism, the maritime pioneers of Portugal deserve credit. They laid the foundation of modern trade between the Occident and Orient. Until the eighteenth century, Portuguese was the trade language in far eastern waters, and it is one component of that lingual hash, the business patois of the East, which today is called "pidgin English."

As early as 1517 the first Portuguese, Fernão Perez de Andrade, reached the town of Macao, not far from Canton. His brother Simon was also received in the following year, but was expelled when he erected a fort and allowed violence to be employed against citizens of the Central Flowery Kingdom, as China was called. Nevertheless in 1533 Portuguese merchantmen sailed as far north as Foochow and Ningpo, flourishing ports which declined a few years later. Several embassies were sent from Goa intended to penetrate to the Manchu court in Peking, but none traveled beyond Canton. A fourth mission was sent in 1667, requesting legalized trade relations; the fifth came in 1727, and the sixth in 1753. These failed largely because the Portuguese did not conform to court etiquette. The Chinese and their Manchu rulers were accustomed to receive tribute from abroad, a characteristic of their foreign relations for more than three centuries.

A permanent Portuguese settlement on the peninsula of Macao was secured in 1557 by bribery and the payment of rent. Although Portuguese trade at Macao diminished, it was this city that became the center for China's trade with all foreigners. Even when the "barbarians" were permitted to establish factories at Canton, these posts were to be occupied during the business season only, and then to be evacuated by the mercantile community in favor of Macao.

OCCIDENTALS REACH JAPAN AND THE PHILIPPINES

In 1542 or 1543, three Portuguese merchants were blown off their intended course from Siam to China and landed in southern Japan. This episode marked the beginning of European penetration into the island kingdom. They were followed by Francis Xavier, co-founder of the Jesuit Order, who, in 1549, arrived in the "Land of the Gods" and for twenty-seven months proclaimed a hitherto unknown deity. A generation later the number of nominal Christians in Japan was reported as 150,000. When Oda Nobunaga became *de facto* ruler of Japan by 1568, he saw fit to encourage Christianity as a counter force against rising, arrogant Buddhists.

Relations between natives and foreigners were satisfactory until the last quarter of the sixteenth century when Spanish missionary competition, largely Dominican, resulted in disorders between Christian sects. All foreign clergy were ordered out of the country in 1587, but Hideyoshi, the second of the great Japanese triumvirate, winked at lax enforcement of the decree. Trade and proselytizing continued apace.

The antagonism which the Portuguese encountered from the Spaniards in Japan emanated principally from the Philippines. The Spaniards, preoccupied with exploration in the New World and encouraged by the pope's bull of demarcation, were a half-century later than their nearest European neighbors in sending expeditions to the Far East. Although Magellan touched the southern part of the Philippines, the islands were not placed under Spanish rule until 1543. Only gradually did these Westerners explore and extend jurisdiction over the archipelago. Manila was founded in 1571, and four years later, upon invitation, an embassy was sent to China. It was not long until the Spaniards were allowed to transact business at Canton. Their merchantmen also visited Japan, where they met vessels from other European trading companies, mostly Portuguese, Dutch, and British.

NORTHERN EUROPEANS VENTURE TO THE EAST

English merchants, who had found the commercial company to be effective for business ventures, began to vie with the Portuguese in Indian waters early in the seventeenth century. The East India Company was chartered in 1600. For the next two hundred and thirty-four years this company was the principal agent of British expansion and, for over a century, a profitable enterprise for London shareholders.

Almost simultaneously the Dutch and the French also formed East India companies. It was intrenched Portuguese opposition, however, which the English first met, an antagonism which culminated in the battle of Swally. Portuguese defeat on this occasion made it possible for an English factory to be established at Surat in 1614. Although the British met with reverses in India, within a decade their administration in southern India assumed aspects of permanence, and Madras was founded in 1639.

The French also ventured into the remote Orient. In 1529 a French vessel reached Sumatra. Despite repeated grants of commercial monopolies to French companies, domestic conditions hindered activity, and it was not until 1699 that a French ship called at Canton. But France's primary concerns abroad were in North America. True, her nationals had begun to penetrate India, but they encountered there determined opposition from the English and Portuguese.

THE DUTCH TURN TO THE EAST

Holland joined the search for spices and silks early in the seventeenth century. Hitherto the Dutch had been the chief carriers of Oriental products from Lisbon to northern Europe, but in 1594 the port of Lisbon was closed to them. Their ships engaged in this spice trade were soon sailing to the source of the supply. In 1604 and 1607, these ships applying at Canton were turned away by the exercise of influence from authorities at Macao. Fifteen ships, which Kornelis Rayerszoon led against the Portuguese at Macao in 1622 failed to dislodge them. The agents of the Dutch East India Company settled in the Pescadores Islands, and then moved to Formosa in 1625.

Dutch missions failed repeatedly in their petitions for commercial intercourse with the Chinese Empire. A minor concession was obtained in 1655 when agents of the Dutch East India Company were allowed to send an embassy with four trading vessels every eight years. Europeans generally were required to observe servility and humility in their relations with governments of the Far East. The Dutch co-operated with Emperor K'ang Hsi to suppress the notorious pirate, Cheng Cheng-kung (Koxinga), who dislodged them from Formosa. The naval detachment was followed with petitions which the Chinese considered as coming from a tributary state. It was not until 1762 that a Dutch factory, or trading post, was erected in Canton, and by that time it was only one among many.

Operating from their base in India, the English in 1613 succeeded in establishing a factory at Hirado on the Japanese island

THE BOROBUDOR, A BUDDHIST SHRINE ON THE ISLAND OF JAVA,
DUTCH EAST INDIES

of Honshu. The first Englishman, to reach Japan was one Will
Adams, who piloted a Dutch ship and suffered disaster on the
rugged coast of Nippon in 1600. He became adviser to the
Shogun, Ieyasu, who founded the Tokugawa line of military
rulers three years later.

Adams not only instructed his hosts in mathematics, astronomy, and shipbuilding, but also confirmed their fears of Europeans.
Ieyasu was suspicious of the feverish explorations in Japanese waters, and he feared the drain of metals from the empire. Christian sects periodically came into conflict, and the shogun anticipated an appeal for a foreign alliance against the *bakufu*, or military government. Another source of friction was commercial
rivalry and consequent political scheming for the favor of the
Yedo (modern Tokyo) government.

JAPAN BECOMES A HERMIT NATION

In 1615 a Japanese mission was sent to Europe, but, before its return, persecution of Christians was fully under way. Hidetada, son and successor of Ieyasu, forbade the entrance of Spaniards into his domains, and by 1638 all intercourse with Westerners was proscribed, with one exception. The Dutch, who were prepared to make any adjustment, were confined to the tiny island of Deshima in Nagaski harbor; for two hundred and fourteen years this was the only permanent window which received rays of light from reawakened Europe.

Throughout the next two centuries, however, Europeans by no means forgot the Land of the Rising Sun. Russian, British, Spanish, French, Portuguese, as well as Dutch ships cruised or were wrecked off those shores. Within two years of the framing of the American Constitution, Yankees attempted to trade furs with the Nipponese, and during Napoleon's occupation of Holland the Dutch East India trade was conducted in American bottoms. For a few years Deshima was the sole spot on the globe to fly the Dutch flag.

Exclusion of the Portuguese from Japan occurred at approximately the same time as that at which their fatherland was freed from union under the crown of Spain. During this "imprisonment," which commenced in 1580, colonial control was centralized in Madrid, but the Portuguese successfully neutralized its effectiveness. Dutch pilots were introduced, and in one thirty-year period scarcely more than five ships completed the India circuit safely. This sealed the eventual doom of Portuguese commercial supremacy, especially in the Far East.

CHINA OPENED TO TRADE

Meanwhile the English East India Company had become eager to share in the lucrative trade with the Celestials of Kwangtung and Fukien provinces. Access to Canton was at first (1635-1637) refused, because of the connivance of the Portuguese who later secured a monopoly. It was not until 1685 that imperial decree opened the ports of China to traders of all nations. This decree

TEMPLE OF THE GENII IN CANTON

did not evince a change of China's policy, but merely showed the Manchu fear of becoming solely dependent upon the Portuguese. Actually, foreign trade was for the most part restricted to Canton.

British attempts to open direct negotiations with the Manchu court at Peking met with no success. In 1793, Viscount Macartney failed to obtain commercial privileges, in part because he refused to perform the kowtow. Trade at Canton was, by the late eighteenth century, brisk but not large. Tea, spices, silks, lacquer ware, china, and small amounts of metals constituted, at first, the chief articles of trade. Chinese merchants grew wealthy from the traffic, and in 1720 they formed a guild or Co-hong which by 1782 had become limited to twelve, and later to thirteen, merchants. These Chinese were responsible for all relations with the "barbarians." China, being economically self-sufficient, had little desire to trade abroad. If lesser peoples required intercourse with the Middle Kingdom, it must be on Chinese terms—which meant the Westeners were subject to severe exactions.

RUSSIA EXPANDS EASTWARD BY OVERLAND ROUTES

One other people, though not strictly European, expanded in this period toward the Far East by ancient overland routes. The first Russian embassy, which reached Peking in 1567, failed because it did not bear sufficient gifts. Russian movement into Siberia was started by Yermak in 1581. Utilizing Cossack frontiersmen, the Russians reached the Pacific in 1636. The Amur River furnished them a highway by mid-century, and forts were constructed to meet the requirements of frontier warfare along the ill-defined Chinese boundary. Hostilities were finally terminated when, on August 27, 1689, plenipotentiaries signed, at Nerchinsk, China's first treaty with a European government.

Repeated embassies were sent to the Manchu capital but none succeeded. In 1727, two conventions and two protocols signed at Kiakhta delimited the northwestern boundary of China and confirmed the existence of a Russian ecclesiastical mission to Peking. North of the Great Wall, the Russians expanded farther along the Amur until the Sea of Okhotsk was reached and Irkutsk founded. In 1728, Vitus Bering, a Danish captain in Russian employ, explored northern Pacific waters. Soon Russians were occupying the Kuriles, vainly attempting to rupture the cocoon in which Japan maintained her isolation, and sailing even to Alaska and Oregon. Two Russian ships succeeded in exchanging their cargoes at Canton in 1806, but immediate orders from Peking restrained Sino-Russian intercourse to land frontiers.

In reopening relations with the remotest Orient in the mid-sixteenth century, Europeans were completing a cultural cycle. The fundamental principles behind the very instruments which enabled ambitious navigators to sail from European shores had come from the East with the Moslems and Greeks as transmitters. Following the Crusades, the new learning gave impetus to a Renaissance which now renewed contact with the parental Orient.

The Chinese Empire, however, remained aloof, suspecting the avarice and fearing the implements of seafaring Occidentals. Centuries of commerce with the West prior to the thirteenth century, and the recurring impact of barbaric tribes in the north and west, had accustomed the ministers of China to relations with those quarters; this fact in part explained the moderate successes of the Russians. Moreover, the Manchus, themselves aliens from the north, feared the undermining of their administration and a possible foreign alliance with native malcontents. In the later eighteenth century, the drain of Chinese silver also became alarming and was largely explained by ever increasing importation of opium.

HEADMAN OF THE DON COSSACKS
(Early 19th century)

Courtesy Cincinnati Art Museum

PHILIP II OF SPAIN
(After the painting by Titian)

INTERNATIONAL RIVALRIES

POLITICAL STATES IN EUROPE acquired and lost extensive empires in the three centuries after the discovery of America. The period was one in which Spanish command of the seas was lost to Holland, France, and England. Hapsburg dominions were divided and changed hands. Traders from Holland and England broke down Spanish and Portuguese monopoly. The strong became weak and occasionally the weak became strong.

Strength and ambition to become stronger were sufficient reasons for the appearance of a system of alliances against any dominant nation. The balance of power in Europe was frequently off-center, especially when allies shifted from one major antagonist to another. Spain, Austria, Prussia, and France were constantly maneuvering for an advantageous position in European politics. The bones of contention were generally portions of the Germanies, the Netherlands, Italy, or Poland. England, too, was interested in Hanover for many years.

Alliances made by Spain and France also concerned England because of the struggle for oversea empires in the Far East and the Americas. England eliminated the Dutch from the Hudson valley, but found France a more tenacious opponent in North America and India. A series of wars that lasted for a century finally left Britain the supreme colonial power and undisputed mistress of the seas. England blundered so seriously in dealing with her American colonies that a princely realm was forever lost to the empire. France and Spain, although on the verge of catastrophe, took satisfaction in promoting English disasters.

The degeneration of France finally brought on the Revolution and gave the Corsican adventurer his chance to pick up the Bourbon crown. Yet, Napoleon failed to effect a permanent restoration of French leadership.

His invasion of the Iberian peninsula precipitated the wars for independence in Spanish America. In less than ten years after Waterloo, the Spanish empire was reduced to a faint vestige of what it had been for three hundred years.

ABSOLUTISM AND INTOLERANCE

A popular international sport after the middle of the sixteenth century was to plague and ruffle the proud Philip II. Under the guidance of the great Catholic Monarchs, numerous territories were added to Spanish dominions, territories in Europe, the Americas, and Asia. Charles I, who was also Holy Roman Emperor as Charles V, thus ruled over one of the most extensive empires known to history. This heterogeneous collection of possessions was divided when Charles abdicated in 1556 to seek the solace of monastic seclusion.

Philip II, his son and heir, inherited Spain, the Netherlands, the Sicilies, part of Burgundy, Milan, and the vast American colonies. Over these territories Philip ruled until 1598, guided by two main principles: he would restore Catholicism to the commanding position in the religious world, and place Spain first among nations. While attempting to realize these two grandiose schemes, Philip dominated international affairs to such an extent that the period of his reign, from 1556 to 1598, is properly known as the Age of Philip II.

The Catholic Monarchs, Ferdinand and Isabella, achieved wonders in driving the Moors from Spain and in bringing political unity to the Iberian peninsula. They did not succeed in eliminating the spirit of individualism which still persists as a characteristic of the Spaniard, and it was to this task that Philip devoted much of his time. One of the main dissenting elements in the population was the group of half-hearted Christians known as Moriscos. These people were Moors who gave lip-service to Catholicism while persisting in their own customs. Their practices were so abhorrent to the Inquisition that Philip took measures to reduce the Moriscos to obedience. The result was armed rebellion which lasted from 1567 to 1571 and ended with the expulsion of the Moriscos from Spain. This act, combined with the persecution and expulsion of the Jews, deprived Spain of some of its most energetic groups of people and became an important factor in the economic decline of the kingdom.

Portugal, long independent of Spain, was added to Philip's dominions in 1580 by bribing the House of Braganza to relinquish its claims to the succession. During the sixty years of this captivity, Spain was in possession of the important Portuguese colony of Brazil as well as the eastern territories. Toward the end of Philip's reign, in 1591, the kingdom of Aragon rebelled against the odious absolutism which was being enforced. Again Philip was triumphant, but the Aragonese were by no means resigned to their fate. These measures against the Moriscos, the Aragonese, and the Portuguese, combined with a high-handed treatment of the Spanish parliament or Cortes, consolidated Philip's position in the peninsula. He was to meet with greater difficulties in the attempt to extend his policies abroad.

Only a portion of the gold and silver stream from the Americas found its way into the royal coffers. The many enterprises undertaken by Philip were so costly that oppressive taxation became necessary, a policy which was to have evil effects upon Spanish trade. The revolt of the Netherlands deprived Philip of large revenues which his father had received from those provinces, while foreign attacks upon Spanish shipping were especially annoying and expensive. The expulsion of the Jews and Moriscos deprived Spain of a large mercantile and industrial population, while the Spaniard's traditional contempt for productive labor added a fatal weakness to Spanish economic life.

Philip II was a devout Catholic, secure in the belief that God would not desert the faithful in the hour of need and that Spain was the nation chosen by Heaven to restore the true faith to its commanding position. The Inquisition, that remarkable institution for the suppression of heresy, was encouraged to extend its activities. Even in the Netherlands, where Protestant doctrines

UNIVERSITY OF VALLADOLID, SPAIN, FOUNDED IN THE 13TH CENTURY
At least twenty Spanish universities were founded between 1516 and 1600.

were sweeping away loyalty to the papacy, Philip attempted to enforce a return to Catholicism. This effort brought about a costly rebellion which finally resulted in the loss of the northern provinces of the Low Countries.

SPAIN'S INTELLECTUAL GOLDEN AGE

The Golden Age in the intellectual development of Spain, which came to full fruition in the seventeenth century, really began during the reign of Charles I and received added impetus in the Age of Philip II. At least twenty universities were founded between 1516 and 1600. Valladolid, Salamanca, and Alcalá possessed universities of especial prominence, with thousands of students in attendance. These institutions were allowed a surprising amount of independence in the development of the curriculum. More than four thousand schools for the study of Latin and Castilian were in existence early in the seventeenth century, while numerous Jesuit colleges concentrated on the study of the ancient classical authors. In spite of certain restrictions, the publication of books increased rapidly under Philip II. Libraries were established, and Philip himself founded important archives whose priceless documents are still in the infancy of exploitation by historians.

The great philosopher Luis Vives (1492-1540) advocated "the observation of nature as the basis of knowledge" a century before Francis Bacon. Many of the ideas of Montaigne, Descartes, and other thinkers, found an early expression by Spanish philosophers. Only the necessity of conforming to Catholic doctrine prevented the development of a great Spanish philosophical school.

Spain contributed writers on politics and jurisprudence who laid the foundations of international law before Grotius. In the field of economics Spaniards contributed many ideas which were later to find expression in Adam Smith, Tolstoy, and others. Luis Vives was also far ahead of his age in this field of thought. Vives, together with Páez de Castro, advocated the writing of history from the social point of view, to include an account of all social institutions rather than concentrating attention upon the political development of a nation. In the age of Philip II, appeared great chroniclers, chief of whom were Zurita and Morales. Mariana, the Jesuit historian, deserves mention for his *Historia General de España*, first published between 1592 and 1595. Other writers, many unknown, contributed important works in cartography, geography, metallurgy, mathematics, and engineering. New World explorers advocated a Panama canal nearly four centuries before Theodore Roosevelt.

FINE ARTS AND LITERATURE

Spanish achievements in the fine arts kept pace with other developments under Philip II. The great actor and playwright, Lope de Rueda of Seville, restored the theater to prominence. Cervantes, author of the immortal *Don Quixote de la Mancha*, belonged to this period. Lope de Vega, one of the most prolific writers in the history of drama, achieved great renown before his death in 1635. Periodical literature, the novel, and poetry also received lasting contributions from Spanish authors. Juan de Herrera established a school of architecture that embodied the

COURTYARD OF THE FAMOUS UNIVERSITY OF SALAMANCA,
FOUNDED 1230 A.D.

Spain's intellectual "Golden Age" came to its full fruition in the 17th century. The large
universities were allowed great independence in the development of curricula.

elements which he himself incorporated in the famous Escorial
built for Philip II.

While depending primarily upon Italian painters for inspiration, Spanish artists gradually developed an independent school in
the Age of Philip II—a school which was to produce such masters
as El Greco, Ribera, Velasquez, Murillo, and Goya. In such com-
posers as Morales and Victoria, Spanish music reached new heights.
Although religious music was the most prevalent form of musical
expression during the Age of Philip II, the guitar had become the
most popular instrument by the close of the sixteenth century.

Great as were these achievements in so many realms of activity, and although Spain was the mightiest European power in the
sixteenth century, Spanish prosperity and leadership rested upon
the insecure foundations of absolutism, religious intolerance,
monopoly, and a deteriorating economic order. The international
conflicts of Philip II and his successors resulted in a loss of world

leadership, and the rise of France, England, and Holland as powerful nations threatened Spain with the loss of much of its American empire.

REBELLION IN THE NETHERLANDS

Of all the brilliant jewels in the crown of Philip II, few shone
with greater brilliance than the Netherlands. But the monarch,
in his clumsy efforts to secure his hold more firmly, lost half of
these gems forever.

Charles I was regarded as a native of the Netherlands, but
Philip was a foreigner. Loyalty under Charles turned to hatred
under the oppression and arrogance of Philip. The traders and
shippers of the Netherlands occupied a strategic position to profit
from the swing of trade routes to the Atlantic, but Philip was
persuaded to continue a system of monopoly in favor of Spanish
merchants. The wealth of the East and West Indies was guided
toward Spain, while merchants from the Netherlands were largely excluded from participating in the profits. These restrictions
on commerce were sharply resented by a people capable of erect-
ing a far-flung commercial empire.

Attempts to collect high taxes in the Netherlands added fuel
to the smouldering embers of rebellion. Philip could have won
political support in the Netherlands by wisely permitting native
participation in important political positions, but he neglected the
opportunity and so alienated an influential class. The Spanish gar-
risons, looked upon as forerunners of the Inquisition, aroused more
opposition, especially in the northern Protestant provinces. Even
in the Catholic provinces, now comprising Belgium, opposition to
Philip's policies was strong. Indeed, it was these very Catholic
areas that provided the first leaders for the rebellion against Philip.

THE HATED DUKE OF ALVA

The revolt of the Netherlands against Spanish domination
entered a military phase with the appearance of the hated Duke
of Alva as governor in 1567. His orders were to suppress religious

heresy and execute the leading rebels, measures calculated to prevent the recurrence of riots like those in 1566 which despoiled
Catholic churches. Alva succeeded so well during his six years in
the country that the prosperity of the Netherlands was almost
destroyed. Many of the one hundred thousand refugees from the
Low Countries found a welcome in England where they contributed much to the strength of Philip's great enemy, Elizabeth.

William of Orange, (called the Silent, for no good reason)
became the leader of the revolt and around him centered the
opposition to Spain until his assassination in 1584. William commissioned privateers, collected armies, and kept alive the spirit
of rebellion.

When an unpaid Spanish army perpetrated terrible acts of
vandalism in 1576, the seventeen Catholic and Protestant provinces united in the Pacification of Ghent until such a time as the
Inquisition should be abolished and their former privileges restored. This union lasted until 1579 when Philip's capable governor, the duke of Parma, convinced the Catholic and industrial
provinces that they had more to fear from the Protestant and
commercial provinces than from Spain. The Catholic leaders
signed the Treaty of Arras to effect a reconciliation with Philip.
The northern provinces in the same year, 1579, united in the
Union of Utrecht and continued the war. Henceforth the Catholic provinces, known as the Spanish and then the Austrian Netherlands, were separated from the Protestant north. Amsterdam
soon developed as a great commercial center at the expense of
Antwerp.

The Dutch traders and empire builders penetrated to the
Spanish dominions, established a colony in South America, gained
control over the Spice Islands, captured ports in India, began a
colony in South Africa, and even challenged English and French
supremacy in North America. During the greater portion of this
period the war with Spain was continuing, although a truce was
declared for a time in 1609. Not until the Peace of Westphalia
in 1648 did Spain recognize Dutch independence as an established
fact.

Philip made the great mistake of trying to keep too many pots
boiling at the same time. Any one of the numerous projects in

which he was engaged would have required the complete attention of a great power. He sought, while trying to suppress revolt in the Netherlands, to interfere in the domestic politics of France and Spain. He succeeded in placing his nation on the toboggan for the dizzy plunge that may be said to have ended with the loss of the American colonies in the early nineteenth century.

STRUGGLES WITH ENGLAND AND FRANCE

There were numerous reasons for enmity between England and Spain. The island kingdom had become a strong national state under the guidance of the early Tudors. English commerce was developing, and men like Richard Hakluyt were calling attention to the rich rewards of a colonial empire. The Spanish effort to monopolize the world carrying trade could not go unchallenged by the future mistress of the seas. An important element in the rise of English nationalism was the break with the papacy under Henry VIII. This schism, so hateful to Philip II, challenged the crusading spirit of the Spanish monarch. He had been married to Queen Mary, and for a time wooed Elizabeth, but she scorned his advances and secretly gave countenance to the depredations of Hawkins, Drake, and similar heroic pirates. At the same time Elizabeth looked with more than passive favor on the revolt of the Netherlands. The final result of these circumstances was the building of a fleet which was known as the "Invincible Armada" until English seamen and a bad storm defeated it in 1588. The destruction of the great Armada did not blast Spanish power to pieces, but the Dutch, the English, and the French no longer shivered at the thoughts of Spanish galleons and Spanish infantry.

Philip should have learned a lesson from the disastrous result of his intrigues with Mary, Queen of Scots; instead he became embroiled in the internal politics of France, a country already uneasy because it was hemmed in by Hapsburg possessions. Catherine de' Medici, who dominated French politics from 1559 to 1589, found her power threatened by Philip II, the Huguenots, and the nobility. Most of this period, extending until 1593, was made turbulent by a series of religious wars in which the Protestant Huguenots and the Bourbon family opposed the Catholics and the Guise claimants to the throne. Catherine played first with one side and then with the other, always attempting to maintain her own supremacy. Until his murder during the horrible massacre of Saint Bartholomew's Day, August 24, 1572, the great Huguenot leader was Admiral de Coligny. Under his patronage and encouragement a French colony was begun near the present St. Augustine in Florida, and another at the site of Rio de Janeiro. Philip's agents succeeded in destroying these colonies, but the trespass was not forgiven.

When it became apparent that the strongest claimant to the French throne was the Protestant Henry of Bourbon, King of Navarre, Philip II allied himself with the Duke of Guise, an uncompromising Catholic. The war that resulted saw three Henries fighting for the throne. Henry of Navarre led the Protestants; Henry of France, the reigning king and son of Catherine, led the moderate Catholics, or Politiques. Henry of Guise soon established his influence over Henry of France, while Queen Elizabeth of England gave aid to Henry of Navarre.

The succeeding events in this confused period of intrigues came swiftly. The king underwent a change of heart and caused Henry of Guise to be assassinated, and the next year, in 1589, he himself made his exit in the same fashion. But with one of his dying breaths, the king named Henry of Navarre as his successor. Henry of Navarre became a Catholic in 1593, made peace with Philip II a few years later, and was himself assassinated in 1610

END OF THE TURKISH THREAT

This discouraging account of the failures of Philip II should be tempered by acknowledging his great service to Europe, and especially to Italy, as a result of the defeat of the Ottoman fleet at Lepanto in 1571. The Ottoman Turks not only had a secure hold on Hungary, but also committed annoying depredations on Mediterranean commerce. With the co-operation of Genoa, Venice, and the Papacy, a great fleet was prepared which destroyed the Ottoman armada. Don Juan of Austria, an illegiti-

mate half-brother of Philip II, commanded this Christian fleet
in what has been aptly called the last Crusade. Henceforth the
Mediterranean was to be free from Mohammedan piracy except
for a brief period at the end of the eighteenth century, and western Europe no longer had cause to fear an Ottoman conquest.
Philip II, whose sincere zeal for Catholicism was attended by so
many political disasters, was by no means a complete failure.

SIXTEENTH CENTURY BOOK LABEL (FRENCH)

EUROPEAN RIVALRY
IN NORTH AMERICA
1750

FRANCE AND ENGLAND STRUGGLE
FOR WORLD DOMINANCE

HENRY OF NAVARRE AND RICHELIEU

HENRY OF NAVARRE, whose conversion to Catholicism gave Philip II no little satisfaction, started France on the road to continental supremacy. Bourbon rulers of France in succeeding years contributed much to the further decline of Spain's international power. Henry devoted his attention to restoring France to economic and political health. In this difficult enterprise he had the co-operation of the duke of Sully who, as chief minister of finance, revised the system of taxation and saved large sums for the treasury. Sully gave his attention to encouraging agriculture, which he believed to be the basic French industry. Henry balanced this activity by encouraging trade and commerce. Within a few years large French cities became industrial centers. French traders began to compete with the Dutch and the English for world trade. Factories (trading posts) were established in India, and the French empire in North America began to take shape under the guidance of Champlain.

An assassin put an end to the life of Henry of Navarre in 1610, and for fourteen years confusion again prevailed in France. One of the most colorful figures in European history emerged from this chaos to become the virtual dictator of France in 1624. This remarkable man was Cardinal Richelieu. The cardinal was a great diplomat, unsurpassed in the art of intrigue. Until his death in 1642, Richelieu used every means to make royal power supreme in France, and to make France supreme in Europe. The first of these objects was accomplished by disregarding the French parliament, known as the Estates General, and by abolishing the power of the nobles. Royal officers, called intendants, were appointed to take charge of financial, judicial, and political affairs in different parts of the country. The policies of Richelieu were continued by Cardinal Mazarin, who governed France until 1661 while Louis XIV was growing up.

HAPSBURGS AND BOURBONS

Two great ruling houses were prominent in Europe during the seventeenth century, the Hapsburgs and the Bourbons. Spain and all of her possessions were ruled by one branch of the Hapsburgs. Austria, Hungary, Bohemia, and other territories were ruled by another branch. Against this great house the power of the French Bourbons seemed small indeed. The most terrible wars in history, before the World War of our own time, were the result of this struggle between Bourbons and Hapsburgs.

The first phase in the conflict was known as the Thirty Years War, a series of bloody conflicts which lasted from 1618 to 1648. Cardinal Richelieu did everything possible to help the enemies of the Hapsburgs, and from 1635 to 1648 French armies played a leading role in the war. Richelieu declared war on Spain, and, although the efficient Spanish infantry gave a good account of itself, the French generals were superior. Even after the Peace of Westphalia in 1648, France and Spain continued the war for eleven years. The result was a French victory. French control was extended over Roussillon, Artois, and Lorraine. Metz, Toul, Verdun, and Alsace went to France in 1648; so French gains from the Thirty Years War were of great importance. Louis XIV, in addition to having these territories added to his dominions, gained a Spanish princess, Maria Theresa, as his wife.

The Spanish cup of sorrows was overflowing, and in the midst of these disasters Portugal began a revolt in 1640. The war dragged on for twenty-eight years and ended with complete independence for the Portuguese. Brazil, which had been ruled by the Dutch from 1624 to 1654, was returned to Portugal; but that little country, which had done so much to increase geographical knowledge, lost many of her prized possessions in the Far East as a result of the Spanish dominance.

DECLINE OF THE DUTCH COMMERCIAL EMPIRE

Philip II might logically be considered as one of the Dutch heroes. During the wars precipitated by the policies of that Spanish monarch, the commercial power of the seven northern provinces of the Low Countries developed with astonishing swiftness. The defeat of Philip's great fleet in 1588 broke Spanish sea power, and within a decade Dutch traders were sending fleets into the stronghold of the enemy. Many of the colonial possessions of Portugal, which were captured by the Dutch in the war with Spain, remained in the hands of their new owners after the general settlement in 1648. Dutch prosperity was so marked and Dutch ships were so numerous that the little nation was a genuine threat to England. Dutch and English traders were in competition not only in the East Indies but also in the Hudson valley area in North America.

This Anglo-Dutch rivalry produced a series of short commercial wars in the second half of the seventeenth century. For a time the issue was in doubt, but English supremacy was gradually established. New Amsterdam fell to the Duke of York in 1664, and later naval victories seriously crippled the Dutch carrying trade. The peace concluded three years later confirmed English possession of the former Dutch colonies in North America, as well as some of the Dutch West Indies.

FIRST ADVANCE OF LOUIS XIV

Louis XIV, the Grand Monarch of France, was fired with a consuming ambition to extend the frontiers of his country. Holland was by no means anxious to have the greedy French king as a neighbor; but, when Louis moved his armies toward the Spanish Netherlands in 1667, the Dutch were still at war with England. The conclusion of this conflict was quickly followed by an alliance of Holland, England, and Sweden to prevent Louis from carrying out his design. France made peace, but the Dutch were blamed for the failure of Louis' grand scheme. Louis bribed the English and Swedish kings to withdraw from the alliance with Holland. This country of the dikes was in poor condition to resist the military might of France. Wars with Spain and England, as well as internal conflicts, had made serious inroads on Dutch strength.

Louis XIV declared war on Holland in 1672; but the popular Dutch leader, William III, resorted to a measure which effectively dampened the ardor of the French army. He ordered the dikes to be cut and so flooded much of northern Holland. While the French were wishing for boots and boats, European rulers became alarmed and formed a new coalition which forced another peace. Holland emerged from the water and the war in a better condition than was to be expected. The English revolution of 1688 brought William III of Holland to the English throne; so the colonial empires of the two rivals were combined, at least for the time being.

After this union was dissolved early in the next century, the history of the Netherlands was relatively smooth until the first wave of successes won by armies of the French revolutionists. Then Holland was reduced to the status of a dependency. The unfortunate country became the Batavian Republic in 1795 and remained under French control until the fall of Napoleon. Since England was at war with France during most of this period of captivity for Holland, the Dutch colonial possessions became legitimate prizes for the English fleet. Capetown, which the Dutch East India Company had founded in 1652, fell to the British in 1806. Arrangements at the Congress of Vienna nine years later confirmed English possession of Dutch South Africa, and also deprived the Dutch of Guiana and Ceylon. In spite of these reverses over a span of more than two centuries, Holland retained an important commercial empire. The Dutch colonial possessions at present include about 800,000 square miles of territory, much of which consists of the still important Spice Islands of the East Indies.

Paul's Photo
VIENNA'S STATELY CITY HALL
This Gothic town hall is noted for the beautiful architectural lines of its towers.

PRELUDE TO THE DELUGE

France and England were clearly the leading nations of Europe after the middle of the seventeenth century. England, victorious over Spain and Holland, entered a contest with France for world supremacy. Each of the antagonists possessed an expanding colonial empire which produced considerable friction in the West Indies, India, and North America. England was superior in sea-power, but France had the finest army in Europe. The struggle was by no means an unequal affair, and the outcome was uncertain until the Seven Years War was nearly over. The European wars invariably had colonial counterparts, and, although France retained her continental territories, the colonial empire was lost to England.

Louis XIV practically took France into the grave when he died in 1715. His incessant warfare had consumed the wealth of the country. Trade and commerce were stagnant; famine and pestilence cast their horrible shadows over the land. Bankruptcies were common in a time when taxation was especially oppressive. More curses than tears followed the Grand Monarch to his tomb.

Not even Louis XIV could have healed the wounds he brought to France. His great-grandson and successor, Louis XV, had none of the qualities needed by the ruler of a great country. This unfortunate monarch was only five years of age when he became king. For nearly thirty years France was ruled by the duke of Orleans and Cardinal Fleury. When Louis XV took active charge of the government about the middle of the century, French affairs continued to be mismanaged. But Louis didn't care. France would last as long as Louis—and then the deluge.

It was under the duke of Orleans that the famous John Law formed a huge corporation to make money in colonial enterprises. Unwary investors bought shares in Law's enterprise which was very active between 1715 and 1720. Although the Mississippi Bubble, as this enterprise became known, popped quickly with an attendant shower of bankruptcies, John Law was responsible for adding strength to French possessions in the lower Mississippi valley.

Cardinal Fleury, who succeeded Orleans in control of the government, had more ability than his predecessor; however, France continued to decline. One wonders at the courage and tenacity the French people displayed while faced with almost inevitable defeat. During the interval of peace between 1713 and 1739, French positions in North America and India were considerably strengthened.

WAR OF THE AUSTRIAN SUCCESSION

France might have recovered some of its former prosperity with the passing of time, in spite of Louis XV and his expensive court; but international affairs soon embroiled the nation in other wars. English merchants were responsible for much ill-feeling between England and Spain in the early eighteenth century. Spain had granted England restricted trading privileges with her colonies in 1713, but the concessions merely whetted English appetites. Spain was determined to keep foreign merchants out of her American colonies, and those foreigners were determined to get in.

One of the English traders, a Captain Robert Jenkins, appeared in England with a highly-embellished story of how his vessel had been plundered by Spaniards. In the fray, according to Jenkins, the Spaniards cut off one of his ears but obligingly left the severed member with its owner as a souvenir. Demand for war against Spain was so great that Robert Walpole gave way. This war, which began in 1739, soon developed into a general European conflict known as the War of the Austrian Succession.

Frederick II of Prussia inherited a marvelous army from his father, and developed in his own right a hunger for territory. Although Prussia agreed to respect Austrian territory before the death of Charles VI and the succession of the beautiful Maria Theresa, the promise was quickly forgotten. Frederick made arrangements with France and Bavaria to participate in depriving Maria Theresa of choice morsels in the Austrian empire. France hoped to acquire the Austrian Netherlands. Frederick marched his army into Silesia, control of which would add much to Prussian power and lessen Austrian influence in the decrepit Holy Roman Empire. Hungary and Bohemia rallied to support the beautiful queen of Austria. England, jealous of her trade with the Austrian Netherlands and opposed to any increase in French power, entered the contest for Austria. Holland also was anxious to keep France out of the Netherlands, and so joined the alliance of Austria and England. The alignment, then, was one in which Prussia, France, Bavaria, and Spain were opposed to Austria, England, Holland, and Sardinia.

Maria Theresa could not drive Frederick's armies from Silesia; so she ceded the territory to Prussia in 1745. Frederick withdrew from the war, and thereafter Austria and her allies were successful in repelling the Bavarians, French, and Spaniards, except in the Netherlands where the French penetrated even into Holland.

The war in America between France and England was known as King George's War, and, with the exception of the English capture of Louisburg, a strong French fortress, in 1745, the outcome was not decisive. In India the French leader Dupleix won some initial successes, but the British recovered the lost ground

APARTMENT OF LOUIS XV IN PALACE AT FONTAINEBLEAU

at the end of the war. The conflict ended with the treaties of
Aix-la-Chapelle in 1748. Frederick II was allowed to keep
Silesia, but all other conquests were restored.

THE SEVEN YEARS WAR

Prussia and Austria had begun in the Germanies a rivalry
for supremacy which was to continue until the time of Bismarck,
more than a hundred years later. Anglo-French rivalry had as
its primary issue the fate of colonial empires. During the few
years of peace before the next conflagration, Maria Theresa and
her great minister, Count Kaunitz, concentrated their efforts
toward isolating Frederick on the Continent. Louis XV of France
was persuaded by his mistress, Madame de Pompadour, to desert
Prussia and ally himself with Austria. In the meantime Frederick
came to an understanding with George II of England who also
possessed the German territory of Hanover. This shifting of

allies has been called the "Diplomatic Revolution." France shifted its support from Prussia to Austria, while England shifted from Austria to Prussia. It was in this manner that the European countries were aligned in 1756 when the Seven Years War broke out.

THE WAR IN THE COLONIES

Just as the War of Jenkins' Ear between Spain and England in 1739 expanded into a European conflict, so also did the border warfare between French and English colonies in 1754 develop into an even greater international war. The American phase of this struggle, known as the French and Indian War, occurred as a result of French and English competition for the Ohio valley. French activity in this region after 1713 greatly alarmed the British both at home and in the colonies. A number of forts were built at strategic points before the English in America were aroused to action. The Ohio Company, organized in 1749 in Virginia to colonize the old Northwest, built a small post at the junction of the Monongahela and Allegheny rivers in 1754. The post was captured by a French force from Canada and rebuilt as Fort Duquesne. George Washington was sent into the region to assert English claims, but he met with defeat and retired. General Braddock, who undertook an ambitious campaign against the French in 1755, was defeated disastrously. It was during this same year that the Acadians were torn from Nova Scotia and distributed through various parts of North America.

French successes in America continued until the elder William Pitt came into power in England. Pitt infused new life into British resistance, and with important co-operation from the colonies France was defeated in Canada. Quebec, valiantly defended by General Montcalm, fell before the strategy of General Wolfe in 1759. Montreal capitulated the following year and the French empire in America was doomed.

Dupleix, builder of the French empire in India, met a far greater man in his opponent, Robert Clive. This former clerk executed a series of daring strokes which culminated in the battle of Plassey in 1757. Four years later Pondicherry fell to the British and France was defeated in India.

THE WAR ON THE CONTINENT

Frederick II had his hands more than full with his European enemies while England was defeating France abroad. Armies from Russia, Sweden, Austria, and France marched against Prussia from various directions. Frederick held his enemies at bay The defeat of a French army at Rossbach in 1757 was followed by a crushing blow against the Austrians at Leuthen. A Russian army captured Berlin, but Frederick continued his desperate fight.

William Pitt was generous in his support, especially with money. England could afford heavy expenditures in order to prevent France from sending reinforcements abroad. It was in this fashion that Frederick the Great did much to conquer India and America for England by fighting France in Europe. In spite of the heroic resistance of the Prussian armies, Frederick would have been defeated disastrously had not Russia suddenly changed sides when the Tsarina Elizabeth died in 1762.

Spain entered the war in support of France in 1761, but it was too late for the French Bourbons to save much from the wreckage. Before the conclusion of peace in 1763, France ceded to Spain the French territory of Louisiana west of the Mississippi. This cession more than compensated Spain for the loss of the Floridas to England. Practically all of the remainder of the French empire in North America and India was surrendered to England. Austria definitely renounced all claim to Silesia. The House of Hohenzollern was thereafter to be supreme in the Germanies, a supremacy that endured until the upheaval following the World War which sent William II as an exile to Holland.

British gains from the Seven Years War were so great there is danger in not appreciating their full significance. British mastery of the oceans was secured, the merchant marine increased rapidly, and the British Isles became the commercial center of the world. Territorial acquisitions in North America and India gave Britain one of the greatest empires of all time. France took revenge by helping the colonies during the American Revolution, an act which further weakened the tottering Bourbon dynasty. France was humbled. Let the years bring what they might. Great Britain was supreme in 1763.

ENGLISH COLONIAL POLICY BEFORE 1763

THE TREATY OF PARIS IN 1763 marked a distinct turning point in English colonial history. Former economic and administrative policies were found inadequate to meet the needs of an empire enlarged by the acquisition of the vast American possessions of France.

England, like other European countries, had early accepted the principles of mercantilism. As previously stated, this theory maintained that colonial possessions were valuable only in proportion to the amount of raw materials and markets they furnished. In other words, the mother-country must accumulate gold and silver bullion, particularly by keeping a favorable balance of trade —a favorable ratio of exports over imports.

British legislators sought to accomplish this end by a series of navigation and trade laws passed intermittently from 1651 to the end of the French and Indian conflict.

In general, these acts provided for the carrying of colonial exports in ships owned and manned by British subjects. Certain colonial products, such as tobacco, sugar, cotton, wool, indigo, and dyes were to be exported only to England or her possessions.

The growing dominance of the English landed gentry and merchant middle classes after 1688 explains the gradual tightening of economic restrictions on American commerce. An excellent example of such regulation was the Molasses Act of 1733. This forced the colonies to buy their sugar and molasses from the planters of the British West Indies. Naval stores and furs were added to the enumerated articles, while the manufacture of iron, hats, and woolen cloth was restricted.

The colonists regarded these trade regulations as oppressive and unjust, and in most cases entirely disregarded them. Smuggling became universal, and customs officials received slight co-operation from local merchants.

ROYAL CONTROL OVER THE COLONIES

English colonial officers were perplexed, not only by the difficulty of enforcing trade acts, but also by the threatening political discontent in America. Despite the growing supremacy of Parliament after the Glorious Revolution of 1688, the English Crown still controlled colonial administration. The royal governor acted as the direct representative of the king, having extensive veto powers over provincial legislation which might injure British commerce or interests. Colonial laws could not go into effect until approved by the Crown advisory body—the Privy Council. Royal influence increased steadily in each province. In fact, by the opening of the Revolutionary War, all but five of the original thirteen colonies were placed under royal control.

The colonists feared this growing domination and strove to maintain a position of independence. They quarreled continually with the governor over acts for raising and appropriating money. During the French and Indian struggle, necessary funds and troops were often withheld by stubborn legislators. Inefficiency, graft, and petty disputes between royal and local officers caused general resentment and misunderstandings. One bitter controversy followed another.

To remedy this universal dissatisfaction and lack of co-operation, American and British leaders suggested proposals for joint action. Such a scheme was discussed in an inter-colonial conference called by the British ministry in Albany in 1754. Some practical plan of action was sought to meet the impending French menace. A proposal, known as the Albany Plan of Union, drafted by Benjamin Franklin, failed to pass. The British maintained that it gave America too much self-government, while the colonists argued the Plan did not go far enough in that direction.

CONFERENCE HOUSE, TOTTENVILLE, STATEN ISLAND

Erected by Capt. Christopher Billopp in 1679. It was here that Lord Richard Howe met with Benjamin Franklin, John Adams, and Edward Rutledge, representatives of the Continental Congress, in an effort to prevent the war with the colonies.

COLONIAL SELF-CONSCIOUSNESS DEVELOPS

By the middle of the eighteenth century the colonists had evolved some sense of national consciousness. They regarded America not merely as an English overseas domain but as an equal commonwealth, united with Great Britain only in the person of the king. They were willing to accede in theory to legislative regulation so long as it was laxly administered. By 1763, however, American manufactures and shipping had grown enormously. Colonial merchants and business men, such as Peter Faneuil and John Hancock, insisted that as Englishmen they had a right to a lucrative trade without unjust discrimination on the part of England.

Another factor sometimes overlooked, but very important in this period, is the great westward trek. Thousands of Scotch-Irish, Germans, and English moved toward the frontiers of New York, Pennsylvania, and Virginia. Isolated as they were, amid physical danger and hardship, they developed a spirit of independence which resented all restriction. Also, the non-English groups had no traditional affection for the British Isles and added their influence to the general eastern reaction against the mother-country.

Despite the increased unrest in the colonies, they enjoyed more self-government and political freedom than was accorded to any other European possession. Provincial assemblies assumed more and more control over local legislation and royal enactments. Commerce and business flourished in spite of trade acts.

Yet, the whole system of English colonial administration was based on a false economic theory and stimulated by a narrow nationalism. Dangerous potential grievances lay concealed in the colonial economic and political structure. These were to burst into flame during the next quarter-century.

ENGLISH COLONIAL POLICY AFTER 1763

The victory over the French in 1763 multiplied England's colonial problems. She was faced with a tremendous war debt, a vast unorganized western domain, and a serious Indian revolt known as Pontiac's Conspiracy. The Ottawa chieftain, fearing further advances into his territory, decided to strike in 1763 before the English frontier defense was organized. Fort Detroit withstood the attack, but before order was restored all but two of the English forts in the West were destroyed and the frontiers horribly ravaged.

In order to meet such Indian hostility, the British ministry issued the Proclamation of 1763. This provided for establishing the provinces of East and West Florida in the south, and Quebec along the St. Lawrence River. The large territory west of the mountains was designated as Indian Country. All grants of land to settlers were expressly forbidden for the present. This restriction was expected to quiet the natives and provide for an orderly, supervised partition of the trans-Allegheny region. Officials also hoped to safeguard the fur trade by closing this vast border to hordes of restless settlers.

Storms of protest at this new restraint came from traders, frontiersmen, and land speculators who were operating in this area. At the end of the French and Indian War many land schemes were under way. Among the more prominent promoters of such plans were Samuel Wharton, a wealthy Philadelphia merchant, and Benjamin Franklin. Their organization, known as the Vandalia Company, sought a grant of land, roughly coinciding with West Virginia and eastern Kentucky. Permission for this colony was withheld until just before the Revolution. This was due to the hostility of Virginia, which maintained that the territory lay within her charter claims. Also, many of her leading citizens, including George Washington and Henry Lee, wished to obtain exclusive grants in the same general area.

WESTWARD MOVEMENT

In 1768 the Treaty of Fort Stanwix was negotiated by the northern Indian agent, Sir William Johnson, with the tribes known as the Six Nations. It opened for settlement a large tract east and south of the Ohio River. A second purchase, by John Stuart, the southern agent, allowed settlers to move into the West Virginia and eastern Kentucky districts.

Frontiersmen began to pour into these regions where, before 1763, only a few squatters had built their tiny cabins along the lonely trails. By 1770, a number of fortified stations dotted the banks of the Watauga and Holston Rivers on the boundaries of Virginia and North Carolina. Here in 1772 came the Scotch-Irishman, James Robertson, from the Carolina frontier, and John Sevier, the Virginia Huguenot. As early as 1772 these settlements drew up a written compact of government, the first one west of the mountains.

The natural highway to the "dark and bloody ground" of Kentucky was known as the Wilderness Trail. Over its narrow pathway, hunters and scouts, such as Daniel Boone, made their way to the rich blue-grass hunting grounds of the Indians. Trained as he was in the use of the gun and the knife and accus-tomed to the dangers of frontier life, Boone has come to symbol-ize for us the characteristics of the sturdy pioneer of the period.

Just a few weeks before the historic clash on Lexington Common, Judge Richard Henderson of North Carolina, head of the Transylvania Company, negotiated a treaty with the Cherokees. Through it he acquired title to much of the land included in the present states of Kentucky and Tennessee. Hunters and pioneers had already found their way into this area. The tiny settlements of Boonesborough and Harrodsburg had been made here a few years earlier. A written constitution was drawn up at Henderson's behest, with the hope that Transylvania might become the fourteenth colony. The scheme failed, for Virginia and North Carolina were not ready to surrender their western lands.

Continued Indian raids kept the frontiersmen in a state of perpetual alarm. Nearly every family that trudged over the famous trail, or pushed down the Ohio River, had lost some loved one at the hands of the hated "redskins."

To meet this situation, England determined to provide for frontier defense by establishing troops at strategic points. The erection of such an extensive military organization meant heavy financial burden. The attempt to pass on a portion of this expense to the colonies led directly to financial and political controversies. These in turn led to the break-up of the empire. The colonists insisted that this new program for western defense was but a pretext to get revenue for a depleted British treasury.

RESISTANCE TO NEW COMMERCIAL POLICIES

George Grenville, as Prime Minister, determined to bring some order into the chaotic American administrative system. Early in 1764, he proposed a number of acts designed to increase colonial revenue. The first of these measures was known as the Sugar Act. It had a dual purpose: to provide revenue and to tighten the enforcement of the earlier trade regulations. The act reduced the duty on molasses from the West Indies, but levied additional duties on sugar, wines, coffee, silks, and linens.

The prospect of such a duty, collected by a reorganized customs service, caused consternation among the New England merchants. For over a generation they had disregarded the Molasses Act of 1733, and had become wealthy from illicit trade with the connivance of dishonest revenue officials. The most unfortunate feature of the Sugar Act, however, was the implication stated in the preamble. This expressed the theory that Parliament had the right to tax for purposes of revenue. The colonists had early accepted the idea that the British legislature had the power to tax for the purpose of regulating imperial trade. They were not willing, however, to accept its right to tax for revenue only.

Merchants, assemblies, and town meetings protested against the law. Colonial lawyers, like James Otis, Patrick Henry, and Samuel Adams, found in it the first suggestion for their dynamic phrase, "no taxation without representation." Other measures of the Grenville program, such as the Currency and Quartering acts, only added to the general reaction against English rule. The former enactment forbade the issuance of colonial paper money, while the latter compelled the colonists to furnish lodging and supplies to British troops.

THE STAMP ACT

Organized opposition was crystallized when the Grenville government passed the Stamp Act on March 22, 1765. Every legal paper, bill of lading, newspaper, or book was taxed under the act. This tax, the British felt, was more equable, and fell on all groups of people.

The violent reception of this measure in America astonished British officials. Merchants, business men, lawyers, journalists, and clergymen of all sections were aroused. Respectable citizens organized the "Sons of Liberty." Mobs, harangued by Samuel Adams, paraded in Boston, ransacked the home of Lieutenant-Governor Hutchinson, and destroyed his remarkable library.

American hostility took unified form in the Stamp Act Congress, held in New York City on October 1, 1765. This was the first inter-colonial meeting called by the colonists themselves definitely to oppose English policy. The resolutions and petitions drawn up by this body are representative of colonial opinion of the time. The colonists willingly gave their allegiance to the Crown. In return, they insisted that they were entitled to all the rights and privileges of English subjects. Chief among these opinions was the theory that no taxation could be levied without their consent.

The constitutional issue centered about the question of representation. In America there had developed the tradition that the representative must live in the geographical district he was chosen to represent. It was impossible then, from the colonial viewpoint, for Americans to be represented in Parliament. The English held, on the other hand, that their system of stratified representation, by class and estate rather than by geographical unit, represented all interests and groups in the empire.

REPEAL OF THE STAMP ACT

To bring pressure to bear on Parliament, the Stamp Act Congress resolved to refrain from buying, using, or selling English goods until the obnoxious measure was removed. This boycott was so effective that soon English merchants, fearing bankruptcy, bombarded Parliament with petitions asking for the immediate repeal of the stamp duty. Repeal was effected in March, 1766, but only after the passage of the Declaratory Act which reaffirmed parliamentary right to tax the colonies.

POST ROAD BETWEEN NEW YORK AND PHILADELPHIA
(About 1790)

Few Americans stopped to worry about the implications of this last decree. They celebrated the repeal of the Stamp Act with extravagant demonstrations of loyalty and gratitude. Changes in the trade laws, which made them no longer regulatory but clearly revenue-raising schemes, were scarcely noticed. If England had been able to take immediate advantage of this favorable colonial reaction, the Revolution might possibly have been postponed or even avoided.

Unfortunately, American rejoicing was short-lived, for the matter of taxation was reopened. The brilliant and injudicious new Chancellor of the Exchequer, Charles Townshend, in temporary leadership of the government, soon brought about a second crisis in colonial affairs. He showed at once that he was in accord with the Grenville policies. Using admirable cleverness, he attempted to straddle the colonial distinction between duties for revenue and duties for trade regulation. Townshend proposed to reduce the cost of Indian control and to retrench in military appropriations. Colonial revenue was to be increased by import duties on paint, lead, paper, and tea. The customs service was reorganized, and new admiralty courts were established, writs of assistance or general search warrants were authorized, and offenders were to be tried by the new courts with no jury.

To the Americans, the most insulting feature of the whole program was the provision to use the revenue to make the royal governors and judges independent of the colonial legislatures. The colonists saw in this another threat to their liberties, for their assemblies had, by the control of colonial finances, kept the governor in check.

REDCOATS SENT TO BOSTON

Massachusetts took the lead in opposing the new restrictions. Her legislature sent out a circular letter in 1768 to the other colonial assemblies. This called for united resistance, and stated that the people of each colony could be legally taxed only by its own provincial legislature. When Massachusetts refused to rescind her action, Parliament ordered the assembly dissolved and radical agitators brought to England for trial. The only result was heightened feeling against English policy. When customs officials attempted to collect duties from John Hancock's vessel "Liberty," they were badly treated by a Boston mob.

Such action brought two regiments of British troops to the Massachusetts capital. The presence of "redcoats" led to irritating clashes, which culminated in the famous "Boston Massacre" in 1770. When the affair was over, four Bostonians lay dead. Such radicals as Samuel Adams and Joseph Warren shrewdly seized upon the incident further to inflame the populace against British "tyranny." Prominent among the liberal agitators in the other colonies were the young Virginians, Thomas Jefferson and Patrick Henry. They represented the democratic philosophy of the frontier counties, and reflected that section's dislike of the eastern planting aristocracy.

BOSTON TEA PARTY

Under the leadership of Adams and the southern radicals, Committees of Correspondence were organized throughout the colonies. These bodies acted as the propaganda machine of this insurgent group. They continued their activity even after the Townshend duties were repealed by Lord North. As a gesture of maintaining Parliamentary supremacy over colonial taxation, however, a tax of threepence was kept on tea. The powerful East India Company, facing bankruptcy at this time, appealed for a government subsidy. Instead, it was given a monopoly of all tea imported into the colonies. This unwise and ill-considered act threw the conservative colonial elements in with the more radical groups. Now the interests of the commercial classes and the provincial policy against taxation for revenue were both challenged.

American reaction took various forms. In Charleston, Philadelphia, and New York, East India agents were forced to resign. Several ships were compelled to sail back to England with their tea cargoes. In Boston, however, Governor Hutchinson refused to allow the ships to return without unloading. The radicals decided to take the next step, and on the night of December 16, 1773, a number of them disguised as Indians, boarded the vessels and dumped the whole cargo, worth $75,000, into the Boston harbor.

THE COERCIVE ACTS

The liberal Whig groups in England immediately withdrew their support from the colonial cause. Such disregard of property rights, as exhibited in the "Boston Tea Party," was abhorrent to them. English opinion almost universally demanded stern coercive measures. The erring colony must be forced to return to the fold of respectability and reason.

Early in 1774, five punitive acts came from an outraged Parliament. They were labeled at once by the colonists the "Intolerable Acts." The first proposal, known as the Boston Port Bill, closed the port to commerce until Bostonians repented of the infamous "Party" and agreed to compensate the East India Company for the destroyed cargo.

The next measure, the Massachusetts Government Act, disregarded what the provincials had come to hold as their most cherished political safeguard—their charter. They looked upon this document as a contract which could be abolished only when one

Courtesy Boston Chamber of Commerce

FANEUIL HALL, BOSTON
"Cradle of American Liberty"

Courtesy Boston Chamber of Commerce

OLD STATE HOUSE
Where Declaration of Independence was
proclaimed in Boston.

party broke its provisions. Since it was granted by the king, the colonists insisted that only the Crown could abolish it. Naturally, then, a storm of angry protest arose when Parliament revoked the Massachusetts Charter of 1691, and substituted a royal government. The council and judges were no longer to be elected by the people, but appointed by the Crown. What struck at the foundation of the personal liberty of all classes, however, was the prohibition of town meetings. These strongholds of Samuel Adams and his cohorts were regarded in British eyes as centers of treasonable propaganda.

The third irritating act provided that persons charged with murder in connection with law enforcement should be transported to England for trial. A fourth measure compelled Massachusetts towns to provide quarters and food for British soldiers. The last parliamentary enactment, the Quebec Act, particularly inflamed the Puritan fathers. This plan extended the boundaries of the province of Quebec to the Ohio River, disregarding colonial claims to that area. Perhaps the most significant feature of the act, however, was the provision granting religious and civil toleration to Catholic French-Canadians.

Still smarting under the restrictions of the Proclamation Line of 1763, the colonists were incensed by this new prohibition. Extravagant speculation and magnificent land-promotion schemes faced destruction. New Englanders felt especially offended by the extension into their western claims of the hated French Catholicism, laws, and customs.

In order to make this coercive program more effective, Parliament issued supplementary administrative acts, one of which resulted in the appointment of General Thomas Gage, head of the British army in America, as civil and military governor of Massachusetts.

Some of the more conservative groups in the disciplined colony were anxious to reinstate themselves in British favor by paying for the tea. The radicals, however, would not consent to this and seized the opportunity of capitalizing on the universal anger against Britain. The movement for resistance developed rapidly under their skilful guidance. City workingmen, frontiersmen, merchants, and planters—all clamored for action against their common oppressor. Samuel Adams, Patrick Henry, and James Madison, in legal and extra-legal assemblies, insisted that immediate steps must be taken to relieve the distressing plight of Massachusetts.

The day the Boston port was to be closed, June 1, 1774, was designated by the Virginia legislature as a day of fasting and prayer. When, on account of this, the governor dissolved its session, some members of the assembly gathered in the famous Raleigh Tavern, in Williamsburg. They resolved to invite the other colonies to meet in a continental congress. The acceptance of this invitation by every colony, except Georgia, proved conclusively that the crisis was no longer local but national in character.

TOWN CRIER, PROVINCETOWN, MASSACHUSETTS
(Posed in our days. Pilgrim Memorial monument in background.)

AMERICAN WAR FOR INDEPENDENCE

REBELLION!

WHEN THE CONGRESS MET IN PHILADEL-
PHIA, September, 1774, it dispatched a petition to
the king asking a return to the political status of
1763, which the colonists felt to be the true constitutional division
of imperial and provincial power. It also urged that the colonists
abide by the rules of the proposed Association, whose provisions
forbade the importation of British goods. A Declaration of
Rights and Grievances, an ultimatum stating the American position, was also drafted. Finally, after providing for another Congress the following year, the members adjourned.

Within the year, however, war had been precipitated. Pitt
and Burke in Parliament had urged conciliation, but the majority
in England realized that the revolutionary movement in America
was led by radicals who were really asking for a return to non-
enforcement of law; hence they supported the king, who urged
General Gage to be firm.

When Gage tried to seize Samuel Adams and John Hancock
as rebel ringleaders and to destroy colonial military stores, the
quarrel broke into open conflict, and the "shots heard 'round the
world" were fired on Lexington Green and Concord Bridge.
Thereupon, militia from New England flocked to Boston, and,
although driven from one height in the Battle of Bunker Hill,
they harried the British and threatened their hold on Boston by
fortifying the surrounding hills. The die was cast. About one-
third of the colonists had forced the war. Another third hoped
and continued throughout the war to hope for conciliation. Now
the middle third had to make their choice.

The Second Continental Congress met on May 10, 1775. It recognized that a state of war existed by appointing George Washington commander in chief of the colonial army, and by issuing a "Declaration of Causes for Taking up Arms."

MOVEMENT TOWARD SEPARATION

Conservative groups in America were slow to support any movement toward separation. Such a step meant severing the sentimental ties to the mother-country, and economic interests dictated hesitation. Not only would commercial privileges within the empire be lost, but there was danger that the resulting revolution might bring on anarchy or military rule, more to be feared than parliamentary taxation. The Whigs in England tended to support the liberal demands of the colonies and to aid them in reducing the royal power. However, patriotism and the whole background of the mercantile system, which would keep the colonies subservient to England, influenced the majority of Parliament—perhaps as much as did royal patronage—to vote support for the war. Lagging enlistments forced the English government to adopt the common practice of purchasing the services of soldiers in other countries; the German principality of Hesse supplied England with mercenaries.

In the colonies, resentment against this hiring of Hessians, as well as the reputed incitement of Indians on the frontier, added fuel to the revolutionary propaganda being poured out. Press and pulpit recited tales of British spoliation of American territory. Thomas Paine's *Common Sense* and John Dickinson's *Letters of a Pennsylvania Farmer* were two of the more influential pamphlets published.

DECLARATION OF INDEPENDENCE

By July 1, 1776, representatives of nine states in Congress were ready to support a resolution of independence. Later the vote was unanimous, and on July 4 a formal declaration was adopted. Jefferson prepared the document which asserted the principle earlier developed by John Locke—that men have certain inalienable rights. This was followed by a list of acts of the king in opposition to these rights. Finally appeared the statement

THE SIGNING OF THE DECLARATION OF INDEPENDENCE
From the painting by John Trumbull.

that hence "these colonies are, and of right ought to be, free and independent states."

This Declaration marked a definite turning point in the war. Henceforth, "Loyalists" were not thought of as individuals who merely differed in opinion. Now they were branded as enemies of the new nation, and were punished accordingly. Imprisonment, banishment, detention camps, tarring and feathering, and confiscation of property made the life of the Loyalists wretched and dangerous. It must be remembered that this group comprised a third of the population.

Secret aid in the form of money and supplies came from France, which was glad to assist in the disruption of the British Empire. France, as a government, had no love for, nor interest in, the colonies. Frenchmen and liberals from other nations, who were interested in the democratic philosophy of the Revolution, flocked to America. While some of these caused much embarrassment and gave little service, others, like Lafayette, De Kalb, Von Steuben, and Kosciuszko, were invaluable to Washington and his army.

Reproduced from *The Pageant of America*. Copyright and permission Yale University Press.
WASHINGTON CROSSING THE DELAWARE, CHRISTMAS NIGHT, 1776
From the painting by Emanuel Leutze.

WASHINGTON'S STRATEGY IN THE FIRST PERIOD OF THE WAR

The scene of the war shifted to New York after the colonial troops evacuated Boston. Washington was dislodged from Long Island, and escaped with his army only because Howe decided to wait until the next morning to bag the "sly fox."

The next four months after the New York campaign, from September through December, 1776, allowed Washington to exhibit his talents as a clever and efficient general who displayed unusual strategical ability. He realized that his task was to keep the small colonial army from dispersing, and to keep it out of reach of the superior English forces. He seized every opportunity to retreat after making sudden and unexpected attacks. These maneuvers made it impossible for his less able opponent to take advantage of British numbers.

Such tactics were necessary. A decisive defeat or capture of the small American army, which was supported by only one-third of the colonial population, would put an end to the Revolution. At least some victories, no matter how small, were necessary as arguments if American ministers abroad were to secure the foreign aid which seemed to be essential for final victory.

Washington continued to prove his ability as a general by the manner in which he carried on his maneuvers. From New York he retired across New Jersey, keeping just ahead of the British forces. On Christmas night in 1776, knowing that attack would be unexpected, he crossed the icy, dangerous Delaware River, and won decisive victories over detachments at Trenton and Princeton. Before the startled Cornwallis could gather his wits, as well as his army, Washington went into fortified winter quarters at Morristown, New Jersey.

SARATOGA AND FRENCH AID

The next year the British planned to cut off New England from the rest of the colonies by capturing the strategically important Hudson River. Three armies were to co-operate. However, Howe took his army south instead and captured the seat of government, then at Philadelphia. A second army, commanded by St. Leger, was defeated by the Americans in the Mohawk Valley. The third army, under Burgoyne, advanced from Canada and was harassed on every side by New England and New York militia. Finally, Burgoyne's long line of communication was cut behind him. Frantic appeals to Howe for aid went unanswered by that Philadelphia-bound general. On October 17, 1777, Burgoyne surrendered his army of five thousand men to General Gates at Saratoga.

The battle of Saratoga put an end to the military plan of the British to divide the colonies. Colonial aspirations, then at low ebb, were revived. More important still, Saratoga proved to be the decisive victory upon which the hopes of Washington and other Americans rested—the victory destined to bring foreign aid.

Benjamin Franklin, the American agent in France, had reason to rejoice when he heard of the victory at Saratoga. Beaumarchais, the French playwright and amateur diplomat who had acted as the agent in bringing secret French aid to the colonies, was also encouraged. These men realized that Saratoga was a convincing argument to promote an open alliance between France and the rebellious colonies. In fact, Beaumarchais was so excited that on

Courtesy The Art Institute of Chicago

THE SURRENDER OF GENERAL BURGOYNE
At Saratoga, October 17, 1777.

his way to the court with the news he wrecked his carriage and broke his arm!

A treaty of alliance was soon signed. Although military aid in the form of land and naval forces did not arrive immediately, ammunitions, clothing, shoes, and other necessities, as well as money, flowed steadily from France. Later Spain and Holland declared war on England and sent some financial assistance and supplies across the Atlantic.

FINANCING THE REVOLUTION

The importance of this foreign aid in the field of finance alone can be deduced from the fact that $8,000,000 was secured from Europe in the form of loans, while the states contributed a total of only $6,000,000. For additional money to carry on the war, Congress resorted to the printing presses. By 1780, $240,000,000 in paper money was issued and depreciation naturally became an acute problem.

REVOLUTION IN THE WEST AND WAR IN THE SOUTH

Just before the Revolution began, a continuous stream of colonists flowed into the valleys of the Virginia and Carolina frontiers. Led by Daniel Boone, James Robertson, and John Sevier, a large number of settlers entered Kentucky and Tennessee during the Revolution. These settlements, as well as the frontier communities of the colonies north of the Potomac River, suffered from British-inspired Indian raids. There was, in addition, the constant threat that the British would succeed in their attempts to form an Indian confederacy and attack the colonies from the West.

To forestall this eventuality and to end British control over the Indians, Virginia sent George Rogers Clark and a small detachment into the West. Surprise attacks and the willingness of Clark's volunteers to march through waist-deep water, won the British posts in the Illinois country and established the American claim to the region.

Clark's victory was almost the only encouraging note for the Americans in the military campaigns from Saratoga to Yorktown. In 1778, the British transferred the war to the South, capturing Savannah as the first step of a new plan. They proposed to march north, taking and controlling one state after the other. This "rolling up of the South" was successful for the most part, although on the frontiers of these states, guerrilla warfare, led by Marion, Sumter, and Pickens rendered British rule ineffective as rapidly as it was established. Along the coast the British plan was successful and was stopped only by the defeat of Cornwallis at Yorktown in 1781.

ENGLAND LOSES CONTROL OF THE SEA AND THE COLONIES

Throughout the world, England was facing the combined forces of France, Spain, and Holland. In 1781 a hostile Armed Neutrality League was formed by Russia, Denmark, and Sweden. No longer did Britain control the sea. Two centuries earlier, when Spain lost this power to England, she had to give up hope of maintaining her American colonial monopoly. Now, when England lost control, the success of the Americans was only a matter of time.

By 1781, Cornwallis had reached Yorktown, Virginia, in his process of "rolling up the South." A rapid march from New York by Washington, and a co-operating expedition under Lafayette and the French general, Rochambeau, closed the neck of the Yorktown peninsula. Admiral de Grasse, with a French fleet, cut off hope of escape or reinforcement by sea. The control of the sea was the deciding factor, and Cornwallis was forced to surrender his army.

That ended the Revolution as far as America was concerned. Her European allies spent the next two years trying further to weaken the British position on the Continent and in the Orient. However, England maintained her position at Gibraltar, in India, and defeated a French fleet in the West Indies. So important had become the world phase of the war that, by 1782 England was willing to concede American independence.

ENGLAND RECOGNIZES AMERICAN INDEPENDENCE

France, Spain, and Holland entered the war not because of any love for Americans or their philosophy of government; they sought only to weaken England and had no wish to see a great nation arise on the North American continent. In the last analysis, France was willing to sacrifice American interests rather than those of her close ally, Spain, which feared the influence of the Revolution on her colonies. Sensing the attitude of France, the American ministers, Jay, John Adams, and Franklin, disregarded the treaty of alliance which bound them to keep the French informed of the progress of peace negotiations, and signed a preliminary treaty with England in 1782 without French knowledge. In the following year, a definite treaty was signed by all the warring nations.

By this treaty, the United States was given all the territory between the Atlantic and the Mississippi River, from Canada to Florida. The right to fish on the Newfoundland banks was granted. In return, the United States promised not to put any legal impediments in the way of collection of British debts and to recommend that the states return the confiscated property of the Loyalists. British generosity in this treatment of her former colonists was an attempt to woo the Americans from the side of the French.

AFTER THE WAR

Social and economic development usually quickens in any period of stress. America was no exception to the rule. During the Revolution, manufacturing was stimulated as a result of the increased demands of the war and the removal of British restrictions. Privateering and war profiteering created a new moneyed class. Changes in the laws of inheritance and confiscation of Loyalist property caused smaller estates and wider property holding.

The philosophy of the Revolution extended into religious and social life. Toleration had been developing slowly during the colonial period. Now the last steps were taken, and freedom of religion became almost universal. Even suffrage requirements were made more liberal in the older states, and in the new western commonwealths, manhood suffrage was written into the constitutions.

Courtesy Metropolitan Museum of Art

GEORGE WASHINGTON
(From the portrait by Gilbert Stuart)

THE ARTICLES OF CONFEDERATION

Courtesy Chicago Historical Society
BIRTH OF OUR NATION'S FLAG

SOLVING OF THE PROBLEM OF FEDERATION

THE REVOLUTION was mainly a result of Britain's failure to solve the problem of federation—that is, there was a failure to distinguish between the rights, interests, and duties of the individual colonies on one hand, and the central government of the empire on the other. The outbreak of war turned this problem over to the Second Continental Congress, which came into session in May, 1775. A central government had to be set up to take the place of government from Britain. It was the problem of Congress to work out a division of powers, satisfactory to the individual colonies and yet granting enough power to the central government so that it would be effective. If Congress failed, the Old World would see across the Atlantic thirteen jealous states, easy prey to European intrigue.

A committee of thirteen was appointed by the second Congress to draft a satisfactory plan of government. They found the solution as difficult as had the British Cabinet. The Articles of Confederation, drawn up by this committee, proved to have grave weaknesses even before the last state, Maryland, ratified them in 1781, four years after they were drafted. As in the case of the British administration, the central government was given power over foreign diplomacy, Indian affairs, and disputes between states. Matters of taxation, control over courts, the right to regulate commerce, in fact those questions which had been in dispute between the colonies and Britain, were all left to the states.

The central government soon found itself ineffective. The states refused to vote money to support it, and there was no power to enforce its demands since an executive department had not been provided. Nor was there a judicial system to interpret the laws of Congress uniformly; instead, the courts in each state interpreted federal law to suit their own interests.

There was little possibility of remedying these defects because a unanimous vote was needed to amend the Articles. In fact, the passage of any law was difficult, for each state had one vote and all important laws needed the approval of nine of the thirteen states. Attempts to correct the most serious omissions of the Articles—the lack of a federal executive and judiciary, of the power of the central government to enforce its laws, to regulate commerce, and to levy taxes—failed repeatedly.

Within two years after the war, the prestige of the Congress had fallen so low that state legislatures often neglected to choose delegates, members failed to attend Congress, and sessions could not be held because of the lack of a quorum. The first American solution to the problem of federalism had failed.

LAND CLAIMS

Maryland refused to ratify the Articles of Confederation until 1781, because of the immense territorial claims of Virginia, Massachusetts, and the Carolinas. She feared not only that these states would in time have an overwhelming voice in federal councils, but also that they would profit by the migration of Maryland citizens to the West. Her ultimatum was that those states which claimed western territories should cede them to the central government. The other states without western lands, including New Hampshire, Rhode Island, New Jersey, Delaware, and Pennsylvania, naturally supported Maryland. They argued that the lands thus ceded could be sold and the proceeds used to pay off the national war debts which, as Maryland pointed out, had been incurred in a common cause.

Another reason for the necessity of such cessions was the dispute between the states over the extent of their overlapping claims. New York, with a weak claim based entirely on Indian treaties, was the first to agree to Maryland's proposal. Virginia had extensive claims based on charter provisions and Clark's conquest. She agreed to cede her lands to Congress, and Maryland announced her willingness to ratify the Articles. The last cession was not made, however, until 1802. Common ownership and interest in this federal domain acted as a strong bond in holding the new states together.

After providing in 1785 for the survey and sale of the lands northwest of the Ohio River, Congress passed the most important legislation of the entire period of the Confederation. This famous act, the Northwest Ordinance, provided for the government of the territory and its admittance to the federal union. Used as a basis for all future territorial organization, it provided for a governor with ample power, assisted by a popular assembly. Provisions were included for the creation of three to five states when warranted by sufficient population, for the support of public education, and for full religious toleration. In addition, slavery was excluded.

EUROPE AND THE CONFEDERATION

Control over this region by the United States was insecure because the British refused to give up the posts they held at Niagara, Detroit, and other places along the Great Lakes. England justified this breach of the peace treaty because of the refusal of Americans to return Loyalist property and to pay pre-Revolutionary debts to British merchants.

Spain held the mouth of the Mississippi River and refused to grant American shipments free access to the sea. Kentuckians and Tennesseans, whose very existence depended upon the free navigation of the river, threatened secession from the Confederation and talked of capturing New Orleans.

Attempts to reach some diplomatic solution of these difficulties failed because of the weakness of the federal government in international and interstate relations, a weakness well understood in Europe. England, in fact, refused to send a minister to the United States saying that she did not know whether to send one or thirteen. Spain, too, realized the impotence of the new federal government, and was deaf to its demands for free navigation on the Mississippi.

DEPRESSION

Congress was not allowed to levy taxes and was dependent upon contributions from the states, each of which jealously watched lest it pay more than its share. In time, money ceased entirely to flow from the states for the support of the government. Borrowing had to be resorted to, even to pay the interest on former debts. As a result, exorbitant interest rates were charged on government loans. Bonds and paper money continued to drop to new lows. One of the after-effects of war is depression, a fact which was soon impressed upon the American people. In the 1780's, conditions were made worse by the lack of gold and silver, the lack of a uniform currency, and the uncertain value of paper money. American foreign commerce was destroyed since the right to trade with the British colonies was lost when the states left the British Empire.

In addition, trade wars developed between the states. One after the other passed customs laws aimed at its neighbors. No control over foreign commerce was possible because as soon as one state passed a customs act, its neighbors reduced all corresponding duties in an attempt to win trade.

Trying to remedy a hopeless financial condition, Rhode Island inflated its currency. Massachusetts farmers advocated the same policy. When state officials attempted to foreclose farm property, the rural districts rose in Shay's Rebellion, demanding cheap money. Printing-press money was made legal tender for payment of debts, and it was so worthless that the creditor actually hid from those who owed him money. If he were found he might have to acknowledge payment of a hundred-dollar debt with paper money that would perhaps buy only a dozen eggs.

DEMAND FOR A NEW GOVERNMENT

These conditions caused certain economic groups to unite with those who saw in the state rivalries and the ineffective central government the destruction of the infant federal union. Those who held government securities, manufacturers, financiers, and landowners, wanted a government able to control radical groups in the states, able to demand concessions from foreign nations, as well as one able to stabilize domestic economic conditions.

Delegates from Virginia and Maryland met at the home of George Washington in 1785 to discuss navigation of the Potomac River. They decided to invite all the states to meet in 1786 at Annapolis to confer on commercial problems of the Confederation. The representatives of the five states who attended this conference adopted Alexander Hamilton's resolution, which called for a meeting of all the states in May of the next year at Philadelphia to consider desirable and necessary changes in the Articles of Confederation. A second attempt to solve the problem of federalization, of the relationship of state and central government, was to be made.

THE FEDERAL CONVENTION

Delegates from all of the states except Rhode Island arrived in Philadelphia in 1787. Not all of them came in May, the month designated, and not everyone remained during all the sessions of the convention. The average age of the group was about forty and it was the younger delegates who did most of the work, although the tempering influence of the few older men must be recognized. The membership, in general, was from

JAMES MADISON
Delegate from Virginia to the Federal Convention in 1787, and later the fourth president of the United States.

the propertied and conservative classes. While these men were not demigods, their average of competence and ability was probably higher than in any other group which has ever met in a convention. Most of them had served their states or the nation as governors, congressmen, judges, or diplomats, and came to the convention convinced that the very existence of their nation depended upon their labors.

From Virginia came James Madison and George Mason, while James Wilson and Gouverneur Morris represented Pennsylvania. Others who were to be leaders in the convention were the Pinckneys of South Carolina, John Dickinson of Delaware, Luther Martin of Maryland, and Alexander Hamilton from New York.

George Washington, whose ambition and patriotism were above reproach, was made chairman. The venerable Benjamin Franklin was present among the Pennsylvania delegation, and his wise counsel often calmed the scene when excitement and conflict of ideas threatened to disrupt the assembly.

THE GREAT COMPROMISE

One of the first of these conflicts occurred when the question of state representation in the federal government arose. The large states, headed by Virginia, wished representation according to population. The smaller states, led by New Jersey, wished a continuation of the system of equal representation. Finally, Connecticut suggested two houses of Congress: a Senate in which the states were equally represented, and a House of Representatives based on population.

Another compromise settled the question of the counting of slaves. The South wished them included in enumerating the population for apportioning representation, but not when taxes were levied. The North took an opposite stand. The final compromise provided that three-fifths of the slaves should be counted both for representation and taxation.

SUBORDINATION OF STATE GOVERNMENTS

Since the greatest defect of the Articles of Confederation was the inability to enforce the acts of Congress, several remedies were suggested in the convention. It was proposed that the army be available to coerce the states into line with federal policy, and that Congress have the right to nullify a state action. The logical and purely peaceful solution of this problem is contained in two clauses. The first provides, "This Constitution, and the laws of the United States which shall be made in pursuance thereof . . . shall be the supreme law of the land; and the Judges in every state shall be bound thereby, anything in the Constitution or laws of any State to the contrary notwithstanding." This may be thought of as the core of the Constitution. The second coercive clause required that all state and federal officers take an oath to uphold the federal Constitution when they entered upon the duties of their offices.

In this way the national government was made supreme in those powers assigned to it by the Constitution, including control over conflicting state laws, and cases arising over this point could be transferred from state to federal courts.

Since the Constitution was defined as a law, it operated directly on the individual rather than on the states. This principle was perhaps one of the most important departures from the Articles. Since state officers had to swear to uphold the Constitution, even when it conflicted with state law, hampering action by any state official could result in his trial in a federal court for violation of the "supreme law of the land."

POPULAR GOVERNMENT?

There was no attempt to make the government responsible to popular demand and opinion. The president was chosen by electors who, the convention thought, would use their own judgment in selecting the executive and not be bound by parties, which were not in existence then nor foreseen by the makers of the Constitution. Senators were to be chosen by state legislatures and judges appointed by the president with the approval of the Senate. Only the delegates to the House of Representatives were chosen directly by the people.

The Constitution followed the plan of a French philosopher, Montesquieu, to divide the functions of government among legislative, judicial, and executive departments. An attempt to make the three departments equal, balanced, and a check on each other, resulted in giving the president a veto over Congress, and the appointment power over the judiciary. Congress had the power to disapprove all appointments and could impeach both executive and judicial officers. The judiciary in like manner was made independent of the other two departments by providing for life appointment.

JUDICIAL INTERPRETATION AND REVIEW

Some agency was necessary to interpret the meaning of the Constitution. Obviously, this power could not be given to the states or thirteen different decisions might result. Congress and the president were frowned on as judicial interpreters, since they had such great powers in making laws. The logical place to put this power was in the courts, since they would have to pass on cases arising under the Constitution.

No specific clause was placed in the Constitution giving the courts the power to declare unconstitutional laws passed by Congress or the states. There are three reasons, however, which indicate that the framers expected this power to reside here. First, as has been noted, the interpretation of the Constitution and laws most logically falls here. If the courts were to consider the Constitution the "*supreme law* of the land" and a state or congressional law came into conflict with it, they had no choice but to exercise this power.

Moreover, precedents were by no means rare. State courts, and before them colonial courts, had set aside laws as unconstitutional. Finally, if the equality of the three departments were to be maintained, the judiciary had to be given the power to decide on the constitutionality of proposed laws, since the other two departments already had it. Congress could refuse to enact legislation of which it disapproved. The president had the power to make a like decision and veto a law passed. The fact that three agencies might restrain legislation, while only Congress can initiate it, is an indication of the conservatism of the Constitution.

RATIFICATION

The completed document was finally submitted to the states for ratification by conventions in each state, with the provision that as soon as nine states took favorable action it was to go into effect in those states. This provision was made in spite of the Articles of Confederation, which provided that any amendment must be unanimously adopted.

The campaign for the adoption of the Constitution showed, in general, rather definite cleavage between two groups which had existed in America from Colonial days. The conservative, tidewater, creditor, strong-government advocates, who had been in control of the colonial governments, now sought a return to leadership. The backcountry, radical, debtor, local-rights advocates, who had opposed the colonial governments and had seized the helm at the outbreak of the Revolution and maintained control up to this time, naturally threw all their strength against the adoption of the conservative Constitution.

In Delaware, Connecticut, New Jersey, Georgia, Maryland, and South Carolina, ratification was secured with little difficulty. In Massachusetts, Virginia, Pennsylvania, and New York, favorable action was secured by the Federalists only after bitter and close fights and the promise to Anti-Federalists that the main objections would be corrected by amendment. This promise resulted in the Bill of Rights, or the first ten amendments, which were adopted within two years. North Carolina and Rhode Island did not ratify until after the new government had been set up.

As soon as nine states had ratified the Constitution, Congress set dates for the election and inauguration of the new government. Federalists were busy in the resulting elections, for they realized that, if the new government were to succeed, its friends must be in office to see that it started in the right way. Fortunately, they could count on Washington's popularity and the popular realization of his ability and honesty, to carry him into the presidential chair. In addition, they obtained a majority in Congress.

Courtesy Chamber of Commerce, Richmond, Virginia

VIRGINIA STATE CAPITOL
Oldest state capitol—designed by Thomas Jefferson. The scene of the Aaron Burr treason trial.

AN EXPERIMENT IN PLANNED DEMOCRACY

Courtesy of and copyright by U. S. N. A., Annapolis, Md.

BATTLE BETWEEN "CONSTELLATION" AND "L'INSURGENTE"
(From the painting by Charles R. Patterson)

HAMILTON AND FEDERALIST POLICIES

THE NEWCOMER to the society of nations made its debut April 30, 1789, in New York City when George Washington was inaugurated President of the United States, thirteen years after the Declaration of Independence. Alexander Hamilton, the financial wizard of his day, was appointed Secretary of the Treasury. He favored a strong central government. "Let the Union," we can imagine him saying to himself, "take over the war debts of the states as well as the Confederation. Let the Union collect the revenue and pay the full amount to the creditors, who held the states' notes. The federal government then will be looked to as a rightful taxing agency and as a savior in time of need—savior of the states which could not pay, savior of the creditors who had expected to get only thirty cents on each dollar owed them." He also felt that the government should pay the holders of continental notes one hundred cents on the dollar, even though speculators had purchased most of them at very low rates. This is the first instance of the desire on the part of federal officials to take over responsibilities which people had expected the states to handle, and is evidence of the so-called tendency toward centralization.

A second of Hamilton's recommendations was a protective tariff to encourage American infant industries. Finally, the Secretary of the Treasury proposed establishing a Bank of the United States with $10,000,000 capital stock, one-fifth bought and held by the government, the rest sold to the public. The bank was to issue "sound" currency, that is, only as much was to be issued as could be backed by the government's gold and silver.

These three policies, assumption and full payment of debts, a protective tariff, and a sound currency, were supported by the Federalists, the group who wished to see a strong federal government. In general those making money from commerce, banking, foreign trade, or manufacturing, and the holders of the state and continental notes, followed Hamilton's leadership, carrying with them the commercial towns, and the tidewater plantations of the South.

JEFFERSONIAN AND REPUBLICAN DEMOCRATIC IDEAS

Hamilton's proposals were not without bitter opposition. Washington appointed Thomas Jefferson Secretary of State. He was the philosophical, democratic, country gentleman who wrote the Declaration of Independence. Although a friend of the Constitution and the federal union, Jefferson had always held republican or democratic ideals. He spent the troubled period of the Confederacy in France and retained his ideals after most of the revolutionary leaders had decided that a strong government, dominated by educated and propertied people, was necessary. This Virginian felt that the ideal America would be a society of small free farmers, very small towns, with as little government as possible and what there was directly controlled by the people. Jefferson was supported by the farmers, craftsmen, laborers, and small shopkeepers, mostly in the rural areas of the North and the frontier parts of the South.

These beliefs were in direct opposition to Hamilton, who wished to aid commerce and industry, in which he felt the real

THOMAS JEFFERSON   ALEXANDER HAMILTON

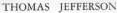

vigor and safety of the new nation would lie. This meant the growth of cities and the rise of at least two classes, laborers and capitalists, and it also meant a restricted ruling class, the very thing that Jefferson feared.

FEDERALISTS AND DEMOCRATS UNDER WASHINGTON

Washington attempted to keep the peace between the followers of Hamilton, known as Federalists, and the followers of Jefferson, known as Republicans (later called Democrats), for two terms, though he was too worn out by the effort to run for office again. At first Hamilton had somewhat the better of the struggle. Jefferson allowed him to put his debt-funding plan through Congress, in return for Hamilton's support of a southern location of the future national capital. Congress also passed a tariff law and authorized the bank suggested by Hamilton.

Temporarily, also, Jefferson's group lost power as a result of foreign affairs. He had sympathized with the French because of the republican principles proclaimed by their early revolutionists.

The Federalists, in opposition, tended to favor the conservative, industrial English, upon whom American commercial life depended. A general European conflict broke out, in which most of the monarchical nations were aligned against revolutionary France. By the terms of the treaty of alliance with France, made during the American Revolution, the Jeffersonians felt the United States was obliged to help the French. However, the French emissary to America, Citizen Genet, behaved so rashly before his official reception that Jefferson with his French sympathies had to take to cover; the Federalists won their point when Washington issued a proclamation of neutrality in 1793.

A BRIGHTER OUTLOOK FOR JEFFERSON

Eventually, however, the Jeffersonian party won public approval. The Federalists sent John Jay to London in 1793 to negotiate a treaty. His instructions were to secure the removal of the British fur posts in the United States Northwest Territory, in accordance with the treaty of 1783; to end Britain's policy of keeping the Indian tribes hostile to the Americans; to end the impressment of American seamen into the British navy; to stop British seizure of American ships trading in the French West Indies; and to secure the opening of British West Indies ports to American trade.

Jay, however, had little to offer in return, and, in the treaty which he brought back, the English agreed only to surrender the fur posts in 1796, to open their East India ports to American shippers, to be somewhat more liberal with American ships in the West Indies, and to let commissions arbitrate certain other matters. The seizure of American ships and the impressment of sailors were not even mentioned. The treaty was ratified in the Senate, although popular feeling appeared to be opposed to it.

Despite the unpopular Jay Treaty, the Jeffersonians were not able to place their leader in the presidency. The Federalists still remained in control by electing the aristocratic New Englander, John Adams, with a majority of only three votes in the electoral college.

X, Y, AND Z

One event in his administration was an undeclared war with France. News that the Americans had signed a treaty with England so angered the French that Adams decided to appoint a commission of three able men to confer with officials in Paris. There Talleyrand, the French foreign minister, sent three agents to negotiate with them, known to history as Messieurs X, Y, and Z. They intimated to the American envoys that for a bribe they might secure a favorable treaty. When Americans heard the news they were furious. Such an insult must be avenged! Fortifications and warships were built, French vessels were seized by privateers and by the navy, and Washington was recalled to command an enlarged army. "Millions for defense, but not one cent for tribute!" was the war cry. Luckily, war was not formally declared, as the officials in both France and America saw the folly of conflict. A new commission was sent to France in 1800. Napoleon, who had just come to power, received them courteously and agreed to end the old military alliance and to sign a friendly commercial treaty.

Meanwhile there was growing indignation in the trans-Allegheny region. The western farmers disliked the tax on distilled liquors, and the Whiskey Rebellion resulted. The unpopular Alien and Sedition laws, passed in 1798 as war measures, were also causing great annoyance in the West and in the South where Jeffersonianism had its greatest support. The most drastic clauses of these laws permitted the president to remove aliens from the country merely by declaring them dangerous, and proposed fines and prison terms for those opposing the execution of laws, or criticizing the president and government. Such laws, so obviously in contradiction to the spirit of the Bill of Rights, have been passed under war pressure, even by liberals like Lincoln and Wilson, and are frequently left on the statute books long after the crisis is over. It is evident that Adams and his party were unduly alarmed, for war was never declared.

The Republican newspapers, however, continued to attack him and raised a hue and cry over fundamental liberties and freedom of the press. Indignation was so great that Jefferson wrote a set of resolutions passed by the Kentucky legislature, condemning the Alien and Sedition Acts, and claiming that the states should prevent the federal government from exercising too great powers. Madison prepared a similar one for passage in the Virginia legislature. Using these resolutions as a platform, Jefferson successfully waged his campaign for the presidency in 1800.

JEFFERSONIANS IN POWER

This election marks the emergence of the West as a factor in national politics. The democratic tendencies of the adventurous pioneers were outraged by the aristocratic leanings of the Federalist party. They eagerly joined the mechanics, laborers, small farmers, and non-propertied classes in their struggle to gain suffrage and political recognition. All these groups heartily endorsed Jefferson's philosophy of government, and were elated at his election. America for them now gave promise of being a democratic republic, instead of an eastern aristocratic oligarchy.

Although the Federalist party had definitely lost its control except in New England, the Republicans accepted the groundwork laid by Washington and Hamilton. They adopted the financial and credit system, the tariff laws, and continued the foreign policy along lines proposed by the Federalists. Cities, commerce, industries, and foreign trade all continued to prosper.

Even Jefferson's dislike of the "loose construction" interpretation of the Constitution gave way under the pressure of his great interest in the Louisiana territory. The growth of centralized government, given its start by the Federalists, continued in the Republican regime as interstate and international relations became more complex and important.

One phase of Federalist policy, however, caused Jefferson grave annoyance. Adams had bequeathed to his administration courts filled with judges of Federalist leanings, including a large number of last minute political appointments. Jefferson greatly resented the presence of these men on the bench and he recommended that Congress repeal the Judiciary Act. Republican ire went so far that impeachment proceedings were started in Congress against certain judges and, as a result, John Pickering, an aged and incom-

CHIEF JUSTICE
JOHN MARSHALL
"Father of the Su-
preme Court"

petent federal judge in New Hampshire, was removed. When
Justice Chase of the United States Supreme Court was brought to
trial, however, he was not convicted; his acquittal discouraged
prosecution of the man who finally did most to strengthen the
court and oppose Jeffersonianism, Chief Justice John Marshall.

Aside from judicial appointments, Jefferson was able to accomplish many of his aims, for he was an able politician as well as a
philosopher. Much of the ceremony of an aristocratic government
was abhorrent to him, and instead of riding in a coach he walked
to his inauguration. However, his supposedly radical ideas did
not create the revolutionary violence which the conservatives had
feared. Instead, as has been said, "he out-Federalized the Federalists."

Albert Gallatin, whose financial genius approached Hamilton's,
was appointed Secretary of the Treasury. He pursued a policy of
economy in order to reduce tariffs, eliminate internal excises, and
balance the federal budget. James Madison, a fellow Virginian
and a close friend of Jefferson, was made Secretary of State.

PURCHASE OF LOUISIANA

The most important domestic event of Jefferson's administration was the Louisiana Purchase. Since the Northwest Ordinance

of 1787, settlers had been moving rapidly into the trans-Allegheny region north of the Ohio River. Land was cheap, wages were high, and in a few years a laborer could earn enough to purchase his own farm. The area south of the Ohio River was so well settled that by 1792 Kentucky was ready for admission to statehood, while Tennessee followed in 1796. Ohio also was sufficiently populated by 1803 to be admitted into the federal union.

With an enlarged western population came a corresponding need for manufactured goods and markets for their agricultural products. Unfortunately, the mouth of the Mississippi River, their most logical and accessible water highway, was in the hands of the Spaniards. Repeated diplomatic protests and sporadic intrigues and armed outbreaks finally resulted in the Pinckney Treaty of 1795. This agreement with Spain opened the river and gave the frontiersmen the right to deposit their produce at New Orleans. Naturally, then, Jefferson was alarmed when rumors came that Spain had retroceded Louisiana to Napoleon in 1800 in the Treaty of San Ildefonso.

Congress, duly aroused, appropriated $2,000,000 for the purchase of New Orleans and named James Monroe and Robert Livingston as American agents to the French court. Napoleon's plans for rebuilding the French empire in North America had been defeated by native uprisings and disease in Haiti. Fearing the collapse of his European policy also, the French dictator astonished the American agents by offering to sell the entire Louisiana territory extending from the Mississippi River to the Rocky Mountains. Livingston and Monroe hastened to accept the offer before Napoleon might change his mind. The sum of $15,000,000 was agreed upon, and thus for a relatively insignificant sum the young republic more than doubled its area. Jefferson put aside his constitutional scruples and urged Congress to ratify the purchase at once.

His interest in western expansion was further proved by his sponsoring of the Lewis and Clark Expedition (1804-1806) which ascended the Missouri River, crossed the mountains, and entered the Columbia River valley. These explorers laid the foundation of later American claims to the Oregon territory.

OPPOSITION TO JEFFERSONIANISM

Jefferson's second term was not as popular as was his first one. Not only did he break with a faction of his own party, headed by John Randolph of Virginia, but he also faced renewed opposition from New England and New York Federalists. A radical faction of this group, fearing complete loss of political influence, even suggested the formation of an eastern federation. To accomplish this, they backed Aaron Burr for governor of New York in 1804. Largely through Hamilton's efforts, this plan failed. The antagonisms aroused in the incident resulted in Hamilton's death in a duel with Burr. For Burr it meant the end of his active political career in the East, and the beginning of his colorful and unfathomable quest for power and dominion in the West and in Mexico—finally ending in his conspiracy trial in 1807.

JEFFERSONIAN NEUTRALITY

Perhaps the most serious foreign problem that Jefferson had to meet was in his struggle to safeguard American maritime neutral rights. With both England and France engaged in the Napoleonic struggle, American commerce was greatly hampered. English admiralty courts held, in the famous Essex case in 1805, that neutrals could not carry on trade with France even if the enemy cargo were landed in a neutral port and then reloaded and reshipped. This struck a deathblow at the American West Indies trade. England further antagonized the United States' commercial interests by issuing Orders in Council which closed the northern European ports and forced all continental trade to go through the British Isles. The English practice which irritated the United States' pride most of all, however, was the halting and searching of American vessels for deserters from the British navy.

Napoleon struck back at Great Britain in the Milan and Berlin Decrees, which in effect prohibited commerce with England and provided for the seizure of neutral vessels that obeyed the English regulations.

Jefferson was in a dilemma, with both European countries so materially restricting neutral trade. He felt that the most effective way to force the belligerents to respect American neutrality was

MONTICELLO—HOME OF THOMAS JEFFERSON

to issue a non-intercourse act. In 1807, Congress passed such a measure, in the Embargo Act, forbidding all foreign commerce with the United States. Unfortunately, it did not have the reaction Jefferson had hoped. In fact, English and French merchants paid little attention to the act, while New England merchants protested vigorously at their loss of markets and profits. This protest became so alarming that even Jefferson admitted the failure of his theory of economic sanctions, and in March, 1809, the act was repealed. American ports and commerce were opened to all nations except France and Great Britain.

This was the situation that Jefferson turned over to his successor, James Madison. The latter, hoping to end this perplexing commercial plight, listened to the unauthorized proposals of the British minister in Washington. According to them, England promised to revoke the hated Orders if the United States would reopen trade with her. Madison ordered trade relations resumed with Great Britain on these conditions, and forbade commerce with France. England, however, refused to ratify the agreement. Congress, still perplexed, decided to restore commercial relations with both Great Britain and France. It proposed that, in the event either country rescinded its edicts against the United States, it would forbid trade with the other.

Napoleon saw in this action an opportunity to stir up war between his British enemy and the United States. He announced that he intended to repeal the French decrees. Madison, not questioning Napoleon's sincerity, immediately announced the revival of nonintercourse measures against British goods. America unwittingly had joined Napoleon's continental system, aimed at stifling British trade. As a matter of fact, France had violated American neutrality repeatedly, seized and confiscated American ships, and frequently submitted their crews to indignities in French ports. The French dictator was clever enough to see that he could use American complaints against Britain to his own advantage.

England was not anxious to add the United States to her list of enemies. Her merchant classes protested against the continuance of the Orders in Council, and Parliament finally yielded on June 16, 1812—just four days after the American Congress had declared war against England.

THE "WAR-HAWKS" IN POWER

The commercial groups in the United States were not anxious for war because they were receiving handsome profits in evading the French and English trade regulations. Other Americans, however, smarted under England's insolent treatment of their trade and the imprisonment of American seamen. Perhaps the primary urge for the War of 1812 came from the frontiersmen and southern planters. The western "war-hawks," led by Henry Clay of Kentucky, and Felix Grundy of Tennessee, were anxious to acquire more free land and the control of the fur trade. They looked longingly on the Indian lands and on Canada. On the other hand, the southern "war-hawks," led by John Calhoun of South Carolina, hoped to gain Florida from Spain, which was then an ally of England.

"War-hawk" enthusiasm for war reached a high pitch after Tecumseh's Indian rebellion was crushed by William Henry Harrison. It was universally believed that the savages fought with English guns and ammunition. War hysteria finally carried away even Congress, which embarked the United States in June, 1812, on a struggle for which she was totally unprepared.

DISASTERS OF THE WAR OF 1812

With a small, untrained, and poorly equipped army led by incompetent officers, the American land campaigns were far from successful during the first year. The attack on Canada in 1812 was a failure. Hull surrendered at Detroit; Smythe and Van Rensselaer at Niagara; while Dearborn's army mutinied before it got to the Canadian line, enroute to Montreal. The next year, however, Perry's victory on Lake Erie and Harrison's success at the Thames River re-established the original American military frontier in the Northwest. On the sea, for the first few months, American vessels had brilliant success; but Britain's superior naval forces finally completely blockaded the American coast. Privateers, however, captured over 300 British merchantmen as prizes.

England now determined to push the war to a close by invading the United States on four fronts: Niagara, Lake Champlain, New Orleans, and the Atlantic coast. At Niagara the Americans under General Jacob Brown forced the surrender of the fort, while the American fleet under Commander MacDonough in the battle of Plattsburg won control of Lake Champlain. The British plan to strike at the Chesapeake Bay regions along the coast was also doomed to failure, although General Ross did burn Washington. Andrew Jackson, the Tennessee Indian fighter, who had been quelling the Creek Indian raiders near Mobile, hurried to New Orleans to meet the British forces. In a signal victory fought, ironically enough, after the peace treaty had been signed, Jackson inflicted a disastrous defeat on the British and completely endeared himself to the West.

New England hostility continued during the duration of the war. Both financial and military aid were refused to the national government. Farmers and merchants living along the Canadian border smuggled goods to the British forces. Finally, in October, 1814, the Hartford Convention assembled to draw up some plan to limit the powers of Congress and the president, and to restate the principle of state sovereignty. Delegates were on their way to Washington with this report when news of the Treaty of Ghent came. This dying gesture of the New England Federalists was lost in the general rejoicing over peace.

END OF A FUTILE WAR

The British at first made excessive demands regarding the Canadian boundary, the control of the Great Lakes and fisheries, and the creation of a northwestern Indian territory. As news of each successive American victory came, and upon the advice of Wellington, who practically refused to take over any command in America, however, the British diplomats gave way. The final treaty provided merely for a return to conditions before the war. Nothing was said about impressment, blockades, or rights of neutrals. Vital matters, such as boundaries and fisheries, were left to future commissions, setting a notable precedent for treating Anglo-American disputes.

Although the War of 1812 was not a decisive one from a military standpoint, it did have far-reaching effects. No longer was American policy to be dictated by European diplomacy—by a French emperor or a British Parliament. Divorced from Old World domination, the young republic could now turn its attention to internal development and expansion. Industries grew rapidly, American commerce expanded to the far corners of the globe, and the United States was ready for the first time to take an independent position among the nations of the world. For three quarters of a century America looked to the West, turning her back on Europe. Domestic concerns, rather than foreign affairs, were of prime importance thereafter.

VOLTAIRE

PART V

ENLIGHTENMENT, REVOLUTION, AND REACTION

THE AGE OF ENLIGHTENMENT

RENAISSANCE INFLUENCES IN ART AND LITERATURE

WHILE THE NATIONS OF EUROPE were engaging in their titanic struggles for power during the eighteenth century, significant changes took place in European culture. Indeed, the foundations of modern science and thought had been laid by 1815. One field in which this progress did not occur to any considerable extent was that of the fine arts. Here the admiration for classical models and masterpieces, characteristic of the preceding years, continued and even increased during the eighteenth century. Regularity and finish were praised highly, and the art of the Middle Ages was scornfully termed "barbaric."

One notable new strain of culture was introduced from China and affected many of the arts. There was great interest in the paintings, furnishings, and architecture of China, and many porcelains, embroideries, and similar wares were imported. It was fashionable to include some Chinese atmosphere in building, and even Frederick the Great built an oriental pavilion at Sans Souci.

The influence was felt in gardening, and it also appeared in literature as descriptions or imaginary tales of oriental life, or as impressions of Western life as it might appear to an oriental visitor.

In literature the devotion to Classicism is especially clear. In the seventeenth century Italy and Germany produced little of importance. Spain, however, was more distinguished with Cervantes' great study of human nature in *Don Quixote*, the hundreds of plays by the great Lope de Vega depicting contemporary life, and later in the century with the less significant poems and dramas of Calderón. In the eighteenth century, Italy's most important writer was Alfieri, who continued the classical manner in his fiery dramas.

Eighteenth-century German writers, led by Lessing, demanded a "pure" Classicism, rather than a slavish imitation of French models. His *Laocoön*, a treatise on Greek aesthetics, and his classical dramas illustrate this direct connection with ancient Greece. About the same time, there was an opposite reaction in the direction of imitating nature. This "romantic" movement began with imitating Shakespeare, Ossian, and medieval folk poetry, while ignoring classical rules. Klopstock, Herder, and, somewhat later, Schiller, were leaders in creating a great national literature. The dominant figure of the romantic and classical movements was the great statesman, poet, scientist, and dramatist, Johann Wolfgang von Goethe. An ardent Romanticist during his early years, he became a thorough Classicist for the rest of his long life. He wrote a number of polished plays in the classical tradition. His greatest work, *Faust*, is perhaps the highest expression of the innate longing for infinity.

CLASSICAL ENGLAND AND FRANCE

In England, Milton's great poetry followed the ancient classic models, with baroque elaboration and colorful detail. John Dryden, in elegant classical poetry, expounded the political and religious ideas of the time. Later, Alexander Pope not only expressed the philosophy of his time, but also wrote light, penetrating satire in his polished and witty poetry. The eighteenth century contributed some great prose, from the political and economic works to the literary criticism of Samuel Johnson, best known for his dictionary. The dramas of the time portrayed the elegant manners of contemporary society. This was also the period in which the novel first became popular, with the portrayal of contemporary life by such men as Fielding and Sterne. The eighteenth century also witnessed the beginnings of newspaper publication and popular essays.

In French literature the height of classical poetry and drama was reached during the time of Louis XIV, in the work of Corneille and Racine. Equally great was Molière, though his work was less classical and portrayed more of the actual life, particularly the follies, of the time. Another great figure was Boileau, whose classical poetry and criticism had wide influence. Even later in the eighteenth century, Classicism was important, with all the orators modeling their speeches upon ancient masterpieces. As in England, this was a great period of prose, which was the medium of Voltaire and other great thinkers. One type of prose literature was the novel, the growing importance of which is illustrated by the popularity of such works as Prévost's *Manon Lescaut*.

ROMANTICISM

Toward the end of the century, discontent with the classical restrictions upon subject-matter and manner of writing led to a freer, more natural treatment of every day subjects and scenes. This romantic movement in Germany has already been noted. In England, Thomas Gray praised simple, poor people in his poetry. Robert Burns wrote poems about the humble Scots in their own dialect. There was also a group of poems supposedly by an ancient Scot named Ossian, and, although they were proved to be a hoax by a young man of the day, their continued popularity shows the interest in this type of poetry.

The great pioneer in French Romanticism was Rousseau, who expressed in many works a love of nature and man, while praising the "noble savage"—the simple primitive man uncontaminated by what we consider civilization. Although classic ideals had governed most of the period, there had begun a romantic trend which was soon to achieve dominance.

THE PALACE AT VERSAILLES
The baroque style of architecture continued to be popular in the 18th century.

Classical and baroque styles continued to be popular in eighteenth-century painting. English portrait painting reached its climax in the grand works of Reynolds, the more realistic ones of Raeburn, and the more delicate ones by Gainsborough. Watteau painted classically the gay, elegant aspects of French aristocratic life. In addition to this type of painting, there developed a group of artists who avoided this beautiful and elegant manner and sought rather to paint things as they actually appeared to be. The English Hogarth went so far as nearly to caricature people, so unfavorable were his representations of them. The great Spanish painter Goya combined satire and realism in his portraits of nobility as they appeared to his peasant eye.

The baroque style was principally evident in architecture, represented by the palace of the French monarchs at Versailles, the added ornamentation of St. Peter's at Rome, the Jesuit churches in Spain, St. Paul's Cathedral in London, and the structures which

Peter the Great erected in his new capital. The simpler forms of classical pillars and other details were found in American colonial architecture, notably on Washington's estate at Mount Vernon.

Music also reflected the admiration of Classicism. A graceful, cultivated phase is represented by the dances of the French composer, Rameau. More impressive were the symphonies, string selections, and Masses of Haydn. Gluck used Greek subjects and style in opera in an effort to achieve the "pure Classicism" which Lessing advocated in literature. The tendencies of the period are personified by Mozart, who wrote all types of instrumental and vocal music, including opera, sometimes lofty, sometimes gay and graceful, with the charm, elegance, and good taste which characterized the period.

ACHIEVEMENTS IN THE SCIENCES

Seventeenth- and eighteenth-century scientists made great contributions upon which our modern sciences rest. Bacon and Descartes in the seventeenth century paved the way for future progress by insisting that man should learn not from books, but from observation of the facts around him. Descartes stressed the need of testing systematically all material things of the world. In addition to this theory, Descartes made practical contributions to mathematics and physics.

The greatest physicist and mathematician of this age was Sir Isaac Newton. He experimented in light and discovered that all color is found in white light which, when broken down, reveals the series of rainbow hues. His most important contribution was the theory of gravitation, which explained not only the falling of objects, but the reason that the earth, stars, and planets move and yet retain the course and relationship which they have.

Newton's work in turn inspired others to study natural phenomena. Halley observed the movements of heavenly bodies and discovered the comet which bears his name. Leibnitz worked out a system of calculus which proved valuable in engineering. During the two centuries other contributions were made to the knowledge of physics, such as the principle of the barometer, worked out by

Torricelli; the invention of the air pump; and the improvement of the mercury thermometer by Fahrenheit. Important contributions were made to the knowledge of electricity by Franklin's work on conduction through "lightning rods," by Volta in his work with batteries, and by Galvani on reactions to electricity.

Modern chemistry also began in the period of the Enlightenment. Robert Boyle made a valuable contribution in the seventeenth century when he developed the theory of the relation between pressure and volume of gases. Boyle also wrote a book in which he distinguished between chemistry and alchemy. He developed the modern idea of chemical elements, and devised many practical laboratory processes. Chemical science was further advanced through the discovery of carbon dioxide by Black, of hydrogen by Cavendish, of oxygen by Priestley, and the composition of air and water by Cavendish. The Frenchman Lavoisier perfected and systematized many of these experiments.

Some advances were also made in the field of medicine. The Italian Malpighi, an expert in the use of the microscope, contributed to the knowledge of blood circulation and anatomy. The work of von Haller, a Swiss, was so significant that he has been called the founder of modern physiology. Jenner developed a vaccine to prevent the dreaded smallpox, and an able Dutch maker of microscopes, van Leeuwenhoek, discovered protozoa and bacteria.

The first important work in geology was done by the Scot, James Hutton. After studying minerals and rocks, he propounded in 1785 the theory that in the earth's crust lies the history of all that has happened in the past and that the age of the earth is much greater than that suggested by the story in the Bible. The full import of the doctrine, however, was not realized until the nineteenth century, when further progress was made.

There were also gains in botany and zoölogy. In the former field, Carl von Linné, a Swede known by his Latinized name Linnaeus, made a new classification of plants which superseded the work done before his time. A new classification in zoölogy culminated in the works of Buffon, the French scientist.

Geographical knowledge was extended through the travels of Captain Cook to Australia and of de Bougainville in the South Seas.

SPREAD OF SCIENTIFIC INFORMATION

These scientific contributions are in themselves interesting, but they gained added significance because of their great popularity in this period. In the first place, scientific knowledge was exchanged and disseminated by scientific academies. Several of these academies were established in Italy during the early part of the seventeenth century. Two of the most famous scientific societies were founded later in the century—the English Royal Society, chartered in 1662, and the French Academy, organized in 1666. Both academies, and academic groups in other countries as well, published journals through which scientific information reached the educated upper and middle classes. Even royalty was interested in and encouraged science. Observatories and museums began to flourish; Paris and Greenwich observatories were founded in the sixties and seventies, and the Oxford Museum to house curiosities was established in 1683. These measures increased the popularity of science and made possible further progress.

PHILOSOPHY PUTS ITS FAITH IN MAN

The progress of scientific thought also involved a development of philosophy. Philosophy had rested upon theology during most of the Christian era. As natural science developed, however, it began to displace theology as the basis of thought. An important step was taken by Descartes, who distinguished between mind and the things it could perceive on the one hand, and matter which could actually be measured, on the other. Then such men as Hobbes, Leibnitz, Locke, Berkeley, Hume, and Kant successively took up the problem of man's mind and body, their relation to each other and to the universe. They differed about the details— thus Hobbes said there was only matter, Berkeley said only the mind is important, and Hume denied the importance of the mind. But all of them ignored the theology of the Bible and Christianity and thought in abstract terms. The philosophers all believed that they were "enlightened," in contrast to the superstition and misunderstanding which preceded them, and soon people in all classes stressed the importance of being enlightened. The main points of

THOMAS HOBBES

this new philosophy, as typified by Kant, were these: (1) Natural law and science were substituted for the all-powerful God and and theology as the guiding force of the world. (2) Man's reason was regarded as the highest thing in the world, and only the facts he could discover need rule his life. (3) If man is supreme, then by seeking to improve his lot he may progress and eventually become perfect. (4) If man is so important, then his care and protection are the main concern; in other words, a humanitarian attitude should prevail.

CONTEST BETWEEN RELIGION AND REASON FOR POPULAR FAVOR

In religion too there were important changes. There was a spiritual revival, and different groups maintained that men should stop quibbling about dogma and try to find true piety through experience. One of these groups was the so-called German Pietists; another was composed of the followers of Swedenborg, a Swedish Pietist.

At the same time in England the Friends, or Quakers, led by George Fox, preached similar opposition to formal doctrine, emphasis upon personal inspiration, and opposition to war. An extremely important phase of this general trend was the Methodist movement, led by John Wesley. He too emphasized personal experience above formal observance, and while he did not originally intend to break from the English national church, it was inevitable that he should. Similar stress upon feeling rather than reason occurred in other denominations. Even the English church, which had for a long time neglected the lower classes in its contentment with cold formalism, was spurred to spiritual revival and a drive to inspire and convert more people.

In France, the emphasis upon the inner spiritual life was advocated by the Jansenists, who thereby gained the enmity of the Catholic Church and were subsequently banned. Even in Russia, stronghold of Orthodox Christianity, there were similar movements. Meanwhile the other Protestant sects, which had arisen during the Reformation, continued to grow without diminishing the strength of Catholicism.

While the movement toward greater piety and religious feeling gathered strength, there was a strong movement in the opposite direction. Many intellectuals, and those who desired to be classed with them, were discarding mystical or "revealed" religion. Influenced by scientific thought and the exaltation of reason in philosophy, they felt that reason should rule in religion also. These skeptics doubted and criticized the doctrines set forth in the Bible. Some of them discarded traditional belief and acknowledged only that there is a God of Nature. Prominent among this group called Deists, were Hobbes and Pope; Pierre Bayle, who expressed his beliefs in his *Dictionary;* and Diderot and the Frenchmen who compiled the great *Encyclopedia.*

Voltaire was the outstanding Deist, philosopher, and advocate of the Enlightenment. A brilliant thinker, he poured out many volumes on different subjects, of which his essays and letters are most interesting. His keen mind investigated numerous phases of life, and his support of Deism contributed greatly to its importance. Deism was also strengthened by the rise throughout Europe of Free-Masonry which had similar doctrines. Some thinkers went to the full extent of atheism—the belief that there is no God at all.

The result of this freedom of religious thought was an increasing tendency toward toleration. Signs of this broadened attitude were the decline of belief in witchcraft, the beginnings of greater freedom for the Jews, and the suppression of the Jesuits, who had been accused of fanaticism and temporal interests.

HISTORY BECOMES ENLIGHTENED

The growth of the scientific spirit, which had revolutionized the natural sciences, also revealed itself in the writing of history and in the development of the social sciences. Historical narratives before the seventeenth century had been semi-theological in character and were concerned chiefly with the fortunes of kings and battles. Historical occurrences were not described dispassionately as natural events, but rather as if guided by a divine will. For example, a victory in war was often ascribed to God's aid, and a defeat might be pictured as a punishment of His people. The new historical writers were more skeptical and rationalistic. They regarded history as a series, not of rewards and punishments, but of natural consequences. The method of the natural sciences was applied to history.

Thus Gibbon in his noted work, the *Decline and Fall of the Roman Empire*, attributed the destruction of Roman pagan civilization to the growth of what he scornfully called Christian barbarism. David Hume, in his *History of England*, placed less emphasis on politics and wars, showing the historical importance of the social life of the people. Herder, a German clergyman, in *Ideas on the Philosophy of History*, emphasized the humanitarian aspect of society and human nature and accomplishments as revealed in literature, science, and social affairs. The historical works of Voltaire and Raynal were even more popular at that time. Their works consisted of rationalistic and sarcastic attacks on contemporary royal despotism, comparing it with conditions in countries, real or imaginary, where actual liberty prevailed.

POLITICAL THOUGHT BECOMES LIBERAL

There were also important developments in political thought. Thus far political philosophers had spun themes designed to explain and defend either papal or monarchical authority and absolutism, often thereby ingratiating themselves with their rulers. Of royal abuses and extravagance, of the exploitation and ignorance of the people, little was said; and the common people were regarded as incapable of having a hand in their own government. Thus Hobbes believed that man, by nature bad, had entrusted his welfare to absolutist rulers, to whom he was forever subjected.

John Locke developed a different approach in his political writings. He was the first philosopher to make popular the idea that sovereignty does not ultimately reside in the monarch but in the people, and that the king's power is derived from a grant of power given to him, by the people. When the king abuses this power the grant may then be revoked. This theory of social contract became of great significance in Locke's day and thereafter. It was the theoretical backbone of the English Revolution in 1688, and had great influence on the American and French Revolutions.

JOHN LOCKE

A different approach to the problem was made in France by the great lawyer Montesquieu who, after studying history, argued that government, instead of being built upon some general abstract theory like a social contract, must be fitted to the particular country and time. Oddly enough, his praise of English government caused many people to do just what he argued against: to assume that the English system should be used in France and in the American colonies.

Rousseau, whose best-known political work is *The Social Contract* (1762), held an opinion similar to Locke's, and greatly influenced his age and subsequent times. His praise of natural man, his interpretation of popular sovereignty, and his concept that government depends on the consent of the governed, were among the ideas which were regarded as so revolutionary that he was forced to flee from France.

Also advocating reform, but from a different approach, was Jeremy Bentham. He stressed Utilitarianism, the idea that an act should be measured by the happiness of its doer, a selfish standard.

JEREMY
BENTHAM

Yet in the long run, in order to be happy a man will act in a way which also makes others happy. The aim of society, therefore, becomes the happiness of the largest possible number of people or in other words, "the greatest good of the greatest number"—a phrase already used by the Italian reformer, Beccaria.

RADICAL CHANGES IN ECONOMIC THOUGHT

There were also attempts to develop economics into a science as mercantilism suffered a loss of popularity. The great exponent of the new economic theory was Adam Smith. In France the Physiocratic school of economic thought, led by Quesnay, already had expounded the theory that economic wealth is not the product of rigid government regulation; that such regulation, instead, hampers economic production. Adam Smith, in his memorable work, *The Wealth of Nations* (1776), elaborated on this idea. He argued that labor was the basic source of all wealth and that it alone created capital. The entire productive process was governed by rigid natural laws, which automatically determined the importance of the various factors of production. That labor received little, and lived in misery on the verge of starvation, was deplorable but should not be remedied by government action. Nothing should interfere with this inexorable natural law which, as by an invisible hand, governed the economic process. Because it demanded a hands-off policy, this school of economic thought became known as laissez faire, which means "let alone."

Adam Smith thus revolutionized economic thinking. His ideas were also to have great practical consequences. The manufacturing and commercial interests soon advocated the complete elimination of tariffs and monopolies, which was carried out to the fullest extent in England. For the same reason, these classes also opposed any legislation aimed at alleviating the lot of the working class. Both of these factors were to be significant in future world history.

HUMANITARIAN AGITATION

The principle of Enlightenment, besides making for change in the fields already mentioned, gave rise to Humanitarianism. One phase of this movement was a growing demand for the abolition of negro slavery, begun early in the eighteenth century by the Quakers, and favored by various individuals in both England and America. Likewise the Quakers, and such writers as Abbé Saint Pierre as well, raised their objections to the horrors of war. They offered various plans for courts or leagues of nations to achieve international peace.

Horrified by the deplorable treatment of criminals, such leaders as the Italian writer, Beccaria, and the English economist, Bentham, advocated the improvement of prison conditions, and a decrease in the use of torture and of capital punishment.

The other principal problem which faced humanitarians was that of education. Both Catholic and Protestant groups in European countries founded day schools and Sunday schools in which the poor received elementary instruction, while in America the colonies provided for education which they regarded as basic for good citizenship.

ENLIGHTENED DESPOTS

The pervasiveness of these doctrines of Enlightenment is perhaps best illustrated by the fact that their influence extended even to the rulers of the day. These so-called enlightened despots aspired to exercise complete power in the best interests of their people.

An outstanding ruler in this respect was Frederick the Great, whose broad education fitted him for his position, and whose own active life was a model for his people. He had read widely, and as a ruler he enacted many reform measures which have already been discussed. Throughout his life, he continued to interest himself in scientific and artistic progress, enjoyed discussing them, and greatly encouraged German activities in these fields. Thus both theoretically and practically, he was the personification of enlightenment in all fields.

Maria Theresa in Austria was less brilliant and thorough, but in addition to centralizing government, decreasing the power of religious groups, and in other ways increasing her power, she improved the educational system and patronized the arts.

SANS SOUCI—POTSDAM, BUILT BY FREDERICK THE GREAT

Her son, Joseph II, was well read in the works of the enlightened writers and aspired to apply their theories. Unfortunately, he lacked administrative skill. He failed to acquire desired territory. A true believer in reason, he tried to reduce the power of the Catholics and increase the rights of the Jews, two projects which rapidly aroused opposition. Furthermore, his attempts to decrease the powers of the nobles and improve the lot of the peasants were bungling and were opposed throughout the empire. He died convinced that he had failed.

The attempts at enlightened despotism by Catherine the Great, on the other hand, were insincere since she was, in reality, a tyrant. In contrast to her were Charles III of Spain and Joseph I of Portugal. The former, by measures similar to Frederick's, increased the population and prosperity of Spain, while the latter appointed as minister Pombal, who likewise promoted education and the welfare of the lower classes. Some of the other minor rulers followed similar policies.

Thus the principles and theory of eighteenth century leaders, from the rulers on down, pointed toward a powerful, intelligent, and perhaps a happy mankind.

GATE OF HONOR, VERSAILLES

ST. CLOUD FOUNTAIN, VERSAILLES

EUROPE IN FETTERS

UNFORTUNATELY, the enlightened theories of the eighteenth century were not translated into action. The theorists stressed the importance of liberty, yet Europe was governed by absolutist rulers who believed in the divine right of kings. There were all-powerful kings in France, Spain, Portugal, Prussia, Sweden, and Denmark; emperors in Austria and Turkey; and petty but equally absolutist rulers in the little German and Italian states. As we have noted, even the rulers who claimed to be enlightened were, nevertheless, despotic, and absolute. A rigid class system prevailed throughout Europe in spite of pleas for freedom and admiration of the "noble savage" who lived unfettered by society.

In a Europe professing liberal ideas, yet ruled by despots, bound by class distinctions, and hampered by economic regulations, England was the only relatively free country. However, the situation in France is especially interesting, since France was the cultural center of Europe and was to be the political center of European activities for the next twenty-five years. What will be said of France was also, at least partially, true of all Europe.

PRIVILEGED NOBILITY

Far above the mass of the people stood the clergy and the nobles, the members of the First and Second Estates, relatively small in number, but having enormous power. Conspicuous in the social scale were the nobles of the Second Estate. Most of them had great landholdings, from which they received large incomes enabling them to live in leisure and luxury. Some also held important church offices, from which they derived additional income.

A minority of these nobles in France were called the nobility of the gown (*noblesse de la robe*). They were wealthy middle-class men who either inherited titles or who acquired them by buying a position in a law court, which carried with it a title and a judge's robe, whence came their name. The majority, however, were nobles of the sword (*noblesse de l'épée*). They had inherited their titles from medieval ancestors and still owed feudal allegiance to the king.

It is true that not all the nobility were in the same position: some had relatively little property and were forced to live upon their estates in a none too prosperous condition. Frequently this group treated their tenants well and took a neighborly interest in their welfare. Others were wealthier and lived in the country by choice. Many held government positions, but they were also members of the highest social class. On the other hand, many nobles were immensely wealthy and lived a life of indolent pleasure and vice at the court. There, in addition to their own wealth, they received money from the king in the form of high-salaried positions for which no work was required. They were absentee landlords with efficient but uncharitable managers who ran their estates and extracted as much money as possible from the peasants.

There was some desire for reform, but as a group the nobility led a life devoid of useful activity. They collected feudal dues from the peasants; yet, despite the great wealth they possessed, they paid almost no taxes. This privilege was inherited from the Middle Ages, when the nobles were expected to contribute to the protection of their inferiors, and, though they no longer did much for their people, they still enjoyed exemption from taxation.

PRIVILEGED CLERGY

Ranking even higher, since they constituted the First Estate, were the clergy. As in the case of the nobles, the clergy varied greatly in wealth and character. There were many priests who were truly concerned over the condition of the poor people, and who devoted their time and what little money they had to the relief of the unfortunate. On the other hand, the higher clergy were wealthy, powerful men, men with vast lands, who lived luxuriously and, because of the similarity of their interests, co-operated with the nobility. In fact many were also nobles. The clergy also enjoyed the privilege of exemption from taxation.

THIRD ESTATE—OPPRESSED PEASANTS

In contrast to approximately 280,000 nobles and clergy stood some 24,750,000 members of the Third Estate. Some of these were artisans, city workers in trades and industries, hard working, poorly paid people who were under great restrictions and had practically no political rights.

Far outnumbering them were the peasants, about 21,000,000 in all, for agriculture was still France's main activity. In France, it is true, there were only about 1,000,000 serfs—people, tied to the land, whose lives were completely at the mercy of their lords, and who owed the lords half their laboring time—in contrast to the almost complete serfdom in other European countries. Some peasants owned their own land, yet most of them were subject to old feudal regulations. They were forced to work upon the roads. They paid rent to their overlords, and in addition paid fees for the use of the mill, the bridge, and the oven. The kind of farming they might do was limited to the cultivation of strips of land under old medieval customs. There was no progressive farming with crop rotation, fertilization, and improved methods such as English gentlemen farmers used. If a peasant owned a few farm animals and managed to raise enough for bare existence and payment of fees and taxes, he was fortunate. If not, he might starve to death.

Not only did the peasant have to pay fees to his lord, but he also was forced to make a contribution of somewhat less than a tenth of his produce, for the support of the Church.

The royal government imposed an especially odious tax burden on the unfortunate peasants. Taxes were levied with complete disregard for justice or the ability to pay. There were land taxes, poll taxes, and income taxes. Theoretically at least, the land tax was supposed to be proportional to the value of the property; but the tax collector followed the practice of getting all he could from his victims. Even the necessities of life did not escape the insatiable government. Salt, pots and kettles, paper, cards, starch, and alcohol all paid tribute to the Old Regime.

Bad as were the principles of the tax system, even more intolerable abuses were prevalent in the manner of collection. A person or company could buy the privilege of collecting taxes by paying a fixed sum to the government. The difference between the cost of the privilege and the amount collected represented the profit of the collector.

LEADERSHIP OF THE BOURGEOISIE IN THE THIRD ESTATE

Members of the middle class, or bourgeoisie, were the leaders of the Third Estate. Capitalists and financiers, lawyers, doctors, writers, artists, tradesmen, and wealthy farmers belonged to this Estate. Their importance increased steadily throughout the eighteenth century as towns, industry and commerce grew. This growth had occurred in spite of the fact that surviving guilds still restricted industry. Mercantilism regulated foreign commerce, and poor transportation and internal duties hampered domestic commerce.

The wealth of the bourgeoisie lessened the severity of the tax burdens they shared with the peasants, but these exactions were far from popular. Particularly annoying to the business men were

GARDEN OF LOUIS XIV IN FONTAINEBLEAU
Typical of the extravagance of early rulers.

the internal customs duties, tolls, and levies at the gates of the cities. Their business also suffered because of French wars and colonial losses. Naturally they resented the discrimination against them. Since they constituted the bulk of the reading public, they were familiar with the advanced scientific and philosophic ideas of the day; sought to put some of these principles of enlightenment into practice. It is not surprising that the bourgeoisie led the opposition to the king.

The problem of public finance was aggravated by the fact that money once collected was squandered upon the royal family and the court, with no real benefit to the nation. Added to this deplorable situation was the confusion in political and legal organization. The government, because it had grown in a haphazard fashion, was badly organized as well as arbitrary, and plagued with overlapping powers. There existed side by side six different political divisions: judicial, ecclesiastic, educational, and three administrative divisions. Each had its own officials supported by taxes. Then, too, the towns elected their councils in different ways. Weights, measures, and coins differed through the country. There were even many different law codes.

ROYAL WEAKNESS

In spite of all these difficulties, France might have continued for years, if really able kings had been on the throne. Unfortunately, the successors of Louis XIV were not only inefficient, but, perhaps, the most wretched possible under the circumstances. Louis XV was too young to rule when he succeeded to the throne in 1715. There was no efficient body to take charge because Louis XIV had kept all government in his own hands in the latter part of his reign. The ministers of Louis XV ruled in their own interests exclusively. When Louis XV finally assumed control, he was so interested in a life of pleasure and so completely controlled by his mistresses, most of whom were hated by the people, that upon his death in 1774 there were cheers rather than sorrow.

Louis XVI proved to be well meaning but weak and rather unintelligent in state affairs. Unwilling to see any of his immediate family or friends discontented, he reversed national policies to please them. His marriage to Marie Antoinette was unfortunate because she was an Austrian and was considered an enemy by the French, who traditionally regarded Austria with suspicion.

FINANCIAL CONFUSION

The incompetence and increasing unpopularity of the royal family was aggravated by the growing disorder of the public finances. The king chose as minister of finance the admirable Turgot, an expert theorist who wished to put laissez faire principles into operation. Industry and commerce were to be allowed unrestricted activity, finances were to be reformed, and taxes lowered—a program necessary to the preservation of the French monarchy. Naturally, however, he was opposed by all persons who would have lost their privileges and even the peasants, who misunderstood his intentions, were aroused.

BOUDOIR OF MARIE ANTOINETTE

Necker, a practical middle-class man, then succeeded to the ministry of finance. He made a step in the right direction by publishing a report on the hitherto unknown condition of French finances. All business men welcomed this information, but Necker was ousted because he tried to force economy upon the court. Marie Antoinette refused to have her friends lose their pleasures and, to placate her, Louis replaced Necker with Calonne. Instead of trying to economize, Calonne borrowed even more money and at high interest. He spent large sums in an effort to make France appear solvent. Intervention in the American Revolution was a very unprofitable venture, for, although France had the satisfaction of humbling England, the expense was enormous. The treasury was bankrupt when Calonne resigned in 1787.

At this point Louis called a meeting of the Assembly of Notables, a group of about 150 of France's most important men, to consider the finances. The nobles would agree to surrender only a few privileges, and recommended that the Estates General handle the tax problem. A new finance minister began by making beautiful promises of reform, but soon resorted to making loans. The Parlement of Paris, the Supreme Court, refused to assent to new loans or taxes, and demanded the meeting of the Estates General, the national legislature, which had not met for 175 years. Annoyed at its impertinence, Louis XVI dissolved the Parlement of Paris, thereby causing much indignation in Paris.

Having asserted his authority by dismissing the Parlement, the king was, nevertheless, forced to call a meeting of the Estates General for May, 1789. Elections were held during the winter of 1788-1789. The Estates General was composed of the three Estates: there were 308 clergymen, 290 nobles, and 598 commoners. This meant that in number of representatives the Third Estate equaled the two upper groups. Since some of the upper classes sympathized with the Third Estate, the latter would have an excellent chance to control the Assembly if all three Estates met together and voted by individuals. On the other hand, if each Estate voted as a unit, the upper Estates would lead two to one, since the nobles and clergy usually voted on the same side.

Before the meeting, groups of each Estate presented their grievances and suggestions, formally drawn up in petitions known as *Cahiers*. Unfortunately, the ministers of the king, instead of studying the *Cahiers* and outlining a program for the Estates General, did nothing and had no leadership to offer.

THE CRISIS

When the Estates General convened, therefore, confusion reigned. At once there arose the question of how the Estates should vote. The king in his opening speech, which said very little, indicated that he favored a vote by order—that is, he wished each Estate to vote as a unit. The Third Estate objected because it would be outnumbered two to one. It preferred a vote by head because, they said, the nation would be truly represented that way. Practically, of course, as has already been pointed out, they would have at least an equal chance this way.

The Third Estate consisted largely of the bourgeoisie, who desired greater power. They had the advantage of two excellent leaders. Mirabeau, a noble whose sympathies drew him to the

Third Estate, was a brilliant orator and a wise and courageous man. The Abbé Sieyès, less outstanding, was nevertheless prominent, especially because he had written a pamphlet in favor of the Third Estate just before the assembly of the Estates General.

Under these leaders the Third Estate carried on fruitless debate for a month. During this time tension increased because the peasants and city proletariat were on the verge of starvation. Finally, since the clergy and nobles showed no signs of yielding, the Third Estate declared itself a National Assembly on June 17, 1789. The king tried to make them subservient to his wishes by barring them from the chamber in which they were to meet; so they assembled instead at a place where tennis matches were held. Here they took the "Tennis Court Oath," swearing that they would not separate until they had drawn up a national constitution. Thus they assumed the task of providing a constitutional government for France, and made the first move of the French Revolution.

The king had failed to enforce his will: the Third Estate, backed by some members of the other two Estates, continued to insist on their rights. After a week, in his usual timid fashion the king submitted and the Estates General met together on July 1, 1789 and voted by head.

VIOLENCE

When troops were brought into Paris from the frontier, it was feared that the royal government would use force against the Assembly if necessary. The Assembly's request for removal of the troops was refused; and the people of Paris, desperately hungry and seeing their only hope in the Assembly, began to riot. The rioting continued for three days until, on July 14, 1789, the mob destroyed the Bastille, an arsenal formerly used as a prison for political offenders and regarded as a symbol of Bourbon tyranny. Its destruction made the upper classes realize at last that revolution was under way. The middle-class people of Paris established a local government of officials chosen by popular election. This Commune, with Lafayette in charge of the National Guard, for the most part controlled the city without royal approval.

But quiet and order did not last long. The peasants in the provinces had taken up the agitation, destroying property and organizing armed groups and local governments. While the Assembly met at Paris and began the program of reform, the dire distress and threatened starvation of the mob continued. The unrest was increased by news that new troops had been brought to the royal court in Versailles and at a lavish entertainment had expressed their enthusiasm for the king.

Finally on October 5, a mob of the women of Paris marched to Versailles and, nearly maddened by hunger, rioted for bread. After a night of terror, during which Lafayette barely succeeded in protecting the royal family, the king and queen consented to move to Paris, as a guarantee that food would be provided for the mob, and the middle class might exercise power. The people in many towns throughout France had refused to pay taxes and had assumed control of local affairs. Under these chaotic circumstances the royal government had collapsed, and the royal family's removal to Paris made them virtually prisoners. The mob was in command.

At last the people had an opportunity to put into effect the principles of liberty—freedom of property, of religion, of speech, of press; equality—the end of all class distinction; and fraternity —a nation of men working together for the good of France.

REVOLUTIONARY LAWS

During these months of chaos, the pressing problems of finances, which had originally caused the crisis, became increasingly complicated because no taxes had been paid. The Assembly therefore undertook taxation reform, and relieved the situation by the issue of paper currency or *assignats*. As security for this issue, the Assembly confiscated large blocks of church lands, in partial return for which the clergy were to be paid salaries. Thus in an attempt to ease the financial strain, the power of the Church was reduced.

The subjection of the Church was furthered by confiscation of church property and the suppression of the monasteries. In 1790, by the Civil Constitution of the Clergy, the number of the higher clergy was reduced, and they were made a civil group, elected by the people and forced to take an oath of allegiance. Many of the clergy fled rather than take this inferior position. As a result a large number of devout Catholics, who had thus far favored the Revolution, now turned against it.

Meanwhile the National Constituent Assembly, as it was now called, continued to work on reform. During the August days, the nobles, frightened by the violence of the mob, and perhaps moved by generosity, surrendered their feudal rights. Serfdom was ended, servile fees ceased, and ecclesiastical privileges were discontinued. By these and other enactments the lower classes were relieved of many grievous burdens of taxation and service. However, the nobles were to be reimbursed, and it was not until 1793 that the feudal abolition was made without indemnity.

As a statement of their basic principles, the Assembly adopted the "Declaration of the Rights of Man," guaranteeing rights of liberty, property, and security of the individual. Important administrative reforms were also made, and the French Revolution was well under way.

MONTIGNY CHATEAU
Typical of the extravagant splendor of the French nobility.

COLONNE DE JUILLET (Column of July)
Monument on the site of the Bastille, French prison-fortress demolished
by an angered populace on July 14, 1789.

DEMOCRACY ON TRIAL IN FRANCE

CHATEAU OF DAMPIERRE
Another example of the lavish display of the power in eclipse.

FRANCE UNDER A NEW GOVERNMENT

MOST OF THE IMMEDIATE PROBLEMS in connection with a new system of government were solved by the National Assembly in 1791. The results of its labors appeared in a written constitution for France. Ther was to be a separation of powers, with the executive function vested in the king and the legislative power vested in an elected assembly. The king's executive capacity was limited primarily to the exercise of a suspensive veto. The assembly was controlled by the middle classes because only property owners were allowed to vote.

Thus were made in two years sweeping changes which had not been achieved in centuries. However, as might be expected under such conditions, few people were satisfied with what had been done. The nobles, many of whom fled from France and were called emigrés, naturally wished to recover their prop-

[353]

erty. Many devout Catholics resented the revolutionary attacks on religion and their discontent was expressed in a riot at La Vendée. The royal family could not be expected to enjoy its new fetters. Louis XVI and Marie Antoinette made an attempt to flee from their rebellious subjects, but they were recognized and compelled to return to Paris.

This attempted flight increased the wrath of radicals, a group which was growing rapidly in numbers. The middle classes, motivated by the desire for power and genuine sympathy with the proletariat, led the radicals. Their activities centered in Paris where political clubs had come into existence. Chief among these clubs were the Cordeliers who were radical from the beginning, and the moderate Jacobins who later became extremely radical. Three great leaders appeared among these extremists. Marat was a brilliant and vigorous advocate of direct popular rights. Danton was a deliberate agitator, calm, practical, and a good orator. Robespierre was a scholar who believed ardently in popular rights. All three of these men met violent deaths early in the Revolution.

UNITED OPPOSITION OF EUROPEAN MONARCHS

France was seething with discontent, but the immediate cause for the downfall of the monarchy came from abroad. The first incidents of the Revolution were observed with sympathy in England where liberal Britons approved the limitation of monarchical power. But British alarm was aroused by unbridled radicalism in France, and by 1790 many influential Englishmen agreed with Edmund Burke in his opposition to the Revolution across the Channel.

On the Continent, however, the feeling was clearly against the French people from the beginning of the Revolution. The Bourbon family, ruling in Spain and the two Sicilies, were united by family compacts with the rulers of France, and their wrath was aroused. Worse still, the sympathy of Leopold II of Austria was alienated from the revolutionists. As a Hapsburg he was expected to protect his sister, Marie Antoinette. As a ruler of Austria, he feared that revolt in the Austrian Netherlands, recently suppressed with difficulty, might break out again. As Holy Roman Emperor he wished to keep ideas of revolution out of the German States.

Co-operation of Austria and Prussia, enemies for many years, would have been impossible had Frederick the Great been alive, but his weak successor, Frederick William II, was willing to act with Austria. The two rulers proclaimed their views in August, 1791, when they stated that the restoration of monarchy and order in France was the common interest of all European sovereigns.

The possibility of war was welcomed by many groups in France. The court group believed that should the allies win, its supremacy would be re-established, and even if the French won, the victory would so add to royal prestige that their position would be improved. The middle classes saw in war a factor to unify all France, now so divided in sentiment. Even the radicals, with the exception of a few who feared that a military dictatorship would follow, regarded war as an opportunity to achieve a truly democratic government.

Therefore the question of war became the main interest of the Legislative Assembly. About half of the deputies, who represented many shades of opinion, at first voted independently; but as time passed they tended to side with one of the two groups which constituted the balance of the members. They were the Feuillants, who favored a monarchy restrained constitutionally, and the radical Girondists, whose leaders came from the department of Gironde, who desired a republic. Although these groups opposed each other in internal problems, they agreed on the foreign problem, and in April, 1792, Louis XVI was persuaded to declare war.

The people were united in enthusiasm for their cause, but they were wretchedly equipped and badly organized. Furthermore, members of the royal family, although supposedly loyal to France, were naturally fearful of the growth of Republicanism. They regarded the foreign armies as possible deliverers and were even suspected of revealing French plans to the enemy. It is not surprising that when the French suffered a series of defeats, they blamed their king and became increasingly bitter and violent.

ROYAL CARRIAGE OF THE OLD REGIME

THE END OF THE MONARCHY

At this point once again an incident abroad incited action at home. Late in July, 1792, the duke of Brunswick, commander of the allies, issued a proclamation declaring his intention to restore order in France and threatening to destroy Paris completely if any of the royal family was harmed. This proclamation roused the proletariat and extreme members of the bourgeoisie to fury, and on August 10, 1792 they revolted. They displaced the Commune by a new revolutionary body headed by Danton; broke into the palace, killed the Swiss Guards, and forced the royal family to flee to the Assembly for protection. Under the influence of the Paris mobs the weakened Assembly suspended the king and called for an election of a new National Convention by universal suffrage.

When the Convention assembled on September 22, 1792, it declared that France was a republic. The Convention was supposedly elected by universal suffrage, though many of the lower classes had been kept away. However, many degrees of opinion were represented. On the right were the Girondists, who were theoretically democratic but actually feared the proletariat. On the left were a smaller number, the Jacobins, members of the middle class but thorough disciples of Rousseau and sympathizers with the proletariat. Their leaders included Robespierre, Danton, Carnot, and St. Just. Between them was "The Plain," the majority, who had no set policy; but as the course of events revealed the strength of the proletariat, they tended more and more toward the left.

The Convention was faced with the necessity of running the war, continuing the work of the Revolution, and improving organization at home. One of the first problems confronting them was the disposal of the king. Louis XVI was tried in January, 1793, for betraying his people. He was convicted and executed. Among those who voted for the execution was the king's cousin, the duke of Orleans, who had turned Revolutionist, taking the name of Philippe Égalité.

THE TERROR

Meanwhile the tide of the war had turned. The news of a French victory had been received on the day the republic was proclaimed. Success continued as the French under Dumouriez not only drove the allies out of France but actually conquered Belgium. The proclamation of the French intention to spread the revolution to all countries aroused Great Britain, Holland, Spain, and Sardinia to join Austria and Prussia in a coalition against France. Even within France there was some reaction against revolutionary policies, and Dumouriez himself deserted to the Austrians.

Military success continued in spite of this desertion. Carnot, one of the Jacobin leaders, took command, drafted and drilled men, devised such new features as making the division a military unit, and perfected plans of strategy. Under his brilliant leadership the French broke up the coalition. By the treaties of 1795,

Spain made peace; Prussia granted France a free hand on the left bank of the Rhine; William V was deposed and Holland was transformed into the Batavian Republic; and France held the Austrian Netherlands. France, in controlling the territory east to the Rhine, had accomplished what Louis XIV with his great organization had failed to do. Only Great Britain, Austria, and Sardinia continued the armed opposition.

Meanwhile violence increased at home. Danton had become virtual dictator, and in the September massacres of 1792 the royalists were ruthlessly executed. Still there was opposition from the middle classes and the people of the provinces. The military machine built up for the foreign war was used to stamp out this opposition. The Jacobins had become supreme, with Robespierre, St. Just, and Carnot directing the Committee of Public Safety, the supreme executive organ of France.

The year of their rule, 1793, is frequently termed the "Reign of Terror," so bloody were its results. The Committee felt that terrorism was the only way in which to deal with their many enemies. To facilitate their activities they decreed the liability to arrest of anyone unable to prove his citizenship. The Revolutionary Tribunal was empowered to try and convict suspects. Most famous of the many victims of the Terror were Marie Antoinette and Philippe Égalité, whose desertion of the royal cause in favor of the Revolution did not save him from the fate of other nobles.

REVOLUTIONARY LEGISLATION

In addition to these violent activities, the Convention enacted much in legislation. It began the task of unifying the law code and adopted some radical social reforms: the abolition of imprisonment for debt, of negro slavery in the French colonies, and the protection of women's property rights. Primogeniture was abolished so that property, instead of being willed to the eldest son alone, was divided among the nearest relatives. A step toward commercial reform was taken with the adoption of the metric system of weights and measures.

An interesting experiment which typified the desire to sweep away all manifestations of the old regime, was the calendar reform. The year was to be divided into twelve periods with new names, each in turn into three weeks of ten days each, with every tenth day set aside for rest, and the remaining few days at the end of the year to be holidays. The calendar began with the birth of the republic, September 22, 1792.

The Convention likewise turned its attention to religion. In 1792 it had decreed an entirely new religion of reason to be expounded in the churches. Later, under Robespierre, Deism, including belief in a Supreme Being, was substituted. Finally, at the end of the "Reign of Terror," the Convention decided that religion was a private matter in which the state should not interfere.

Extreme economic measures were enacted, whereby further confiscations of property occurred. Land was divided into small parcels and sold. Furthermore, laws were enacted fixing maximum prices.

The radical nature of this legislation, and particularly the bloodiness of the "Reign of Terror," inevitably led to reaction. Danton, wearying of violence, now favored moderation and consequently was guillotined. Finally Robespierre, after a short dictatorship, was executed, together with St. Just.

This decline of radicalism, known as the Thermidorian Reaction, because it occurred in the month called Thermidor, marked the end of terrorism. Bourgeois groups were once more in the ascendancy, but they continued their homage to republicanism. The Convention, called to draw up a constitution that had never gone into effect because of the Terror, now provided one in harmony with the prevailing bourgeois spirit. Effective in 1795 and known as the Constitution of the Year III, it provided for two legislative chambers elected indirectly: a lower house to propose the laws and an upper house to examine and enact them. Executive power was delegated to a Directory of five persons elected by the legislature. The Directory was to appoint ministers and supervise law enforcement.

THE DIRECTORY

The four years of the Directory were characterized by domestic dissension and dissatisfaction. With the exception of Carnot, who was expelled in 1797, the members of the Directory were of mediocre caliber. Interested mainly in the amount of profit they might acquire, they paid little attention to the welfare of the country. Political and social dissension continued. On the one hand there were many royalists and reactionaries in the legislature, who were restrained only by illegal force. At the other extreme were such men as Babeuf, a socialist radical leader, whose indignation at the still unimproved lot of the underdog caused him to lead an insurrection for which he was subsequently executed.

An increasingly serious problem was the financial situation. The issue of the *assignats,* or paper currency, which had been instituted as a temporary measure, was continued until by 1796 three hundred livres in *assignats* were required for one livre in cash. In 1797, a partial bankruptcy was declared and the *assignats* repudiated. The financial situation was no better than it had been in 1790. In fact, inflation and repudiation had made it worse.

THE CORSICAN OVER EUROPE

ARC DE TRIOMPHE, PARIS
Built as a memorial to the victories of Napoleon Bonaparte.

RISE OF AN UNKNOWN CORSICAN—NAPOLEON BONAPARTE

THE CHIEF THREAT TO THE POWER of the Directory was the increasing popularity of Napoleon Bonaparte. The man who molded the destiny of Europe by his own personal power, was born on the small Mediterranean island of Corsica in 1769. The Bonapartes were an old and honored family, prominent in Corsican politics. Charles-Marie Bonaparte had some political influence at the French court, and obtained an appointment for his son Napoleon to attend the military academy at Brienne. Four years of military training were followed by a year of specialized preparation as an artillery officer at the École Militaire. Then, like any other soldier in his class, the future master of Europe was commissioned a sub-lieutenant and detailed to a provincial post.

There was little that distinguished the young Bonaparte from other lieutenants of artillery except his short stature and his interest in the ideas of Rousseau. The outbreak of the Revolution and the subsequent reorganization of the army gave Bonaparte ample opportunities for advancement. As tactical adviser in the siege of Toulon, a town on the Mediterranean coast that rebelled against the Parisian authorities, he established a reputation as an artilleryman and strategist. His superior officers next honored him, so they thought, by giving him command of the infantry in western France. Bonaparte refused the dubious honor because of his pride in believing himself an authority in the use of artillery, especially as applied to the peculiar conditions of warfare in southern France and northern Italy.

Left without a command and disgraced because he had refused one, Bonaparte lived in poverty and disrepute until called upon to assist in suppressing a royalist uprising in Paris in 1795. The ambitious young Corsican saved the Convention with a "whiff of grape-shot" and at the same time caught the scent of power. Raised to the position of a hero, Bonaparte was eventually rewarded with the command of the army in Italy.

ITALY AND EGYPT

The French military strategy called for two major campaigns. One army was to move in a northeasterly direction, and the other was to advance into Italy against Sardinia and Austria. This latter campaign was entrusted to Bonaparte. In a series of brilliant maneuvers through the Alps into Italy, he swept away the armies of the Sardinians and the Austrians. By the Treaty of Campo Formio in 1797, France was given the Ionian Islands and the Austrian Netherlands. As partial compensation for the loss of the Netherlands, Austria was given the Venetian Republic, but only on promising to stay out of other parts of Italy. Both Austria and Sardinia were thus removed from the conflict and only Great Britain remained to oppose France.

Members of the Directory realized the danger to their position in having a military hero in Paris. Bonaparte himself favored an Egyptian campaign as a means of striking at England and his wishes were followed.

Bonaparte's soldiers won new laurels in the shadows of the pyramids and suffered terrible hardships on a futile Syrian campaign. But Lord Nelson defeated the French fleet and maintained the supremacy of English sea power in the Mediterranean. The most significant accomplishments of the Egyptian campaign were scientific rather than military. Bonaparte encouraged the study of Egyptian antiquities by the archaeologists who accompanied the expedition and returned to France with many Egyptian treasures.

Bonaparte was well aware that his Egyptian adventure was a military failure; but the French people were willing to believe that their remarkable young commander had won new honors for the republic. When he received the news of French reverses in Europe, Bonaparte decided to desert his army in Egypt and return to France. He managed to escape capture by a British fleet and landed to receive a tumultuous welcome which was by no means wholly deserved. But the French people were looking into the future as well as toward the past, and Bonaparte was expected to save France from an uncomfortable position.

COUP D'ETAT OF 1799

The Directory had decided that the best protection for France would be a ring of dependent republics around the country. Holland became the dependent Batavian Republic in 1795. The Swiss Confederation became the Helvetic Republic. The Duchy of Milan, the city of Genoa, the Papal States, and the Kingdom of the Two Sicilies had all become republics. But the enemies of France formed a new coalition. Great Britain, Austria, and Russia made an alliance in which the British statesman, William Pitt, was an important leader. Armies of the coalition won victories over French troops, and in France itself there was domestic chaos. No wonder then that Bonaparte's return was regarded with so much favor!

For a few weeks after his return from Egypt, Bonaparte lived in conspicuous retirement in Paris. During that time he was plotting with the Abbé Sieyès for the downfall of the Directory and the establishment of a military dictatorship under three consuls, two of whom would be Sieyès and Bonaparte. A coup d'état was scheduled for November 9, 1799, and was to be accomplished in one of the sessions of the legislature. When the time came, the coup all but miscarried. One branch of the legislature, the Council of the Ancients, agreed to the proposed changes on November 9. But the Assembly, strongly Jacobin in membership, violently opposed modifications in the government. The conqueror of Italy fainted at a critical time in the proceedings on November 10, and the whole plot would have failed had not Lucien Bonaparte saved the day by dispersing the Assembly with a force of grenadiers.

FIRST CONSUL

Bonaparte himself became the First Consul in the reorganized government. There were two others, but they became mere phantoms when the powerful personality of Bonaparte began to make itself felt. His popularity and the prospect of a capable government overcame the momentary distaste for the dictatorship. Although France under the Consulate was nominally a republic, it was not long until First Consul Bonaparte adopted the pomp of royalty. Before long, too, occurred the psychological transformation of Citizen Bonaparte into Napoleon, Emperor of the French.

Early in 1800 Bonaparte saw his enemies of the second coalition seriously weakened by the withdrawal of the Russians from their ranks. Only England and Austria remained in arms to threaten France. He sent one army into German territory and personally undertook an expedition to humble Austria and drive her armies out of northern Italy. The campaign was a distinct success. Italy was bound securely to France, and Austria was again defeated. In the Peace of Lunéville (1801) which confirmed the conquest, Bonaparte assured the security of France by establishing a series of friendly Italian republics, the Rhine River as a "natural" boundary, and a respite in the war with Austria. England, the only power remaining at war with France, ceased her hostility in the same year. The speed, with which Bonaparte was able to bring peace, clearly proved him a genius in handling international affairs.

BONAPARTE AT THE BATTLE OF RIVOLI (1797)
(After the painting by Philippoteaux in the National Museum of Versailles.)

PAULINE BONAPARTE BORGHESE (by Canova)

HALL OF THE EMPERORS, THE LOUVRE
"The Louvre was enlarged to house the precious booty of Napoleon's campaigns"

BONAPARTE'S ADMINISTRATIVE GENIUS

When he grappled with the internal problems of France, the First Consul showed an equal genius for administration. In short order he solved monetary problems, thereby restoring confidence in his central government and a measure of prosperity to the people of France. Almost overnight he wiped out the republican government of the provinces and substituted *prefects,* appointive officials who were responsible to him alone. He knew how little the uneducated people of the provinces cared to exercise their voting power. The system of prefectures, so efficiently administered, brought provincial France into the closest union that had ever existed. Thus Bonaparte was always in contact with the minds of his people.

The status of the church was the next problem to be solved. Catholicism, although in official disfavor, had remained a powerful force throughout the Revolution. Restoration of order under the Consulate required that the relations of church and state be established on a permanent basis. Negotiations with the papacy finally resulted in the mutually satisfactory concordat of 1801.

The legal problems of France were simplified by the preparation of a concise code which was published in 1804 and took as its popular name the *Code Napoléon.* Paris was beautfied and France was given a system of good roads. The Louvre was enlarged to house the precious booty of Napoleon's Egyptian and Italian campaigns. Everywhere France blossomed anew under the stimulating personality of the First Consul.

EMPIRE—1804

Subject states, such as the Italian republics, were also included in the general reorganization which Bonaparte brought to France. One after another they were brought under his personal power. In a similar manner he built up a colonial empire. Spain ceded to France the vast trans-Mississippi region known as Louisiana, and a French army took the island of Haiti in the Caribbean Sea.

Building an empire, Bonaparte waived republican principles aside. In 1802 he had himself elected consul for life. Late in

1804, he dropped all pretense of republicanism and assumed the title of Emperor. Amid all the pageantry that was characteristic of his public appearances and those of Pope Pius VII, who came from Rome to grace the occasion, Napoleon placed the crown on his own head.

France's foreign enemies were alarmed by the growing power of Napoleon. The imperial designs of the little despot became a matter of international concern. England induced Austria and Russia to join a new coalition of powers to curb the increasing might of France. Napoleon was not unmindful of his responsibilities to his people and to his own ambition. In 1803 he had sold Louisiana, his greatest American possession, to the United States to raise money for the impending war. Although Napoleon began to build a navy, he became convinced of the impossibility of carrying the war to the British Isles, so he attacked England's continental allies.

His genius did not fail him. In less than six months his citizen army and Bavarian allies captured the Austrian capital and dealt the combined Austrian and Russian armies a crushing defeat at Austerlitz. He next turned on Prussia, another of the allies, and drove its army from the field at Jena and Auerstadt on October 14, 1806. Of the continental members of the coalition, only Russia remained to be humbled.

The march from the Prussian battlefields toward Russia was impeded only at Friedland, where the French army signally defeated a Russian army augmented by a remnant of Prussians. Tsar Alexander of Russia did not risk further defeat but agreed to meet Napoleon on a raft in the river to sign the Treaty of Tilsit. More than a peace was concluded, since Alexander soon appeared as an ally of France and an empire-builder in his own right. Sweden, in spite of feeble aid from England, lost Finland to the Tsar in 1809. In only two years Napoleon had asserted his mastery over continental Europe.

THE "CONTINENTAL SYSTEM"—A BOOMERANG

Unable to cope with England directly, the master of Europe devised an indirect war on Britain. The French navy, which had

MONUMENT TO NELSON AT TRAFALGAR SQUARE, LONDON

been reconditioned and augmented, lost its effectiveness in the battle of Trafalgar in October, 1805, and so in a single stroke, Napoleon's chief weapon against England was taken from him. His plan of indirect war on Britain was to strike at her trade with continental Europe. As master of the continent, he closed all of its ports to British goods, hoping thereby to starve Britain of her life's blood—trade and commerce. Further decrees, after 1806, even allowed confiscation of English goods found on the continent. England, unable to attack Napoleon on the continent, issued counter-decrees prohibiting the world's trade with France, and ordering the seizure of vessels that complied with French decrees.

Napoleon's plan, which has come to be known as the "continental system"—economic war of the continent against England —was intended to injure Britain. Instead, his decrees worked hardships on his continental subjects and on the neutral powers whom Napoleon expected to supply Europe. Among the latter was the United States. American merchants were subjected to both French decrees and English counter-decrees. The difficulties of legal traffic with the combatants were a major cause of the American war with England which began in 1812. It was the despotism of Napoleon, typified in the Continental System, that contributed to

his ultimate failure. Its application from 1806 onward turned Europe's thoughts from Napoleon the liberator to Napoleon the tyrant.

NAPOLEON'S EUROPE

The French invasion of Europe was at first viewed by the European peoples as a liberation from the tyranny of their own monarchs. Everywhere the Napoleonic army was welcomed as the herald of a new day.

When Napoleon entered a European state, he intended to stay there. The newly enlarged France was administered by his prefects; the lesser states of Europe were given over into the hands of persons who could be relied on to give Napoleon support when needed. Close relatives of Napoleon and trusted generals were raised, in many instances, to the positions of highest authority in some of the European states. Holland, the principalities of the east bank of the Rhine River, and Italy were among the states that were placed in the hands of his relatives and favorites.

Napoleon's policy was to keep his subject states so weakened that none could rise against him. Groups of smaller states, such as the Confederation of the Rhine, were banded together to balance the power of Austria and Prussia. The reorganization of Europe was accomplished at the expense of the old Holy Roman Empire, an organization which had been superfluous for more than a century. Napoleon merely laid its ghost and thereby compelled the Emperor, who was also Emperor of Austria, to restrict his power to his Austrian possessions.

Russia was the only continental power that did not feel the force of the Napoleonic program for Europe. The fickle Tsar escaped its rigors because he had, by chance, become the ally of the master. For a short time Portugal, too, held out against the new order. But, although supported by England, the country fell before Napoleon in 1807. When Portugal and Spain fell, all continental Europe was in the hands of Napoleon or his friends.

Spain, ruled by a Bourbon who had bowed to the inevitable and become friendly to France, suffered without fault on her part. In order to secure the Portuguese conquest, Napoleon took the crown from the Spanish king and gave it to his brother, Joseph. It was an insult to Spain, and the Spanish people took it as such. A revolt broke out and England hastily sent a force to aid the fighting Spaniards. The stubborn resistance of the Spanish forces could not be overcome. Other European peoples, seething under the heel of the oppression, took heart and made ready for the day when they could also rise. Napoleon had lighted the fuse to the keg of powder on which he sat.

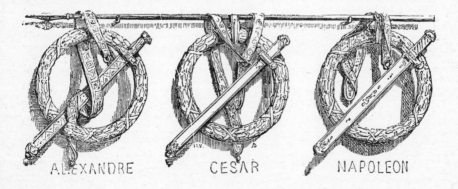

ALEXANDRE   CESAR   NAPOLEON

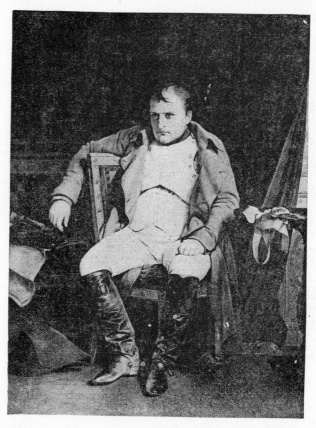

NAPOLEON BONAPARTE AT FONTAINEBLEAU ON MARCH 31, 1814
(Painting by Paul Delaroche)

END OF THE NAPOLEONIC ERA

THE ISLE OF ELBA TO WHICH NAPOLEON WAS EXILED

DISCONTENT IN LATIN AMERICA

NAPOLEON'S DIFFICULTIES in Spain were important in bringing about his final downfall in Europe. Moreover, he was badly mistaken if he expected to secure control over Spain's American colonies by placing his brother Joseph on the Spanish throne. The colonies were far from being contented under Spanish rule, and they welcomed the opportunity to escape from oppression.

There were many causes for rebellion in Spanish America. Before the reforms of Charles III toward the close of the eighteenth century, the monopolistic trade practices were especially burdensome. However, corrupt officials and greedy merchants developed an extensive system of smuggling to modify the restrictions. Foreign goods found their way into the colonies in spite of efforts to exclude them. Taxation within the colonies was also oppressive, and Spain failed to encourage industrial development overseas. There is danger of overemphasizing these economic reasons for discontent in the colonies, but there is little doubt that they were factors in the loss of the Spanish-American empire.

[373]

EMPRESS MARIE LOUISE AND THE KING OF ROME
(HER SON BY NAPOLEON)

There were religious causes for discontent, centering around objectionable practices of the Inquisition and on the part of a minority of the clergy. Scandalous conduct by unworthy clerics provided ammunition for detractors of the Church which had done so much to civilize two continents. The Inquisition attempted to stamp out heresy and to prevent the introduction of certain publications. These efforts could not fail to arouse the hatred of the people involved, especially among the small educated groups.

Colonial government was largely centered in the hands of native Spaniards, to the practical exclusion of Creoles, as American-born Europeans were called. This Creole group was vociferous in all of the Spanish colonies, and should have found support among the *mestizos*, the numerous offspring of unions between Spanish men and Indian women. Below this *mestizo* caste was the large mass of Indians whose every attempt at self-assertion was severely suppressed. Broadly speaking, the interests of Spaniard and Creole were similar, while the *mestizo* and Indian should have been sympathetic toward one another. The *mestizos* held the Indians in contempt; the Creoles scorned the *mestizos;* and even the most insignificant European Spaniard considered himself far superior to the Creole. These mutual animosities prevented the co-operation necessary to carry the subsequent revolutionary movements to early and successful conclusion.

PRELIMINARIES OF REVOLUTION

Many of the viceroys and captains-general were very capable rulers. Their efforts were largely responsible for maintaining Spanish authority and extending Spanish rule in spite of decadence in the mother country. But all of their efforts, sincere as they were, could not build an impregnable Chinese wall against the revolutionary ideas then current in the European world. Spain gave her colonists dangerous ideas by joining France in fighting England during the American Revolution. Then came the French Revolution and the Rights of Man, with propagandists like Antonio Nariño to spread the new gospel in northern South America. But still Spanish power remained unshaken in her part of the Americas.

Godfather to Spanish-American independence was a colorful adventurer, Francisco de Miranda. This knight errant was intimate with American and British statesmen, a general in the French Revolution, and a favorite of Catherine the Great. After a series of disappointing experiences with English promises, Miranda found aid in the United States for an expedition to carry the torch of liberty to his native land. He sailed from New York in 1806 on the *Leander,* but the people of Venezuela refused to be liberated. Miranda sailed away with those of his companions who had not been captured, and returned a few years later when the outbreaks of 1810 occurred.

The people of Buenos Aires gained valuable experience and self-confidence in 1806 and 1807 when they repulsed British efforts to conquer their city. Sir Home Popham and General Beresford turned from Capetown, which they captured from Holland, to an unauthorized attack on the cities at the mouth of Río de la Plata. Buenos Aires fell in 1806, but was retaken by the colonists under the newly elected viceroy, Liniers. Beresford surrendered his army. General Whitelocke captured Montevideo in 1807, but he met with a crushing defeat in Buenos Aires. Although British arms were sadly tarnished, British goods were introduced in sufficient quantities to increase discontent with Spanish trade restrictions.

THE INFLUENCE OF NAPOLEON

Napoleon Bonaparte more or less unwittingly cut the ties between Spain and her American colonies. The Corsican moved an army into Portugal in 1807, but the British admiral succeeded in pursuading the Portuguese court to take refuge in Brazil. French troops then occupied important positions in Spain. Charles IV abdicated in favor of his son, an almost wholly despicable creature who became Ferdinand VII. Father and son were induced to confer with Napoleon at Bayonne. Ferdinand, too, abdicated, and Napoleon placed his brother Joseph on the Spanish throne.

Local governing bodies in Spain united to oppose the French invaders, and through their guerrilla warfare and English aid, they developed a "Spanish ulcer" which proved fatal to Napoleon. One of the proposals of the Central Junta of Spain was to give Spanish Americans equal voice in colonial government with the European Spaniards. The proposal satisfied few of the influential colonial leaders. Eventually the Spanish colonies were allowed to send thirty delegates to the Spanish parliament, or *Cortes*. Again colonial leaders were disappointed and began to think in terms of independence from Spain.

REBELLION IN THE NAME OF FERDINAND VII

The struggle in Spain and the hateful rule of Joseph Bonaparte gave the Spanish-American colonies a valid political basis for establishing their independence. Sporadic outbreaks in Chuquisaca,

La Paz, and Quito were suppressed by royal troops in 1809. These movements were just a year too soon, for in 1810 a number of separate wars for independence broke out in the Spanish dominions. These armed revolts occurred in so many places that one is justified in stating that rebellion was an endemic political disease in Spanish America. Revolutionary *juntas* or committees were created in various colonies to rule in the name of Ferdinand VII. The most important of these committees were those in Buenos Aires, Chile, and Venezuela. Royal power was concentrated in Peru, from which region armies were sent out to subdue the rebellious *juntas*, since the Spaniards and many of the Creoles knew perfectly well that loyalty to Ferdinand VII was merely a screen behind which the leaders were fighting for independence.

This first period of the wars for independence terminated in 1814 when Ferdinand VII was restored to the throne. By that time royal power had been fairly well secured in most of the colonies with the exception of the modern Argentina. In the very year of Ferdinand's restoration, the great José de San Martín was given command of an Argentine army. This remarkable soldier, who must be given a high place in military annals, was destined to become the liberator of Chile and Peru.

Simon Bolivar, the Liberator, also played a prominent part in the first period of the wars for independence. He was especially active in northern South America between 1810 and 1815, although in the latter year he was forced to flee to Jamaica. Bolivar gained valuable experience as a revolutionary general, and in the second phase of the wars he accomplished more than enough to entitle him to be called one of the greatest sons of America.

An inspired parish priest, Miguel Hidalgo y Costilla, was the leader of rebellion in Mexico. He raised the standard of revolt in September, 1810, and rallied Indians and *mestizos* around his banner. "Long live the Virgin of Guadalupe! Death to the *Gachupines!*" became the battle-cry which threw all Mexico into civil war. Hidalgo and some of his companions were captured and executed in 1811, but José María Morelos continued the fight. A constitution was drawn and independence was declared in 1813. Two years later Morelos, a priest like Hidalgo, was captured and executed. Until the final stroke by Iturbide in 1821, the war in Mexico was little more than a series of guerrilla raids by petty leaders.

SOURCES OF DISCONTENT IN EUROPE

Having seen the results of the combined forces of international politics and economic and social dissatisfaction in Latin America, we now return to the empire of Napoleon, where these factors, working under widely different conditions, had a similar result.

Although the conquests of Europe were first understood by European peoples as an extension of Liberty, Equality, and Fraternity—the three ideals of the French Revolution—it was not long before they felt the tyranny of Napoleon's rule. In the workings of the "continental system," which has already been described, they found themselves subjected to poverty because Napoleon wanted to humble England. His numerous demands for soldiers to fill the ranks of many armies depleted the population and filled almost every continental family with the sorrow of parting or death.

A ray of hope that the day of Napoleon need not go on forever came from Spain. Napoleon's inability to quell that revolt gave the Austrians an opportunity to stimulate the revolutionary spirit in the German states in the hope of a general European clearing of the Napoleonic influence. But the efforts were premature— the states of the Rhine were too closely allied to their master's interest, and the French army was in possession of all strongholds of anti-French influence. In midsummer, 1809, Napoleon easily disposed of the abortive uprising. Austria was again crushed under the heel of despotism.

DISASTER IN RUSSIA

Yet the spirit of the people of Europe was not broken. French armies marched up and down the bypaths of Europe, but the spirit of revolt against Napoleon's despotism could not be suppressed. His Russian ally, the tsar, also began to slip out of his position as

WATERLOO MONUMENT
The battle of Waterloo sealed the doom of the Corsican.

a friend of France. Russia was no longer co-operating with Napoleon by 1810; she opened her ports to British goods. Italian states
were likewise beginning to circumvent the rigors of the Continental System.

Napoleon realized that he needed to mend the situation. He
quickly chastised the Italian states and laid the plans for a Russian
campaign. First, he secured a nominal Austrian alliance by marry-
ing an Austrian princess. Next, he collected the largest army
Europe had ever seen and marched it toward Russia.

One-half million men were in the Grand Army that entered
Russia to find burned villages and a denuded countryside. The
Russians had evacuated their towns, set them afire, and sought the
safety of the hinterland. Napoleon found even Moscow a mass
of ruins. There the victorious army camped amid desolation and
the swirling snows of a Moscow winter awaiting the surrender of
a foe who would not chance open battle. Napoleon might have

been able to defeat the Russians had they fought; but, as it was, his only enemies were cold, hunger, disease, and the maddening raids of elusive Cossack warriors. In the late days of the year 1812 Napoleon began a fateful retreat. Few of the half-million soldiers ever saw their homes again. Napoleon's power dribbled away on the long road home. It was the road to Elba and to Waterloo.

THE FALLING HOUSE OF CARDS

The European countries did not remain idle when they saw their hated master so seriously weakened. Prussia, particularly, was ready to lead the way in a general European revolt. The earlier victories of Napoleon's armies, composed of citizens fired with nationalistic ideals, taught Prussia that the disinterested professional armies were outmoded. Prussian military leaders trained a national army in spite of the various restrictions. As in the case of the army, other national institutions were brought up to date and to the peak of efficiency. Under the stimulus of a rising nationalistic feeling that penetrated to the humblest citizen, Prussia joined Russia in a war on Napoleon in March, 1813. Other European states were making ready to join the two leading powers.

Napoleon struck at Prussia immediately, but, while winning battles, was unable to demoralize his enemies. At this juncture Austria, wavering for a time to see which side would win, chose to risk her lot with that of the allied powers. For the first time in the years of war against Napoleon, the enemies were united in both spirit and purpose. Together they struck at Napoleon's tired army and administered a crushing defeat at Leipzig. Methodically, relentlessly, they followed him into the very heart of France.

In lower France, also closing in on Paris, were the forces of the Spaniards and English led by Sir Arthur Wellesley, later to become the Duke of Wellington. The Spanish forces had not been contented with driving the French out of Spain, but resolutely continued to hammer away at the retreating army. With an enemy before him and an enemy behind him, each stronger in men and fired by a nobler cause than he, Napoleon saw his end was near.

On April 6, 1814, Napoleon abdicated and was given an asylum on the Mediterranean island of Elba. In a few short years the master of Europe had fallen from the greatest heights any man had ever reached in modern times. His own methods, which had carried him into every corner of continental Europe, were taken over by his enemies and were used to drive him from his pinnacle. The enthusiasm for nationalism and liberalism, which he had given Europe, turned on him and drove him whence he had come—to a Mediterranean isle. With an honorary guard of 800 old veterans, Napoleon was interned at Elba.

The victorious powers faced many problems. The overthrow of Napoleon had left many lands without constituted authorities. In many instances the puppets of Napoleon had managed to retain their thrones, but, if the rule of Napoleon were to be set aside, his puppets must be removed from their positions. Problems of territorial division, always thorny, arose when the will of the master was no longer felt.

The problem of providing governments for the regions which Napoleon had ruled was the most immediate problem faced. Having been subjected to the will of a tyrant for a decade, the European states turned to the standard of legal rights. On this basis a Bourbon, Louis XVIII, a brother of the late king, was given the throne of France. The Spanish throne was given back to its former possessors, another branch of the Bourbon family. Having determined the location of national authority, the concerted powers assembled in Vienna a few months later to re-establish Europe on a basis that would afford peace and security to every country. It was a war-tired Europe that was represented at Vienna in the fall of 1814.

THE ONE HUNDRED DAYS

While the leaders of Europe discussed the fate of the world in Viennese drawing rooms, the world was electrified by the sudden appearance of Napoleon in lower France. While all Europe shuddered at the news, Frenchmen again placed their country at the disposal of the exiled hero when he entered France in 1815, less than a year after his abdication.

Louis XVIII, the Bourbon king placed on the throne of France by the powers, sent an army to take Napoleon prisoner, but the army, too, joined Napoleon. Louis fled across the border for safety as Napoleon triumphantly marched to Paris.

The Congress at Vienna acted quickly. Napoleon was outlawed and the generals of the concerted powers, the English Wellington and the German Blücher, were ordered to unite their forces and defeat the army Napoleon was gathering. Napoleon acted even more swiftly. He first attacked Blücher and defeated him. Dispatching a part of his army to chase Blücher, he turned on Wellington near Waterloo.

Wellington was ready for him. All the afternoon of the single day of battle, June 18, 1815, Napoleon attempted to dislodge Wellington from his positions but utterly without avail. Late in the evening Napoleon was startled to find Blücher taking a position on his right, placing the French forces in a cross fire. The unexpected had happened—Blücher had outwitted the French general who was to keep him from joining Wellington at Waterloo. Seeing himself outmaneuvered as well as in imminent personal danger, Napoleon left his soldiers in the hands of his generals and fled to Paris, where he abdicated a second time.

Now deserted by all his friends, he planned to escape to America. But England had been careful to blockade the entire French coast. He found he could do nothing but surrender to the British. They held him in custody until it was decided to place him on the bleak, mid-Atlantic island of St. Helena. There, after six lonely and bitter years, he died in 1821.

He could not stem the tides he had loosed upon Europe. His magnetic personality had drawn men to live and die for him. His despotism and overweening ambition drenched Europe in blood and despair. Yet, in that same Europe made bloody and despairing, he spread the ideals of the French Revolution that still thrive in Europe. He found Europe a poorly organized continent and re-cast its three hundred odd states into thirty-three, each driven by new urges—nationalism and liberalism.

In a few short years Napoleon passed from obscurity to power, and from power to an island prison. His rise and fall were made possible by the blood of millions of men, women, and children and the conscripted wealth of a continent.

CHAPEL OF NAPOLEON'S TOMB
Hôtel des Invalides, Paris.

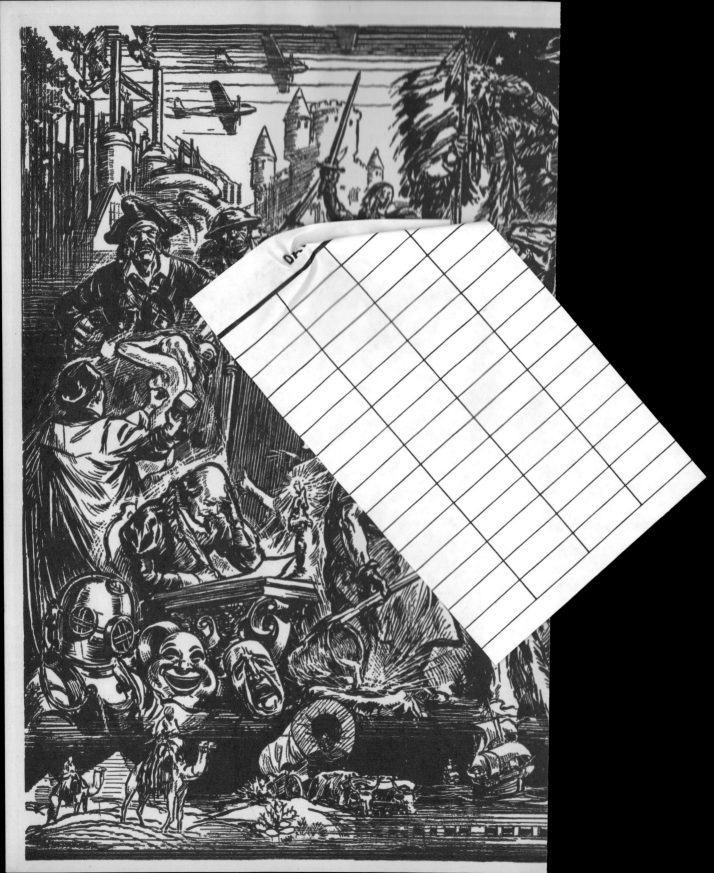